ECOLOGICAL SOLIDARITIES

WORLD CHRISTIANITY

Dale T. Irvin and Peter Phan, Series Editors

Moving beyond descriptions of European-derived norms that have existed for hundreds of years, books in the World Christianity series reflect an understanding of global Christianity that embodies the wide diversity of its identity and expression. The series seeks to expand the scholarly field of world Christianity by interrogating boundary lines in church history, mission studies, ecumenical dialogue, and inter-religious dialogue among Christians and non-Christians across geographic, geopolitical, and confessional divides. Beyond a mere history of missions to the world, books in the series examine local Christianity, how Christianity has been acculturated, and how its expression interacts with the world at large. Issues under investigation include how Christianity has been received and transformed in various countries; how migration has changed the nature and practice of Christianity and the new forms of the faith that result; and how seminary and theological education responds to the challenges of world Christianity.

ECOLOGICAL SOLIDARITIES

Mobilizing Faith and Justice for an Entangled World

Edited by Krista E. Hughes,
Dhawn B. Martin, and Elaine Padilla

The Pennsylvania State University Press
University Park, Pennsylvania

"How We Become," by Crystal Tennille Irby, is used with kind permission by the artist.

"What If?," by Sapient Soul, is used with kind permission by the artist. A recording of Sapient Soul performing the poem can be found at https://sapientsoul.bandcamp.com/track/what-if.

Library of Congress Cataloging-in-Publication Data

Names: Hughes, Krista E. (Krista Elizabeth), 1971– editor. | Martin, Dhawn, 1970– editor. | Padilla, Elaine, editor.
Title: Ecological solidarities : mobilizing faith and justice for an entangled world / edited by Krista E. Hughes, Dhawn Martin, and Elaine Padilla.
Other titles: World Christianity (University Park, Pa.)
Description: University Park, Pennsylvania : The Pennsylvania State University Press, [2019] | Series: World Christianity | Includes bibliographical references and index.
Summary: "Employs academic, activist, and artistic perspectives to explore ecologies of interdependence as a frame for religious, theological, and philosophical analysis and practice"—Provided by publisher.
Identifiers: LCCN 2019025523 | ISBN 9780271084626 (cloth)
Subjects: LCSH: Ecotheology. | Ecology—Religious aspects—Christianity. | Human ecology—Religious aspects—Christianity. | Climatic changes—Religious aspects—Christianity.
Classification: LCC BT695.5.E26 2019 | DDC 261.8/8—dc23
LC record available at https://lccn.loc.gov/2019025523

The Pennsylvania State University Press is a member of the Association of University Presses.

It is the policy of The Pennsylvania State University Press to use acid-free paper. Publications on uncoated stock satisfy the minimum requirements of American National Standard for Information Sciences—Permanence of Paper for Printed Library Material, ANSI z39.48–1992.

Contents

Acknowledgments

Many of the chapters in this volume emerged from the June 2015 conference titled "Seizing an Alternative: Toward an Ecological Civilization." We are grateful to John B. Cobb Jr. and the Center for Process Studies for organizing the conference and for the invaluable dialogue of each participant in our track on "Entangled Difference: Gender, Sex, Race, Class, Etc.!" chaired by Catherine Keller and Monica Coleman. Other works in the volume are original contributions invited from thinkers, activists, poets, and artists we regard deeply. Our ecological efforts have also been bolstered by the personal and financial support that we have received from our respective institutions: Newberry College in Newberry, South Carolina; the Source of Light (SOL) Center at University Presbyterian Church in San Antonio, Texas; and the University of La Verne in La Verne, California. The creative task of tri-editing this volume has itself been one of entangled differences, and we bow in honor to the deepened friendship the process has forged. It is from a place of planetary gratitude and toward visions of an ecological civilization that we dedicate this work.

painting 1 Scott Neely, *The Light That Encircles Nothingness*. Acrylic on paper, 8 × 8 inches. Used with kind permission by the artist. Photo: Mark Olencki.

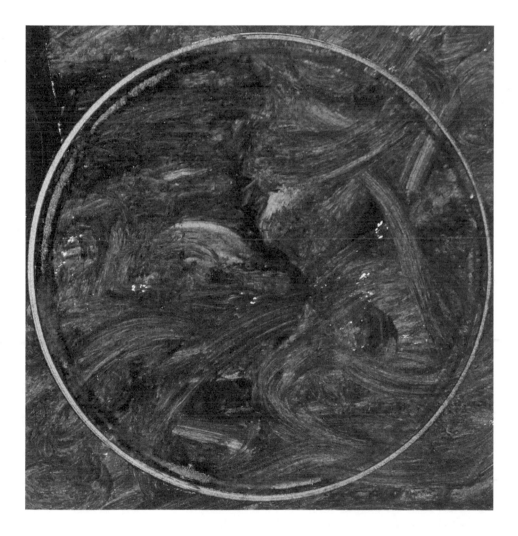

INTRODUCTION

Krista E. Hughes, Dhawn B. Martin, and Elaine Padilla

> Within the interdependence of mutual (nondominant)
> differences lies the security which enables us to descend
> into the chaos of knowledge and return with true visions of
> our future, along with the concomitant power to effect those
> changes which can bring that future into being.
>
> —AUDRE LORDE[1]

What powers and future visions might mobilize the billions who inhabit the third rock from the sun? The blue-green marble of Earth is in crisis, with certain creatures, human and other-than-human, disproportionately paying the price for the destructive habits and self-serving choices of those in power. Here, in the age now known as the Anthropocene,[2] it is easy to despair. As this volume suggests, earth-dwellers—those both responsible for and suffering the consequences of global degradation—must name reality as it is and lament. Yet the offerings here come not from a space of despair but from one of hope, a tenacious, clear-eyed hope that should not be confused with blind optimism. That is, we in this volume affirm with Audre Lorde that it is precisely the interdependence of creaturely differences that can fuel humanity's visions for the future if we honor both the differences and their entanglements.

4

This volume is an invitation to think differently about *entanglement*, the notion that all existence is inescapably and perpetually constituted by relationships with the rest of the cosmos, even when individuals experience their distinctiveness as self-bounded and separate. Blake's poetic call to see the "the [whole] world in a grain of sand" is not mere fancy. Relational entanglement is a fact. Neither good nor bad, it simply *is*.

The concept, and more importantly the *reality* of entanglement, challenges Western drives toward myths of rugged individualism, policies of isolationism, and practices of consumerism that are indifferent to the communities and species they damage. To confess an entangled reality is to confess that the human predicament is thoroughly material, thoroughly embedded in natural processes, and thoroughly bound to ecosystems not of human design. Such materialist confessions are radically egalitarian, embracing all matter as bearing forth wondrous possibility.

Feminist philosopher Karen Barad, who develops *entanglement* as a frame for engaging the world, insists that "matter and meaning are not inseparable elements."[3] Such a frame, wherein basic engagement with the other engenders meaning—be it plant other, animal other, human other, or planet other—leads inevitably to the field of practice and activism. As Barad notes, "questions of ethics and justice are always already threaded through the very fabric of the world."[4] Justice, however, has not always already been the central thread guiding local, national, or global politics.

Indeed, the contributors to this volume work from the premise that it is precisely the failure to recognize the fact of entanglement—instead casting reality as a conglomerate of fundamentally separate and alienated individuals—that has produced the current age, one of planetary peril and creaturely coexistences that are toxic rather than fecund, destructive rather than generative. Human blindness to planetary entanglement, whether intentional or incidental, has so altered the biology, geology, chemistry, and entangled patterns of the earth that "scientists now propose . . . a new interval of geologic time: the Anthropocene."[5] In no other planetary era has one species so determined the present and future conditions of planetary existence. To prevent the unraveling of the fabric of the world, humans, we *anthropoi*, need to track whatever threads of justice and social mobilization remain. Such tracking will call for creative alliances, new ways of being in the world, and a frame for action that engages all life as meaningful.

Entanglement conceived thusly likewise invites those of us weaned on myths of individualism to think differently about *difference*. Aiming to both reflect on and perform difference—of perspective, of voice, and of method—the offerings herein explore difference from theoretical, activist, and artistic perspectives, probing how our creaturely differences shape us: restrict us and free us, divide us and connect us, distort us and transform us, violate us and empower us.

To attend to entangled planetary existences is, then, to consciously engage the collective and communal. As collectives inevitably group around symbols and systems of meaning-making, this volume tracks the theopolitical dynamics present in such entanglements. In a broad sense, then, this tracking reveals both the everydayness and complexity involved in the theopolitical task that is the making of meaning. That is, the volume explores from various angles how religious acts are always political: they have shaped and can reshape again the polis in its urban, suburban, and rural dimensions. Acts of faith, from ecclesial rituals to discourses on God and on interhuman and other-than-human relationships, are not merely private. They have public, communal implications. Conversely, our quotidian embodiments— loves and passions, collective activisms, and socioeconomic choices, whether among kindred or strangers, near or far—are never isolated. Therefore, these embodiments can inform how the sacred is conceived and enacted across societies as they strive to construct meaning.

Meaning-making is an ongoing process, one frequently beset by prejudices or obstacles but one also buoyed by liberating insights and inexplicable wonders. From a technical or theoretical sense, to track the theopolitical within this process is an endeavor both critical and constructive, as the narratives and images of this volume highlight. Process theologian John Cobb describes political theology as "essentially critical theology." Drawing on Cobb's description, the theopolitical models and methods detailed in this volume are critical. They critique systems and symbols, ideologies and theologies, and socio- and globo-political structures that devalue, exploit, ignore, and oppress.[6] These models also create. They envision new individual and collective possibilities, possibilities grounded in a realistic but also hope-infused analysis of the entangled Anthropocene era. The whole of human reality is relational. This means that the social imagination and structures that have constructed adverse realities can yet be de- and reconstructed to promote flourishing rather than toxicity and unaccountable loss. Governments, media, civic leaders, faith communities, activists, and artists of all kinds can choose to develop new narratives and new forms of meaning-making that lean into that flourishing.

This volume in turn witnesses to and seeks to model ecological solidarities. Our contributors advocate for forms of theological, social, and political engagement that bid the reader to consciously participate in meaning-making processes—to build bonds of mutually beneficial coexistences within their own particular ecologies regionally and globally. Each ecology is gloriously unique. It teems with distinctive sets of micro and macro elements, organic and human made, as well as physical, natural, biological, mental, and emotional components. These distinctions are to be celebrated and honored in a manner that views such rich diversities as resourcefully fecund openings both to acknowledge extant interdependence and to create deeper relationships and solidarities.

We offer this volume as a meditation on entangled difference, then, not so much for its own sake but as an invitation for the sake of the planet and its myriad creatures.

Our Purpose

The world stands at a critical juncture. Its human agents can either concretely address the climate devastations and global inequalities pressing in on an ever-evaporating horizon or they can do nothing. In either case, there is no real escape. The planetary degradations caused by the expansions and exploitations of the Anthropocene era make news headlines daily. Food and water shortages are present and future realities. Mass population migrations, driven by both the violence of war and environmental collapse, test the limits of human suffering while challenging the resources of neighboring populations. Profit-seeking investments of capital are destroying noncompliant economies and "nonessential" ecologies alike. Global warming and unpredictable, increasingly extreme weather patterns threaten to destabilize a wide swath of socio- and ecopolitical systems. The picture is bleak.

But it is not inalterably set, *if* we choose to do something rather than nothing.

Admittedly, modernity chose to do something. It sought a global human response to solve dilemmas such as world hunger and lack of education. Where modernity went wrong, however, was to place its trust in progress by means of an increase in capital production—resulting in exploitative uses of natural resources and the impoverishment of global communities. It is now clear how the well-intended motives of *progress* have yielded less than optimum results. Fluid economic borders, transmigrating affluent economies, and democratic capitalisms at the hands of oligarchies have, instead of "lifting all boats,"[7] endangered entire human and other-than-human ecosystems. It is time to do something else—to think new things, to dream new visions, to enact new practices of being with, in, and for the world.

Ideologies of the status quo, however active they may appear on the surface, in fact tend to align with a do-nothing approach. Whether theological or political in tenor, these alignments offer no genuinely alternative practices or visions of renewal for an era marked by technologies of control and mechanisms of exploitation. A direct outgrowth of modernist-capitalist thought, the current era of indifference, rooted as it is in a denial of entangled existence across the planet, has driven diverse ecosystems to the threshold of catastrophe. The primary engines propelling this drive are two dangerous "-isms." *Individualism* and *dualism* function together to perpetuate divisive understandings of transglobal relations, wherein "the one"—be it an individual person or a tribalized collective—is pitted against "others." The exploitative histories of racism, gender discrimination, empire expansion, and neoliberal capitalism attest to the destruction these "-isms" generate. If myths of the detached individual continue to dominate politics and theologies, the status quo and its do-nothing approach just might *progress* the planet's ecosystems toward oblivion.

Despite the power of these isolationist, dualistic, and do-nothing narratives, ecojustice counternarratives persist in their efforts to halt and overturn its bulldozing effects: scientists worldwide, various religious traditions, environmental activists, and concerned global citizens have issued calls to *do something*. Bill McKibben's work with 350.org is developing global networks and grassroots efforts not only to raise awareness about global warming but to resist industries and policies that threaten the environment. Global and interreligious, the Fast for the Climate has attracted influential world leaders as well as folks on the ground giving voice to the planet. Likewise, Pope Francis's *Laudato Si'*, which emphasizes steps to nurture "a new and universal solidarity," has galvanized peoples around the globe.[8] Desires to discover, imagine, and cultivate sustainable ecologies of transformation pulsate from the grassroots to the magisterial. The time is therefore ripe for expanded collaborations across diverse disciplines as a contribution to these movements.

Acutely attuned to the complex interdependence marking all earthly existences, the collected offerings in this volume cross borders, binaries, and belief systems. To describe this multifarious weaving, we adopt the rich metaphor of "entanglement" from the works of feminist theorist Barad and constructive theologian Catherine Keller to signal the most elemental "intra-actions"[9] of life on Earth. *Entangled difference*, then, names the inextricable interplay of distinctive particularity and primordial relationality that constitutes our shared cosmic existence. Working in that spirit, the varied contributions illustrate that effective solidarities require innovation, improvisation, and even *agonism* (a productive tension not to be confused with antagonism). Herein lie no guarantees but instead vibrations of hope in contrast to the apathetic and denialist energies of the status quo. Throughout this volume, the myths of Westernized forms of progress (perpetually in denial about the discarded bodies such "progress" has required) are subverted into narratives of liberation, justice, and sustainable coexistence. In the performative symbols of theology and philosophy, ever in conversation with the social and natural sciences and interwoven with activist and artistic perspectives, this collection suggests a radically relational frame by which we might explore questions of justice, climate change, race, class, and gender alongside alternative ways of engaging the world in all its biodiversity.

As conceived in the West and deployed across colonized spaces, Christian symbols and systems of meaning-making have played complex roles in leading global communities to the current situation. It is absolutely vital that Christianity acknowledge its destructive ecological and economic legacies as well as mine its generative riches for solutions. By locating this volume in Penn State University's World Christianities series, we seek to both learn from the example of such discourses and contribute to the conversation. The United States' theological engagements with postcolonialism and global capitalism are vital, and yet often they fail to listen deeply to the very global voices that can so strongly inform the conversation. In this volume, we seek to contribute uniquely to the ecotheological conversation by mobilizing voices and perspectives from across the globe that can speak to the global-local impact of neo-capitalist systems as well as share alternative perspectives on how to address the inequities and destructions wrought by those systems.

These voices also remind those of us in the United States that Christianity is not isolated, either culturally or religiously. The world Christianities conversation honors a reality too frequently and facilely ignored in the U.S. context, where diversity within Christianity is understood simplistically as conservative versus liberal polarization—and where common ground, in turn, is hard to find. Acknowledging the global scope of religious discourse forces the concomitant awareness that faith is not a singular phenomenon—moreover, that multiplicity is thoroughly entangled. That is, it is one thing to acknowledge the diverse shapes of Christianity that emerge from particular contexts, yet it might also be said that Christianity is a dynamic, multifaceted movement that intertwines all locations. Global and diverse, theological dialogue is characterized more by fluidity and permeability of boundaries than we often acknowledge.

It is precisely for this reason that planetary ecumenism might offer a model for what the contributors are aiming to achieve in this volume on entangled differences. After all, a planetary commitment is the tie that binds, or better the very ground of shared responsibility, that does not allow "privileged" voices to simply exit the conversation. Leaving the proverbial table is simply not an option. Rather, differences must be worked through and seen as resources rather than barriers. Likewise, conversations from a world Christianities perspective are necessarily open to influences from non-Christians and the nonreligious. Although the United States is more globally influenced than ever, communities of faith in the United States too often mistakenly assume their own isolation and function accordingly. The exception to this is more urban areas. Yet, even in megacities, isolationist tendencies remain dominant. Planetary ecumenism at its best models a vital alternative: transreligious dialogue that may also include the nonreligious, as is the case with this volume. While some of the contributors do not identify personally with the Christian tradition, they desire to both speak to that tradition and learn from it.

Finally, this volume shares with a world Christianities perspective that faith is never simply for itself. Rather, it is the trust Christians are called to exercise *for* the world, reflecting our faith's own imperfect ways and seeking to be *with* the beloved other—Creation itself. We therefore offer this multivocal volume in the wise, open spirit of world Christianities, made possible by its own generative transgressions of borders, binaries, and belief systems.

As editors, we have also sought to centrally include both activism and art in what normally would be a purely academic volume. We have interwoven poetry, activist voices, and images among more theoretical chapters. Each essay likewise bears the fingerprints, the entanglements, of activist perspectives with critical theories and theologies emerging out of its encounters with activism. By integrating praxis and *theoria*, the book strives to diversify the lenses by which we human earth-dwellers might interpret our present realities and in turn to inform concrete action. Like a kaleidoscope, where distinctive configurations quickly flow into and out of one another, we juxtapose and weave the theoretical, the activist, and the artistic, convinced that all are necessary to build and sustain coalitions and to inspire a range of acts at once subversive and generative.

A Map

The voices in this volume approach difference and entanglement via diverse avenues as well as methods. In what follows, you will hear echoes of Alfred North Whitehead's process-relationalism, Audre Lorde's academic activism, and Karen Barad's quantum-shaped theories—and many others, resonant yet distinctive and possibly agonistic.

Although we have arranged the volume according to a certain logic, it could have taken many different shapes. The very nature of entangled differences, insofar as one can imagine their breadth, is that they are excessive. Nor do they fit neatly together like a jigsaw puzzle with straight outer edges. We therefore invite readers to engage the volume as they feel drawn. You might begin with those pieces that attract you. But we also encourage you to engage those very titles that may stir discomfort for one reason or another. We likewise invite you to read slowly, even contemplatively in a posture of genuine listening. Whether academic, activist, or artistic, each piece in this volume tells a story. A story of difference, ever entangled.

Each piece reflects on, though does not necessarily offer an answer or solution to, how to live entangled difference generatively rather than destructively. The voices herein celebrate with Lorde, as she voices in the epigraph at the start of the chapter, that it is interdependent differences that provide the unexpected grounds from which we might explore new knowledges and develop both visions for the future and the power to birth such visions into being. Thus, rather than conceive difference as that which necessarily divides creatures into antagonistic relations of destructive manipulation and distorted entanglement, each contribution to this volume invites us all to live into the conviction that difference might just be "that raw and powerful connection from which our personal power is forged."[10]

Our volume opens and closes with circle paintings by artist, pastor, and community activist Scott Neely. *The Light That Encircles Nothingness* (before this introduction) and *Ocean Circle* (at the volume's end) portray the very nonenclosure of entangled differences, alongside their fluidity, their porousness, and the plurality that ever creates yet also exceeds the oneness of planetary life. The paintings, one dark and one bright, likewise echo other contributors' reflections on the spectral range of ecology's colors and its dark, spooky energies.

Catherine Keller sets the stage for the volume with "A Political Theology of Now." She explores how fresh threats of global warming and reactionary capitalism are rapidly contracting time itself. In the face of such frightening developments, Keller uses political theology as a backdrop for her meditation on what she calls the "now time" of planetary contractedness. She suggests that this "now time" might effectively counter the current glorifications of omnipotent power, which while rooted theologically in classic Christian images of God now serve the robustly secular purposes of legitimizing a politics of sovereignty. How might the notion of "now time" open communities of faith or of activism to countervisions?

A pair of poems moves readers from more theoretical imaginings to the concrete realities of violence, public and private. Crystal Tennille Irby's "How We Become" and Sapient Soul's "What If?" usher readers into the realities of gendered and racialized violence. Their images render visceral the terror and pain woven into such mundane moments as children watching Saturday morning cartoons. While Irby's offering illustrates the tragic normalization of violence, Sapient Soul's poem calls her listeners to ask and ask and ask again hard questions, primarily of themselves, that too often escape notice. These poetic voices complicate and implicate theory, driving us into motion.

The volume then turns to two essays that take seriously *intersectionality*, a concept that civil rights activist and critical race theorist Kimberlé Crenshaw coined to convey how various markers of discrimination, mutually informing, shape and position each person uniquely. The essays offer glimpses into the entangled bodies of underprivileged populations in relation to climate change and the globalized market economy while drawing upon biblical and theological resources to deepen their analysis.

Sharon Jacob's "Jezebel and Indo-Western Women" explores the biblical character of Jezebel, who appears in the book of Revelation, as a fitting depiction of how the globalized body of India and the culturally hybrid bodies of India's daughters have been controlled and regulated by means of sexual violence. Jacob shows how issues of race, gender, and sexuality collide with those of nationalism, land, and globalization to produce a destructive ecology of sexual violence. Cynthia Moe-Lobeda's "Climate Change as Race Debt, Class Debt, and Climate Colonialism" explores a distinct yet related global ecological complexity, making a strong case for the intricate links between climate change and both white privilege and class privilege. Who pays the price for the ecological devastations of climate change? Who has access to clean, potable water, and who does not? Moe-Lobeda's unflinching observations ultimately lead her in a constructive direction. She closes her essay by calling privileged earth-dwellers to a moral response that may include practices such as "climate reparations" and primary identities as "climate citizens."

The volume then contemplates powerful instantiations of "deep solidarity." Gail Worcelo, SGM, and Mary Judith Ress both richly describe communities of women who have woven together spirituality, activism, and art in order to cultivate solidarity with one another and with a world in need, including ecological need. Joerg Rieger, theoretically embedded between them, assumes an intersectional approach to "Deep Solidarity" while focusing specifically on the category of class.

Worcelo's "The Mystery of Love in the *Via Collectiva*," written in collaboration with Marg Kehoe, PBVM, reflects on the spiritual practices and insights of thirty-nine women who gather from around the globe through Zoom technology to collectively journey into love, a process and a community they call "Continual Blossoming." Their *via collectiva*, emphasizing connection over oneness, involves meditation through art, inquiry on what is present, and the pursuit of deep connection.

The connectional and communal, as noted earlier, is theopolitical—rich in meaning-making that weaves together narratives of class, race, gender, economics, beliefs, and symbol systems. Unpacking the connectional as political, Rieger argues that the 99 percent, even those in the upper echelons of that group, have more in common with each other than with the top 1 percent. In turn, he calls those who enjoy certain privileges of class and education to engage in practices of deep solidarity rather than put their primary efforts into charity or even advocacy, both of which inadvertently harbor attitudes of separation and condescension. Only deep solidarity, as a disposition and a practice, can fund significantly transformative changes vis-à-vis the global economy and the planet's ecological trajectory.

Meanwhile, in "From Latin America with Love," Mary Judith Ress offers a history of Latin American ecofeminism and the Con-spirando movement/community that has spanned decades—its origins, its aims, its intentions, and its accomplishments. Boldly challenging the violent elements of patriarchal Christianity and joyfully adopting those indigenous perspectives and practices that foster healing, these women, "breathing together," have formed a community at once spiritual and activist. This community addresses some of the most pressing ecological challenges facing Latin America, its peoples, and its land. While the challenges remain dire, like the *via collectiva*, they draw strength and joy from their connections with one another.

The following three chapters engage Pope Francis's encyclical on ecology. While *Laudato Sí* carefully outlines the violent injustices of the global ecological crisis, its inspiration is the very glory, and hence pricelessness, of God's creation. Colorfully celebrating the same, two paintings by José Ernesto Padilla frame the three essays. Expressive of the ecologically entangled differences of creation, the paintings vibrantly depict the exuberance of creaturely interconnection and the fluidity of bodies. In *TitoArt 8*, eyes—whose?—peer out from the coffee plants, seeing yet easily unseen. *TitoArt 12* portrays a body vulnerable yet open, self-possessed yet connected, rooted yet reaching, entangled yet nourished. Together the paintings highlight how creaturely lives, ever bodily entwined, bear pain but also can awaken in us an innate affinity for celebration.

Through Latinx and Latin American eyes, Elaine Padilla's essay, "Spooky Love" invites us into the darkness, proposing for our consideration the kind of love that *spooks*, a normally pejorative term often referring to dark bodies. But, Padilla maintains, such spooky love can awaken us to our own inner cosmos and accompany us through an embodied darkness that may seem far and distant but is, in fact, intimately close. Journeying through this inner darkness can, in turn, affectively stir us toward attitudes and behaviors that nurture rather than annihilate planetary life. Our turning is at once inward and outward. Experiencing the universe as a cosmic lover embracing and being embraced by us, noticing each living thing making manifest its livingness, we can respond with love rather than fright. In listening to nature, bringing to consciousness what is felt, and experiencing anew seemingly remote geometries, we can wage a *fight* in love in order to commonly *dwell* in love.

Teresia M. Hinga's essay, "The Hummingbird Spirit and Care of Our Common Home," also sees loving care as vital to deep and transformative solidarity. Hinga offers an African meditation on the call to practice an integral ecology that is mindful of creaturely interconnectedness and interdependence as expressed in Pope Francis's *Laudato Si'*. Reading the papal encyclical "through African eyes," she places it in fruitful conversation with the indigenous values of awe before God, the centrality of community, the interdependent whole of the universe, and the conviction that all that exists is continually in the process of formation, reformation, and transformation. These beliefs alongside the values of the Green Belt Movement can empower African activists and their allies to develop, disseminate, and sustain practical forms of care for the earth.

Following Hinga, Peter C. Phan examines *Laudato Si'* "with Asian eyes," with particular attention to those aspects of the encyclical most relevant to the Asian context. Noting that scientific, technological, and economic responses to ecological degradation are necessary but insufficient, he insists that cultural, social, philosophical, and religious values have a vital role to play. "An Ecological Theology for Asia" outlines the import of environmental solutions *for* Asia, yet its most compelling contribution is its call for an interreligious ecological theology. Not only is Asia well positioned culturally to model interreligious thinking and practices, but Buddhist and Daoist traditions can complement and correct exclusively Western-Christian perspectives.

14

Padilla's *TitoArt12* colorfully transitions the volume from meditations on *Laudato Si'* to the penultimate pair of theoretical essays. Informed by new materialisms, queer theory, and process-relational thought, these two chapters explore critical theories of identity, change, and meaning-making as resources for engaging the ecological crisis.

Clayton Crockett's essay, "Plasticity and Change," responds to questions of identity and difference through the lens of French philosopher Catherine Malabou. Crockett commends Malabou's notion that plasticity and change are not matters of flexibility and adaptation but much more robustly about resistance, resilience, and the "ability to change conditions, to blow up." This notion of change is, Crockett contends, more helpful than the concepts of identity or difference for negotiating functioning solidarities across gender, race, class, and caste, and can fruitfully serve as grounds for a "political theology of material change and a political ecology of change." Whitney A. Bauman's "Prismatic Identities in a Planetary Context" uses the metaphors of the prism and the color spectrum to widen and deepen reflections on planetary existence. Spectral thinking, says Bauman, enables a homing in on a particular wavelength or problem without abstracting that frequency from the relations that make it particular. It also prepares academics and activists to map how our "ideas, values, and concepts . . . affect actual earth bodies differently and [to] begin to question these unequal distributions of goods and ills." Only from that space can we begin to develop an ethics to address them.

Pivoting once more to praxis, Krista E. Hughes proposes listening as a civic discipline that can strengthen our capacities for mutual understanding. She profiles three technologies of listening created by various community transformation organizations, each with the specific aim of deepening civic life. While sharing commitments to speaking from personal experience, the three models of listening have distinct, if complementary, approaches that range from listening with the body though "resonance practice" to ground-ing conversation in spoken word poetry. Hughes suggests that we can learn from these models as we consider what listening as a civic discipline might entail. Akin to spiritual disciplines, a civic discipline of attentive listening requires that we assume a posture of open receptivity to the unknown, taking the risk of being changed—perhaps even counting on it. Hughes concludes that such a discipline, because it counters prevailing cultural norms of self-protective defensiveness, may be precisely what U.S. culture needs to renew its civic life.

If Keller's essay serves as one bookend for the volume, Dhawn B. Martin's "Xtopia" serves as the other, a complement to Keller's reflections. Drawing on theories of utopianism in conversation with feminist theory, Martin challenges narratives that have become static through convention or caricature. Utopian visions, upon Martin's reading, share many promising qualities: connectivity, contextuality, the asking of questions, the activation of desire, and the balance of creativity and pragmatism. Martin, however, shifts to the language of "xtopias" to capture the best instincts of utopic thinking while (rather literally) creating an open yet unfilled space for the unexpected. The *x* for Martin also serves as a marker of creaturely interdependence (for good and for ill) and a call to work from a space of love. She ultimately proposes that, when approached as multilayered, open, flexible, and provisional projects, xtopias are well equipped to both more carefully diagnose ecosocial injustices and enact practices that engender promising solutions.

Readers might note how *agonism* shapes the structure of the volume's sections. Chapters are coupled or grouped according to resonances, though possibly *agonistic resonances*, as if facing each other in conversation and sharing insights. The volume also unfolds and enfolds geographically. It seeks to thread humans' uneven implications in and responsibilities for the depletion and exploitation of the developing world, which the residents of Global North nations in particular cannot deny. Furthermore, those of us in the Global North must acknowledge, even amplify, the vast contributions and efforts toward an ecological civilization arising from Latin America, Africa, and Asia. Finally, our dialogue in this volume takes us on a journey through multiple dimensions of relationality, where centers and margins become intimately entwined—or better are revealed to have been interwoven all along. Contributors' joint efforts to cross boundaries (racially, sexually, and geographically) compel all of us not only to be *for* fruitful global entanglements but to act—to stand, speak, walk, kneel, sing, cry, shout, pray, dance—in solidarity *with* those whose efforts are calling the planet to live into its entangled reality.

Our Invitation

16   The genesis of this volume was the Tenth International Whitehead Conference, "Seizing an Alternative: Toward an Ecological Civilization," held in Claremont, California, in June 2015. Global in scope, the conference was convened by process scholar–activist John B. Cobb Jr., who has dedicated his life's work to bringing about a vision of "ecological civilization." Central to the conference's structure were "tracks," which allowed sustained, multiday conversations among a small group of people on a focused topic. For four days, about a dozen scholars gathered to share papers and to reflect deeply on the theme of "entangled differences" with a stated aim toward *activist* as much as academic fruits. What you hold in your hands is an evolution of that conversation. Not all the voices here were part of the original conversation, and some of those early voices do not appear individually in this volume. Yet, the volume bears forward the insights and the spirit of that first conversation and all the voices, named and unnamed, entangled therein.

One key thread that emerged in our conversation in Claremont was the transformative power of storytelling. This theme emerged early on as Whitney Bauman critiqued the excessive greening of ecological discourse and invited us to expand our color spectrum in engaging the world. Our last session, facilitated by the Relational Center, led the group in a form of storytelling as a technology for building community, one that involved attuning bodily to resonances. We were all delighted to discover, in a fresh way, storytelling as a vital mode of generatively engaging entangled differences. As the time-bound conversation in Claremont moved toward written form, we editors realized that we wanted to incorporate art of all kinds. Lorde insists that "poetry is not a luxury," and we agree.

Between that first conversation and now, more has happened politically, ecologically, and culturally than we possibly can enumerate. For example, in the span of just a few key weeks of pulling the volume's pieces together for one stage of submission, wild fires were burning out of control in California, Puerto Rico was still facing utter devastation in the wake of Hurricane María, and environmental protections in the United States were being rolled back on a daily basis. Tapping into our entangled differences, working with and through them generatively, is as critical as ever.

We assume we are preaching to the choir. We do not expect among our readers those who deny climate change or humankind's central role in it; those who believe racism, sexism, and homophobia are myths perpetuated to punish the white straight man for his historic success; or those who attribute poverty to laziness or moral laxity. We assume, rather, that our readers are those who consciously *value* difference. We likewise suspect that many of you assume the relational entanglement of reality, for good and for ill. Why, then, do we offer up this range of voices? What is the purpose of this volume?

Quite simply, it is a meditation—multivocal and multiperspectival— on how entangled differences play out in our lives and the life of this planet. And it is an invitation to consider your own perspective and voice as well as your limitations and rough edges in the face of entangled differences. It is this *spirit* of solidarity-building amid entangled as much as any content that we offer to our readers for consideration. To engage in entangled meaning-making is to grapple together with embodying a planetary ecumenism, whether kneeling in lament, marching with ferocity, standing for the water, or telling our story. Ever already entangled, we welcome you to the conversation.

Notes

1. Audre Lorde, "The Master's Tools Will Never Dismantle the Master's House," in *Sister Outsider: Essays and Speeches* (Berkeley, Calif.: Crossing Press, 2007), 111–12.

2. To call our current geological age the *Anthropocene* indicates that human activity has been the dominant shaper of the climate and the environment.

3. Karen Barad, *Meeting the Universe Halfway: Quantum Physics and the Entanglement of Matter and Meaning* (Durham: Duke University Press, 2007), 3.

4. "Matter feels, converses, suffers, desires, yearns, and remembers." Interview with Karen Barad, in *New Materialisms: Interviews and Cartographies*, ed. Rick Dophijn and Iris van der Tuin (Ann Arbor, Mich.: Open Humanities, 2012), 69.

5. Erle C. Ellis, *Anthropocene: A Very Short Introduction* (Oxford: Oxford University Press, 2018), preface.

6. John B. Cobb Jr., *Process Theology as Political Theology* (Philadelphia: Westminster Press, 1982), 10.

7. The image "a rising tide lifts all boats" is meant to suggest that a robust neoliberal market economy ultimately raises living standards and, presumably, quality of life for everyone. Theologian Joerg Rieger, a contributor to this volume, is one major voice among many who have exposed the inaccuracies of this metaphor. See Rieger, *No Rising Tide: Theology, Economics, and the Future* (Minneapolis, Minn.: Fortress Press, 2009).

8. Pope Francis, *Laudato Si': On Care for Our Common Home* (Huntington, Ind.: Our Sunday Visitor, 2015).

9. *Intra-actions* is a term coined by Karen Barad to capture how new materialisms scholars indicate the interrelational complexity that marks even our own internal landscapes—from the subatomic and quantum levels to our affective, precognitive body-consciousness, ever shaped by a certain permeability between the inner and the outer, the material and the ethereal.

10. Lorde, "Master's Tools," 112.

A POLITICAL THEOLOGY OF NOW

Catherine Keller

What happened to our time? How did we lose it?

Whatever the story of our individual mortalities, there extended out from each of us, from us all together, the space of a shared time, the time of a shared space. The sharing was rent with contradiction; we reached no consensus on the fabric of the future, and we could ignore the spatial texture of its temporal bodies or the alpha and the omega of its ages. Our calculations collided, our opposed futures warred, and so left hope drugged or in ruins. But then there was always before us, if we were not fundamentalists, at least a time to rebuild. With the space for a more marvelous togetherness: New Heaven and Earth, utopic horizon, seventh generation, endless rhythm, eternal return, r/evolutionary leap, indifferent timeline or deferred postapocalypse. Or so the stories go. We—"we" the species—had time.

And now we seem to have lost it.

That is what the science of climate unhysterically and relentlessly signals. It appeared, however, that we—"we" the possible public of which you, the reader, are an instance—had a fighting chance of changing course within the narrow window of time that global warming allots. After the 2016 election, however, the window seemed to be slamming shut on a materially viable future for civilization. Politically, we would be too busy responding to the immediate threat to vulnerable human populations—or to the political process itself. With emergencies of white supremacism and other hurricanes, how could we also protect endangered elephants and the Paris climate accord and reorganize the global economy? So, then, am I writing in order to proclaim the window shut?

No, that would perform just the sort of self-fulfilling prophecy of doom that always tempts the Left with paralysis. Conveniently for the Right, we would thus shut ourselves down. And nonetheless: the time is short.

Really I am just quoting 1 Corinthians 7:29: "The appointed time is short." Surely Paul did not mean by "short" some two thousand or so years. Nor was he making an appointment with climate catastrophe. But I did need to make an appointment with Paul—and that is still no easy thing for a feminist theologian with the twentieth-century habit of opposing liberating gospel to sexist/heterosexist/supersessionist/dualist epistle. Nonetheless, in the space of this century, I am in need of ancestral help, of a certain backward depth to time that somehow slows it. And, lo, what did I find but that the New Revised Standard Version's translation ("The appointed time is short") misleads on two counts: the Greek word translated *short* is far more complicated, far more inviting, and indeed far more political: *sunestalmenos* means "gathered in," "contracted."

It was not from biblical scholarship but from the political philosopher Giorgio Agamben's *The Time That Remains*, a meditation on Paul, that I got this clue.[1] Then, also, the appointed of "appointed time" really means "remaining." Agamben does not note that the modifier in his titular phrase may itself be syntactically misplaced and the phrase more accurately translated as "the time is contracted." In other words, Paul is not announcing some predetermined end of the timeline, or programming an imminent appointment with Christ at the Second Coming. This contracted temporality is distinguished from the *chronos* that in its continuum can be calculated, chronologically extended, or concluded. It is instead the time of *kairos*. In Agamben's analysis, "kairos is a contracted and abridged chronos." This captures an intensification through which he channels the political messianism of Walter Benjamin—and so a secularized Jewish "now-time" (*Jetztzeit*), contrasted to the modern homogenization of time and key to current conversations in political theology. The abridgment can be misread as shrinkage. Yet, for Paul, "the kairos is filled full."[2]

As the New Testament scholar L. L. Welborn puts it: "The kairos arrests and suspends chronos."[3] The empty continuity of chronotime is interrupted by a messianic contraction, kin to the gospel teaching of the "kingdom of God": a politico-spiritually charged transformation, imminent and immanent to the now-time of the kairos. So, then, Paul's point will not have been to menace his community with The End but, to the contrary, to dispel the paralyzing affect of doom: "I want you to be free of fears." For as the letter puts it: "For the present *schema* [form, order, schematism] of this world is passing away" (1 Corinthians 7:31). Not the world itself but the existing world order.

In the spirit of fearlessness, may we contemplate together a political theology of *now*? In this Anthropocene moment of mounting crisis, the schema of the world—not the earth itself but the schematism of a civilization based on its long-term stability—does seem to be in political jeopardy. The "political" means first the gathered, the contracted—as *polis*, *civis*, city, the unit of civi/lization. And, as in *The First Urban Christians*, Wayne Meeks classically demonstrated that Christianity has since its urbanization by Paul always been political.[4] It dispersed its theopolitics across the known imperial expanse of its material world. In our time—the chronos of modernity—the mattering world is being degraded by its neo-imperial urban elites into a planet of slums and dumps.

No heirs of either Testament can ignore the material schematism, the economics and the ecologies, densely contracted in the polis: Whore of Babylon, New Jerusalem, or ambiguously vibrant metropolis. *Theology is always already political.*

The Agonistic in Political Theology

And, at the same time but by an inverse theo-logic, *politics is always already theological*. I cannot therefore avoid the following oft-cited postulate from the *Political Theology* (1921) of the German legal theorist Carl Schmitt: "All significant concepts of the modern theory of the state are secularized *theological* concepts."[5] I am, in other words, considering the political in relation to political theology, which itself has not developed primarily as a branch of theology. The phrase *political theology* came into its own as the mockery of a mockery: as Schmitt's sardonic reversal of its earlier deployment by the anarchist Mikhail Bakunin, who had used it in derision of fellow revolutionaries still partially motivated by their Christian faith. The phrase has served in the past couple decades largely as a discursive tool passed among postmodern philosophers of the Left—from Agamben to Žižek.

Indeed, if political theology designated just a room in the edifice of theology, it would now be of little use to theology itself. Inasmuch as the inherently political animus of progressive religion (the first context of this essay) seeks zones of resonance and intensifications of solidarity with massively secular social movements, it cannot simply proclaim its own relevance. But it can welcome the recognition by political theorists of a largely hidden theology already at play in politics. Of course, that political recognition is then complicated by the huge difference between theologies and therefore between the forms of their secularization.

The concept of political theology, however, had been claimed by theologians of the post-Holocaust German left starting half a century ago. In a movement of European solidarity with the fresh voices of liberation theology in the Global South, Johannes Metz, Jürgen Moltmann, and Dorothee Sölle freed the phrase from the Nazi association with which Schmitt had tainted it.[6] But it seems that "political theology" felt too generic, too Eurocentric, to catch on among the progressive Christians of the United States in the following decades. The phrase perhaps threatened to dilute the bursting particularism of the liberation, feminist, Black, sexual, or ecological identities. And so it is now coming back into theology largely by way of secular and non-Christian political theory. I must therefore clarify that I am not having recourse to political theology in order to get finally disentangled from the identity politics of the religious (or any other) Left. I am rather thinking together with any who work to *gather* a de-essentialized, dense, indeed contracted, entanglement of our differences: not solid but solidary. It takes constructive theological form in what Moltmann has in the present century called "the solidarity of hope."

Since the counterrevolutionary Schmitt has ironically provoked a new wave of secular Left interest in theology, his view of the political appears oddly illumining. In the present epoch, one who in the relevant past put his brilliance at the disposal of a fascist state may help us come to terms, from within a certain dark inside, with the unthinkable that we are having, now across a significant swathe of the earth, to think. The powerful waves of an authoritarian populism with neofascist tendencies may not prevail in Europe or even here. But surely that danger will be lowered only to the extent that pluralist and democratic sensibility addresses the felt need for communal identity that is being manipulated into the phobic rage of a racist, ethnoreligious, indelibly sexist nationalism.

Schmitt had in the 1920s defined the political in terms of the formation of a "we." His thinking thus focuses on the construction of collective identities, as formed through conflict and antagonism. As Chantal Mouffe demonstrates, Schmitt poses therefore a "false dilemma." Either the heterogeneity leads to "the kind of pluralism which negates political unity and the very existence of the people," or "there is unity of the people, and this requires us expelling every division and antagonism outside the people."[7] Schmitt, of course, advocates the latter. "The people" cannot be sustained through free discussion but only by decision and exclusion. In this context, as Schmitt proclaims: "A group of people only become a unified and coherent subject to the extent that they share a common enemy." The common good is thus a parasite upon the common enemy. "Tell me who your enemy is and I'll tell you who you are."[8]

For any ethics steeped in Christianity, it is tempting simply to read the Schmittian notion of politics as friend versus foe as itself the foe. *Our* "we"—as in, for example, we friendly religious progressives—wants amity, not enmity. (Hand-scrawled "Love trumps hate!" signs sprouted overnight at seminaries and churches like mine on November 9, 2016.) But I cannot see how to deny that the one in whom this hatred was so effectively embodied in the contemporary moment is properly called an enemy. Nor can I deny the hope that such inescapable enmity can join a critical mass of us in new forms of solidarity—a solidarity that is not just pro-love and justice but militantly *against* the emergent neofascist collective. Love your enemies, okay, amen. But that does not mean that they are not your enemies. Biblically speaking, it is the love of the alien, the immigrant—"You shall also love the stranger, for you yourselves were strangers in Egypt" (Deuteronomy 10:19)—that gets radicalized and, in the Second Testament, directed even at the enemy. For Schmitt's Christianity, however, neither alien nor foe are loveable; rather, both are smoothly collapsed into one Other. He defines "the enemy" as "the other, the stranger; and it is sufficient for his nature that he is, in a specifically intense way, existentially something different and alien."[9] So one sees how in the 1930s, he could support the production of the Jew as unifying enemy. If the political collective comes down to oppositional identity, the religio-racialization of an Other becomes the most effective means to essentialize at once an enemy—and therefore a *we*.

But can *we* then avoid playing a mirror game of antagonisms, opposing the oppositionalism of our foe-producing foes? If, alternatively, we avoid hostility, do we fall back on a disempowering civility, an inclusivism invested in the liberal rationality that Schmitt not without reason deemed a failure in the Weimar of the 1920s? A certain civility may form the very basis of the civic: of the polis, of the political. But did its fusion with secular liberalism and then economic neoliberalism render it increasingly ineffectual in forging its own democratic *we*—indeed, in the United States, in holding together coalitions inclusive of even civically like-minded religious and irreligious citizens?

Mouffe suggests a third way beyond both liberal consensualism and mere antagonism. She calls it *agonism*, which signifies not enmity but struggle. Taking seriously Schmitt's critique of the liberal political expectation of rational consensus, she argues that "a healthy democratic process calls for a vibrant clash of political positions and an open conflict of interests. If such [a clash] is missing, it can too easily be replaced by a confrontation between non-negotiable moral values and essentialist identities."[10] In a parallel vein, the political philosopher William Connolly names as key to a working democracy the practice of "agonistic respect." Such agonism resists the resentment religious or economic—that fuels antagonism and its spirit of retaliation.[11]

Connolly has long warned of the dangers of hubris and resentment in late modern capitalism, demonstrating how this resentment fueled the unlikely fusion of the religious and the political right over several decades in the late twentieth century. The "we" of what he dubbed the "evangelical-capitalist resonance machine"[12] may be now taking odd, self-contradictory turns, but it shows no signs of diminishing political force. Nor does its antagonism. A resentment against fellow citizens who seem to be getting something for nothing—economic entitlement, sexual pleasure, social dignity—fuses, Connolly suggests, with a Nietzschean ressentiment against the fragilities of earthly life, of mortality, and so of time itself, of time's "it was."[13]

As an alternative, the ethic of respectful agonism does not await the cessation of struggle, nor does it depend on consensus for action. So we may infer that it does not erase the agonies of time, let alone those routinely inflicted by systemic antagonism. We might also want to amplify—that is, render audible—the relation of agonism to *agony*. This lets us support the work of grief and foster the practices of lament, in the face of despair.[14] The refusal to struggle and sometimes to agonize together over difference, including the differences up close, means the repression of the political space in which "a vibrant clash of political positions" can take place. Then the possibility of a shared good, a common weal, gets defeated in advance. This is no mere problem of the Right. Beyond its avowed diversity, the Left has failed dismally to struggle faithfully, respectfully, with difference, even with neighborly difference, let alone with enmity.

Critical Difference: On Politics and Power

So it is tempting to define the political—never reducible to politics—quite simply as the struggle for a common good. But the common cannot gather unless the struggle remains open and avows its agonies. Nor does the common have any meaning apart from its materiality. That shared state of embodiment may call for no less than the "earth commons" of Vandana Shiva, in her protest against the Euro-colonial history of the enclosure of the commons. Of course, one asks immediately, "Whose common good?" So an honest commons can only materialize as indissociable from what radical race theory calls "the undercommons": a public that has lost hope in formal democracy but persists in resistance and in self-organization.[15]

Does coalition with those with good reason for their hopelessness (e.g., Afropessimists, or the "no future" of Edelman's queer theory, or *Embracing Hopelessness* as theological gesture) then not oblige one to give up the solidarity of hope?[16] No doubt, from the perspective of an antagonizing purity. Solidarity with the hopeless, however, obliges one not to forfeit hope but to keep it honest and, therefore, struggling. This is to hold its collective accountable to the asymmetrical distribution of the agonies, to differences beyond inclusion,[17] to the failure of the schematism of civilization, to the threat to any commonly mattering world.

More precisely, then, I would characterize the political as *collective self-organization across critical difference*. Self-organization characterizes the open process in which complex systems emerge, if not always from emergency, always at the edge of chaos. The edge of chaos in science refers to a phase transition in emergent systems; complexity requires order but not too much of it, in evolutionary as well as revolutionary assemblages. A collective self-organizes to redirect a given system, or to protest against it, or to shape a new one. But the self-organizing does not stop unless politics does—and with it the creative struggle amid and across difference. This is one reason for theology to read creation as the self-organizing complexity at the edge of chaos, on "the face of the deep."[18]

Connolly often solicits complexity science for political theory, in a universe "far from equilibrium, nonlinear and full of irreversible processes."[19] Its multiple temporalities demand a swarming new planetary public. It allies itself with what *Cloud of the Impossible* inscribes theologically as an infinite complication, a barely speakable *complicatio*, or "folding together," of entangled difference. "We inhabit," Connolly writes, "an entangled world in which the best hope is to extend and broaden our identities, interests, and ethos of interconnectedness as we multiply the sites of political action."[20]

Yet, how shall we—we who recognize our cohabitation—"broaden our ethos of interconnectedness" at this moment in time when time itself is contracting? Or is the question, rather: how shall we *not*? What if in the midst of crisis we read our planetary interdependence precisely as contraction, as a *complicatio*, that does not fold differences down but gathers them together? Does it not suggest a strategy for recapturing political energy, recycling some—perhaps just enough—wasteful antagonism into sustainable agonism?

The time of critical difference signifies the space of rupture: the interruption of a glaze of sameness by the difference that constitutes the relation. The question for political theology is here whether it is kairos or mere collapse that ruptures the calculable chronos of a homogenized history. For while chronos holds to the simplification that drives the identities of antagonism, kairos evokes the agonism of emergent complexity.

It is crucial to recognize that the "critical difference" of political struggle demands the deep sense of *critical*, from the Greek *krinein*, to discern or judge, to *decide*—as linked to *krisis*, crisis. Critical difference refers to a crisis in which it is necessary to act: this is why we gather not just communally but assemble politically. These crises are frequent in any collective, routinely of minor import, often major, but they prevent the illusion that a common good has been established even in theory, let alone in practice. They are the difference of community from itself. Critical differences—of perspective, identity, or situation—create crisis and require decision: they constitute the political.

We have now fallen again under the laconic gaze of Carl Schmitt, who has been waiting to remind us of the other main postulate of *Political Theology*: "Sovereign is he who decides on the exception," meaning in the emergency. Indeed, the power of the sovereign state is contracted into the person of the leader who decides what counts as a state of emergency, the lawgiver who may suspend the law.[21] So it is this exceptional power of the sovereign to decide, in what "he" decides is an exceptional crisis, that proves the rule of sovereignty itself.

It is right here, to the apex of power—to the exception—that Schmitt nails theology. If all modern political concepts are secularized theology, it is because historically "the omnipotent God became the omnipotent lawgiver." This transfer of the exceptional power from above invests theology in the law of the state: "The exception in jurisprudence is the miracle in theology."[22] Schmitt here cunningly paraphrases Kierkegaard: "The exception is more interesting than the rule. The rule proves nothing; the exception proves everything. . . . In the exception the power of real life breaks through the crust of a mechanism that has become torpid by repetition."[23] He thus mobilizes Kierkegaard against universalism—whether Hegelian, liberal, or Marxist. But he fails to mention that Kierkegaard goes on to say, quite dialectically after all, that "the exception is reconciled in the universal."[24] Of course, it is difficult to deny the torpidity of the liberal party machine, which has left "the power of real life" to break through, over and over, on the right (in such moments of sovereign vulgarity as: "At the request of many, and even though I expect it to be a very boring two hours, I will be covering the Democrat Debate live on twitter!").[25]

For Schmitt, the boringly bureaucratic liberalism merges with the democracy of "everlasting conversation" (*ewiges Gespraech*). This modernist political dissipation is for him inseparable from the liberal Christianity that "banished the miracle from the world." Politically and metaphysically, "the rationalism of the Enlightenment rejected the exception in every form."[26] Interestingly, he also blames early twentieth-century experiments in reorganizing gender. So he gets in an early blow against the "anarchists who see in the patriarchal family and in monogamy the actual state of sin."[27] Too much hermeneutics—indeed too much *her*—undermines the potency of the sovereign Christian God and with *Him* the state. Egalitarian disorder disrupts the capacity to act decisively in the time of emergency. That Schmitt soon found his sovereign in the Führer reveals where, in the exception, the racial and sexual politics of antagonism trends.

The point is not, however, that fascism flows inevitably from sovereign exceptionalism—any more than that divine dictatorship is the necessary effect of the doctrine of omnipotence. Rather, when crisis intensifies, authoritarianism has its best chance, precisely as breaking through the torpor of flaccid systems. It is then in pragmatic recourse to the trope of divine omnipotence that *Political Theology* culminates. Schmitt salutes the reactionary Spanish Catholic philosopher de Maistre's "reduction of the state to the moment of decision, to a pure decision not based on reason and discussion and not justifying itself; that is, to an absolute decision created out of nothingness."[28] Anything else for him is torpid universalism—or else anarchy and chaos. Communist, socialist, anarchist, or liberal, these irreconcilable differences are fused by Schmittian sovereignty into one galvanizing foe.

"Decision created out of nothingness" expresses newness, power, the force of will against any odds. It certainly ruptures the rationalized chronos, the homogenized time of a secularized modernity. It mimics the kairotic breakthrough. But its absolute enacts less the Pauline kairos than the *post*biblical presumption of the *creatio ex nihilo*: not an in-gathering now-time but upon a purity of origin. The old doctrine of creation as the sheer exceptionalism of origin does doubtless interrupt a view of time as endless continuum. But it is a mistake to presume that it presents the only alternative spatiotemporality. I have argued elsewhere that the biblical narrative supports neither the omnipotent decision in the void nor the empty continuity of a cycle or a line of time. The decisiveness of the Genesis *Elohim* lacks the purity of the nothingness: indeed, it contracts in itself not a nothing but "the deep"—what Augustine called the "nothingsomething."[29]

A Schmittian political theology can admit no hermeneutics of creation from that oceanic chaos, the dark and indeterminate, indelibly Jewish, *tehom*. Indeed, no straight story of creatio ex nihilo—whatever its politics—will tolerate the counterdoctrine one may call *creatio ex profundis*. For Genesis (which means "becoming") itself begins to read as an "everlasting conversation." Elohim calls, the becoming creatures respond with *decisive* creativity, and Elohim answers back in delight "It is good," drawing even ocean and earth into the evolutionary cocreativity of a self-organizing *chaosmos*.[30] Thus, reading Genesis through the lens of "the democracy of fellow creatures" deconstructs at the same time centuries of anti-ecological reading of the *imago dei*, which we may now call "anthropic exceptionalism."[31]

Creation in its every kairos[32] signifies neither the exception nor the rule. Instead, it performs the *inception*. It is the chance of the *novum*, the possibility that urges us to begin again, at a present moment of chaos, of crisis, of creation, in the imagination of a politics resisting each self-declared exceptionalism and exercising a decisiveness irreducible to sovereignty.

Mindful Mobilization

Without, then, acceding to any secularizations of omnipotence, we may nonetheless borrow Schmitt's recognition of the hidden operation of theological motifs in secularized form. That is political theology, and as such it marks a transdisciplinary back door through which Christian theology today may enter a wider—sometimes secular, sometimes postsecular—political conversation. This does not commit us to his nostalgia for theocracy, nor to the history of exceptionalisms it sanctifies.

Let us note that Schmitt's monarchical sovereignty is recognizable early in Christianity, at least as early as the fourth-century Bishop Eusebius, Constantine's house theologian. "And surely," Eusebius writes, "monarchy far transcends every other constitution and form of government; for that democratic equality of power, which is its opposite, may rather be descried as anarchy and disorder."[33] Eusebius mobilizes the unifying force of monotheism against all multiplicity and equality (in monarchical contradiction, anticipating that of his Catholic defender Schmitt, to the then crystallizing doctrine of the egalitarian trinity).

The theo-logic of the sovereign exception enthroned as the rule of the world yields a long and potent series of political exceptionalisms. It begins with the imperial Christian supremacism, its corollary religious exclusivism (*extra ecclesiam nulla salvus*), and its dehistoricized Christ, who rules precisely as absolute ontological exception rather than by human example. That sovereign Christology powers up the dominion of Man (*sic*), investing in the anthropocentric exceptionalism that would later drive, in secularized form, the whole modern nature-conquering project. And, pressing fast forward, this political Christology of the exceptional people lands right at the antimonarchical and secular origin, ironically, of United States democracy.

Here I turn to the genealogy of American exceptionalism offered by womanist theologian Kelly Brown Douglas. "In an effort to establish the antiquity of the Church of England [in its break from the Vatican]," Brown Douglas writes, "research was encouraged into the . . . history, and politics of Anglo Saxons."[34] For two centuries, this research centered on Tacitus's *On the Manners of the Germans*, which describes the blue-eyed tribes that the English would claim as their ancestors. It nourished, at the same time, participatory governance. "According to Tacitus, within the various tribes 'the whole tribe' deliberated upon all important matters, and most final 'decisions' rest with the people." This proto-democracy fed such radical experiments as the Levelers, Puritans, and Pilgrims. And so the Anglo-Saxon myth came to America through the English reformers: "They considered themselves the Anglo-Saxon remnant [New Israel, city on the hill] that was continuing a divine mission . . . traced beyond the woods of Germany to the Bible."[35] The kairos of exodus stirred—as it did in all the radical movements of Europe—the politics of the new polis: new self-organization across an ocean of critical difference.

Once settled in its New World, Anglo-Saxon exceptionalism soon shifts toward an overt and *secularized* racism. Benjamin Franklin would write that not only is all "Africa black or tawny, Asia chiefly tawny," but that most Europeans including, "Russians and Swedes, are generally of what we call a swarthy complexion; as are the Germans also, the Saxons only excepted, who with the English make the principal body of white people on the face of the earth." So Franklin muses: "I could wish their numbers were increased. And while we are scouring our planet, by clearing America of woods, and so making this side of our globe reflect a brighter light to the eyes of inhabitants in Mars or Venus, why should we in the sight of superior beings, darken its people? Why increase the sons of Africa, by planting them in America?" So, yes, this extraplanetary whimsy offers a *racist* logic for opposing the transatlantic slave trade. A political theology of the Anthropocene moment takes in the *eco*racial takeout of this dream—of a bright and shining nation stripped at once of dark woods and dark people. (Note that "exception" comes from *excipere*, the Latin for "to take out.")

29

Brown Douglas demonstrates that "the narrative of Anglo-Saxon exceptionalism is America's exceptionalism."[36] And we add now that it hooks right into the old Christian and the modern anthropocentric exceptionalism. But its race narrative gathered, in the face of mounting crises of difference, a defining force. The challenge to national unity became the multiplicity of other immigrant stocks, a fact of difference that was felt as emergency by the late nineteenth century: "President Theodore Roosevelt feared 'race suicide.' . . . It was the construction of 'whiteness' that worked to resolve the contradiction between America's anglo saxon and immigrant identity. Whiteness signified that the immigrants were anglo saxon enough." In other words, a versatile religio-politics of race fuels the secularized galvanizations of a *we* versus a *they*—a *we* to be taken out, unitary, purified of the dark taint of diversity. The complexity of the multiple—of African or Latin American or Asian or Muslim provenance—operates in great asymmetrical histories of entangled difference, in which chaos often works creatively. But at any crisis point, sovereign whiteness can curdle into unity. The racial *they* then becomes the object of antagonism inasmuch as they resist their subjection, threatening the *we* with insubordination, intermarriage, or insurrection—they become aliens cast in the role of the foe. J. Kameron Carter shows in *Race: A Theological Account* that it is first the medieval European racialization of the Jew that reorganizes the human in terms of race (rather than language, ethnos, wealth, faith, citizenship).[37] So we might say that the race machine is from the start a modernization of the Christian supersessionism that takes something called Christianity out of its Judaism, someone called Jesus out of his Jewish body, something called *christos* out of its unwhite messianicity.

If, in other words, the take-out exceptionalism works to take the sovereign out of the law, as in *above* it, it at the same time functions to take the religio-racial Other out of the *we*, as *beneath* the law. So the culture of white exceptionalism within our presumptive democracy retains a deep ancestral bond with the antidemocratic exceptionalisms that precede it, and they energize the concept of sovereignty both within and against liberal democratic governance. The point now for a political theology cannot, of course, be that we as a "people" might take ourselves out of all notions of sovereignty—becoming thereby exceptions to the exception. But in the interest of the social and ecological justice we need now, we might mobilize our constitutive impurities mindfully. And so potentially more powerfully.

Charisma, Sovereign, or Messianic

Early in this millennium, it was particularly his attention to a sovereign exceptionalism operative within the European politics of immigration and the United States' "war on terror" that stirred Giorgio Agamben's engagement of Schmittian sovereignty on the one hand and the Pauline messiah on the other. Agamben is, for present purposes, the most fetching of the leftist philosophers who have discovered at once political theology and Pauline epistle. (Feel free to call the genre "Paulitical theology.") Agamben engages Paul by way of such leading Jewish thinkers of the period of the Second World War as Walter Benjamin and Jacob Taubes in *their own* complicated joint engagements with Schmitt and with Paul. In his development of this generative intertextuality, Agamben cuts afresh through the long history of the supersessionist misreading of Paul as at once an opponent of Jewish law and a proponent of unquestioning subordination to "the governing authorities" (Romans 13:1). Agamben can then, with exegetical precision, distinguish Paul's sublation of "the law" not as a disregard but as a fulfilment, pleroma, from any state of exception that would indefinitely suspend it.

Provoked by the United States Patriot Act of 2001 to write *State of Exception*, Agamben explains of that titular state that it "appears increasingly as technique of government rather than an exceptional measure."[38] Regarding the routine United States violations of international law by way of torture and imprisonment, Agamben concludes that "the state of exception has today reached its maximum worldwide deployment." We should not let his fast-response hyperbole conceal the longer-term relevance: "The normative aspect of law can thus be obliterated and contradicted by a governmental violence that—while ignoring international law externally and producing a permanent state of exception internally—nevertheless still claims to be applying the law."[39] Contemplating Schmitt's conception of rule by suspension of the rules, Agamben warns against the collapse of the distinction of two powers into one another: *potestas*, which is "normative and juridical," and *auctoritas*, which names an "anomic and metajuridical" authority emanating from the personality of the leader. When these two fuse in one person, "the juridico-political system transforms itself into a killing machine." So, then, "to interrupt the working of the machine that is leading the West toward global civil war," these potent forces must be kept apart. In this analysis, Agamben is channeling Walter Benjamin, who had written in the face of twentieth-century fascism that the "state of exception had become the rule."[40]

If sovereignty has recently again managed a game-changing fusion of potestas and auctoritas, it lacks the dignity of the Latin but boasts the power of a Caesar with nukes. So in the currency of a more recent "now," a *Lawfare* blog post by legal theorist Quinta Jurecic offered rapid post–election 2016 help. Considering Agamben, she analyzes "the nightmares of those who thought they saw Schmitt in the form of George W. Bush." While the Bush administration certainly saw an intentional turn toward an aggressive view of executive power, Jurecic avers that, however narrowly, the "fundamental structure of the rule of law itself has remained standing." So, she asks, did Agamben cry wolf? "Our new President-elect . . . now poses an interest-ing problem for the Schmittian revival: have we now, eight years after Bush left office, elected our first Schmittian President? . . . The crucial bit of that Aesop fable about the boy who cried wolf, after all, is that the wolf actually does show up at the end. So, is Trump the Schmittian wolf that Bush was not?"[41] Displaying little by way of sophisticated awareness of law beyond the law-and-order campaign slogan, with its racialized, sexualized potes-tas, the forty-fifth president had always been characterized, in admiration or dismay, as one who does not play by the rules. Therein lay his fateful charisma. So he bequeaths to U.S. history its most farcically extreme exam-ple of the aggressive self-authorization of the "exception."

Agamben's notion of auctoritas develops Max Weber's concept of the charismatic leader. Weber had contrasted the charismatic, in religion and in politics, to both the "traditional" (conservative) and the "legal" (administra-tive/bureaucratic) styles of leadership. Charisma characterized the "certain quality of an individual personality, by virtue of which he is set apart from ordinary men and treated as endowed with supernatural, superhuman, or at least specifically exceptional powers or qualities."[42] For Weber, charisma remains in itself ethically neutral. It may work for good as well as for ill. Its theological background is manifest in the originators of religious move-ments. Weber offers the example of St. Francis.

In terms of the temporalities of sovereignty, we might consider that traditional leadership repeats a normative past, whereas democratic or socialist dependence on legal institutions presumes a progressive gradualism. The charismatic, however, leads from an intense present tense—a "now-time" that can rupture the homogeneity of chronos. The "exceptional powers" may excite the fusion of auctoritas and potestas that pumps up the popular strongman and his killing machine. Or, to the contrary, the religious aura may glow through its secularizations as *charis*—"grace," after all. These may manifest in the kairos of a Mahatma Gandhi or a Martin Luther King Jr. On the one hand, it irrupts the sovereign charisma of the bully; on the other, it surges the messianic charism of love.

Messianic Collectivity

Opposed secularizations express opposed political theologies: the exception of top-down omnipotence and the exemplar of its agonizing alternative. In this opposition, however, the messianic charisma does not compete with the potestas of its antagonists. It practices not the pacifying acquiescence often identified with forgiveness but what, in honor of its theological radicalism, I want to call an amorous *agonism*. It lacks potestas but conveys auctoritas. It is gifted with what Benjamin—on the verge of his death in the attempt to flee the killing machine—says every generation has been endowed with: "a *weak* Messianic power, a power to which the past has a claim."[43] It gazes backward with his now-iconic citation of Paul Klee's *Angelus Novus*, the angel of history contemplating in horror the unredeemed losses of the past. The collective traumas, the lynchings, the camps, the bombings. And now we add—the hurricanes, the floods, the fires, the extinctions of populations both human and nonhuman.

If, then, amid chaos this weak power inaugurates the space of a new time, it may signify the barest of beginnings. The exception swerves into the inception. But in that swerve, this beginning does not abstract the present from its past—a charismatic temptation no doubt—but contracts in itself its history and its lament. Nor does the passion of "being moved" sever the struggle from the desire for the not-yet, the eros that inflames an amorous excess.[44]

That weak power has also been encoded, Paulitically speaking, as "God's weakness" (1 Corinthians 1:25) and comes bearing its cross. It carries an agony never quite erased by triumph and its "crucifixions."[45] And so it unleashes a history of struggle that is never quite terminated by power. In fact, the cross performs a double coding, of both the sovereign antagonism and the amorous agonism, the opposed world schemas intersecting. The one inspires a long and fitful struggle for the *basileia tou theou*, the kingdom of the least, and above him hangs a sign that reads "The King of the Jews," in sovereign ridicule of the messianic promise. The ultimate irony came later. As Alfred North Whitehead put it in the final chapter of *Process and Reality*: "The church gave unto God the attributes which belonged solely to Caesar."[46] Of course, Whitehead's early resistance to the doctrine of the omnipotence of the unmoved mover, political and metaphysical, has fomented the movement of process theology, with its impressive ecological, economic, and political practices.

Without reference to his contemporary Schmitt, Whitehead captures the core problematic of political theology: "God is not to be treated as an exception to all metaphysical principles, invoked to save their collapse. He is their chief exemplification."[47] God, in other words, is not the all-controlling creator from nothingness, who, as the absolute exception, lays down the rules and intervenes at will to impose them. God here signifies no longer the immaterial, immutable, atemporal transcendence. Divinity becomes now, instead, the space of all times, the *oikos* of all becomings, itself also becoming. In the process-relational ontology, every now-moment is a materialization and so a recapitulation, of its history, its world—it "repeats in microcosm what the universe is in macrocosm."[48] In other words, each creature can be read as a *contraction* of its past universe.

The world is what is the matter with us. And so the figuration of divinity here exemplifies the cosmology of interdependent creatures in their moment-by-moment processes of becoming. The charis is given as the faint lure of possibility, at any given now-time, and not as the sovereign intervention in its state of emergency. Its messiah preached with auctoritas and without potestas the humble possibility—fitfully realized and in its "weakness" often trumped—of an earthly collective of just love.

We may in effect distinguish between the ongoing effects of two historical styles of self-organization, two great currents of secularization, two political theologies: that of a *sovereign omnipotence* and that of a *messianic collectivity*. The top-down One and its exceptional percent, vacillating now between smooth global control and its "shock creation machine,"[49] faces off against the in-gathering, *sunestalemnos*, of the counterexceptional—but gifted and potentially extraordinary—collective. The latter may collect itself in socially democratic or democratically socialist publics in which self-organization does not omit the undercommons and "the least of these" (Matthew 25). Its contractions may, in the now-time, persist as "birth pangs" of our mattering world (Romans 8), despite our failures or because of them.[50] As the time of our time contracts, the kairos retains its history as its own complexity, in a recapitulation that minds the agonies without essentializing them. It signals—in the face of victorious vulgarity—the undefeated vulnerability of a terrestrial creativity, which is to say, of the creation itself. We may have to start again, even from scratch. But never from nothing: "scratch" signifies a mark or a wound, not a nothing. The messianic collects not around the *nihil* of omnipotence nor around its collapse into impotent nihilism.

One might in the light of its messianicity read against Schmitt another of his contemporaries: Ernst Bloch discerns the biblical eschatologies, earthly apocalypses, and "Christian social utopias" as the source of all Western revolutions, democratic and socialist—indeed of what we politically call hope.[51] But then "true hope moves in the world, via the world," expressing a "not-yet," he wrote, "which in the core of things drives toward itself, which awaits its genesis in the tendency-latency of process."[52] Thus, genesis and eschaton, creation and new creativity, churn up a feedback loop of kairotic possibility.[53] If dislodged from the lingering linearism of a modernist faith in dialectical progress, this possibility does not dislodge itself from its now in the delusional optimism of an assured future. Rather, it grounds itself in the now—the grounding of earth, not a foundation,[54] recycles the past, contracts, and composts its hope as "real potentiality."[55] Therefore, it grows the loving struggle of a vulnerable present, a "hazardous business."[56] Its public urgency requires the recollection of its own sociality and so its new self-collection—for which it does not postpone or predict the not-yet so much as it begins to materialize it—to in-gather, to contract it. So its hope does not pacify—it activates. And as it enfolds in consciousness the political theology that had been lurking in its shadows, it recaptures not just the prophetic eschatology of the First Testament, not just its messianic inception in the gospel kingdom of God; it also rediscovers Paul the militant, the one who has reappeared even in such bluntly atheist Marxists as Badiou and Žižek. It is the prophetic thread of radical futurity that throws open a door for the political theology of now.

The Narrow Gate of Now

Through the door spills the whole history of collective struggles for justice, divergently secularized in breakthrough moments of resistance, revolution, democratic socialism, satyagraha, civil rights, Occupy Wall Street, Black Lives Matter–ing, queer cruisings of utopia, women's marches accompanied by pink pussies across the planet, surging local alliances to contract rather than expand fossil fuel use, and, I pray, new surges, movements, and actions that postdate this publication. The space-time of inceptions continues to pose a political history, endlessly complicated by its own charismatic *kairoi*, alternative to the chronology of sovereign domination.

The inception means actual novelty, not ideological purity. Sometimes the struggle is to shift sovereign power itself back from its killing machines and toward a more common good. Let us remember that the exception takes itself out—out of any human or planetary commons. We must help it take itself right on out of power, and so work beside and sometimes within any institutional and legal authorities that may collaborate. That means to muster the amorous agonism by which we may gather, contract, and so simultaneously grow, our alternative "we."

On this planet, time continues to contract. But crisis need not reduce our critical difference to antagonism (which our foes will always do more effectually). What we are unconditionally against need not define us even when it gathers us; we might just twist emergency into the emergent agonism of a new public. Does it not emerge even now? Something fierce, fresh, promising, a charisma of self-organization at the edge of chaos. Within our Abrahamic branches, as they tangle with one another, might we not more boldly proclaim the messianic commons? And beyond them, as they entangle a growing range of planetary wisdoms, assemblages, and negotiations for new solidarities of hope, the amorous agonism translates deftly through and beyond any particular theological metaphors. The chance of a planetary common good, of self-organization for ecosocial justice, collects across its own critical differences. Its now has come, it has been betrayed, it comes again, now again, as the not-yet of the "wild possibilities."[57] Not that we—any we—will be or will *deliver* the messiah. Our struggle does not await a charismatic exception to take us out of our crisis. But might it *take in* instead the grace of the inception?

Still, at this moment, such hope strains against the impossible. Poisons of racialized-sexualized-financialized-Americanized, climate-degrading, pussy-'n-earth-grabbing neofascism are penetrating our common world, our collapsing *schema*. But when was the biblical notion of hope, for that matter any honest hope, mistakable for optimism? Optimism and pessimism keep chronos straight; hope pumps kairos.

36

We noted in opening that Agamben nimbly traces kairos through Walter Benjamin's hidden Paulinism of the now-time: "History," writes Benjamin, "is the subject of a structure whose site is not homogenous, empty time, but time filled by the presence of the now."[58] As a Marxist, Benjamin found that the homogeneity had, in its absorption in a view of inevitable progress, betrayed the working-class struggle in Germany. He opposes to the chronos of modern temporality the *Jetztzeit*: *ho nun kairos*. The Jews, he writes, "were prohibited from investigating the future," but neither was "the future turned into homogenous, empty time." The final sentence: "For every second of time was the narrow gate through which the Messiah might enter."[59] And that is precisely the moment of what he calls a "monstrous abbreviation"—*ungeheure abbrevatur*, a recapitulation, or the messianic crystallization. It contracts an immense history into itself.[60]

Is this, then, the alternative to the window slammed apocalyptically shut? As in the Pauline *sunestalemnos*, one hears the contraction of time itself not as closure but as dis/closure (*apokalyptein*). If in this imaginary the entire world is undergoing the contractions of a birth, this provides no ready reassurance. There is nothing comfortable about the pressure of those birth pangs of the possible; so much has already miscarried.[61]

So, practically speaking: do we radicalize our voices in more effective intersections between our differences, our burning issues of immigration, race, climate, capitalism, sexuality? Or, differently, do we reach out in more effective populism to that white working class so seduced now into letting racism eclipse economics? Shall we work locally, nationally, or internationally? With what spectrum of a party and its politics shall we collaborate? Indeed, shall we in the United States fight to reassemble our democracy, or to assemble something better? Do we oppose all language of sovereignty or multiply and democratize it, recognizing, for example, its crucial role in the Global South and in the food sovereignty movement?[62] And considering the political theologies in play, in overt conservatism, in progressive pluralism, or in civil religion, when do we stay secular in our discourse? And when, if, for instance, we are Christians, do we inject ritual flashes of the ancient dissident prophetic hope and the amorous gospel imperative?

Dramatic differences of possible strategy will persist among even the likeliest allies. They will verge on contradiction. Within the forcefield of a messianic agonism, they may, however, radicalize democracy rather than end in indecision. The critical differences of identity, perspective, or situation complexify solidarity and so may, precisely under the pressure of contraction, "broaden our ethos of interconnection." Just when we most materially and terrestrially need it. The emergency that drives our excep-tionalisms may instead swerve to the urgency that dis/closes the kairos. That opens that narrow gate.

37

Such a moment was powerfully translated by another, more recent theological ancestor, one fully political in his theology and fully theologi-cal in his politics. In a different moment of national crisis (one of race and of war, just preceding the ecological intensification), Martin Luther King Jr. did not flinch from the contractions of time: "In this unfolding conun-drum of life and history there is such a thing as being too late."

In our now-time, we do not know what emergency, rather than justi-fying an endless state of the exception, may pry open the narrow gait. We cannot know when impossibility will break into the possible. But we—we of this aspirational public—do know that catastrophe can turn into cata-lyst. Any contraction, in the agonistic embrace of its tensions, might trigger the inception. We might begin to collect ourselves as a new public. And adding to the chain of Pauline effects, Martin Luther King Jr. then offers to our moment the supreme paraphrase of the kairos: "We are now faced with the fact that tomorrow is today. We are confronted with the fierce urgency of now."[63]

Notes

Portions of this material were previously published in Catherine Keller, *Political Theol-ogy of the Earth: Our Planetary Emergency and the Struggle for a New Public* (New York: Columbia University Press, 2018). Thanks to my research assistant Winfield Goodwin for his help preparing this draft for publication.

1. Giorgio Agamben, *The Time That Remains: A Commentary on the Letter to the Romans*, trans. Patricia Dailey (Palo Alto: Stanford University Press, 2005).

2. Ibid., 19.

3. L. L. Welborn, *Paul's Summons to Messi-anic Life: Political Theology and the Coming Awakening* (New York: Columbia University Press, 2015), 16.

4. Far from the rural and village sensibil-ity readily associated with the gospels, Pauline Christianity "was an urban cult that spread through the empire," of which the earli-est evidence comes "from the documents

associated with Paul." See Wayne Meeks, *The First Urban Christians: The Social World of the Apostle Paul*, 2nd ed. (New Haven: Yale University Press, 1983), x.

5. Carl Schmitt, *Political Theology: Four Chapters on the Concept of Sovereignty*, trans. George Schwab (Chicago: University of Chicago Press, 2005), chapter 3; emphasis added.

6. For a contextually congruent summa-tion and interpretation of this German theological development of political theol-ogy, see John B. Cobb Jr., *Process Theology as Political Theology* (Philadelphia: Westminster Press, 1982).

7. Chantal Mouffe, *The Democratic Para-dox* (New York: Verso, 2000), 54.

8. Carl Schmitt, "Theory of the Partisan: Intermediate Commentary on the Concept of the Political (1963)," *Telos* 127 (2004): 85.

9. Schmitt, *The Concept of the Political*, trans. George Schwab, exp. ed. (Chicago: University of Chicago Press, 2007), 229.

10. Chantal Mouffe, *The Return of the Political* (London: Verso, 2005), 6.

11. See William E. Connolly, *The Fragility of Things: Self-Organizing Processes, Neoliberal Fantasies, and Democratic Activism* (Durham: Duke University Press, 2013), 133.

12. See William E. Connolly, *Capitalism and Christianity, American Style* (Durham: Duke University Press, 2008), 39.

13. Connolly, *Fragility of Things*, 171.

14. For a deeply political theology of the activist hope that lament makes possible, see Emmanuel Katongole, *Born from Lament: The Theology and Politics of Hope in Africa* (Grand Rapids, Mich.: Eerdmans, 2017).

15. Stefano Harvey and Fred Moten, *The Undercommons: Fugitive Planning and Black Study* (London: Minor Compositions, 2013).

16. See, for example, Frank B. Wilderson, *Incognegro: A Memoir of Exile and Apartheid* (Durham: Duke University Press, 2008); Lee Edelman, *No Future: Queer Theory and the Death Drive* (Durham: Duke University Press, 2004); and Miguel A. de la Torre, *Embracing Hopelessness* (Minneapolis, Minn.: Fortress Press, 2017).

17. For an in-depth analysis of the problem of "inclusion" in liberal Christianity, see Michael J. Oliver, "Limits to Attempted Remedies of the Problem of Exclusion in Christian Discourse: Divine Choice as a Case Study" (PhD diss., Drew University, 2017), forthcoming as a book titled *Discerning Difficult Decisions: Derrida, Power, and Theological Discourse* (Lanham, Md.: Fortress Academic, 2019).

18. See Catherine Keller, *Face of the Deep: A Theology of Becoming* (New York: Routledge, 2003). Key to my thinking of chaos and genesis therein is the complexity theorizations of Ilya Prigogine and Stuart Kauffman, and the related interdisciplinary theological work of Philip Clayton.

19. See Ilya Prigogine, quoted in William E. Connolly, *A World of Becoming* (Durham: Duke University Press, 2011), 96.

20. Connolly, *Fragility of Things*, 193–94.

21. Schmitt, *Political Theology*, 5.

22. Ibid., 37.

23. Ibid., 15.

24. "The vigorous and determined exception, who although he is in conflict with the universal still is an offshoot of it, sustains himself. . . . Consequently, the exception explains the universal and himself, and if one really wants to study the universal, one only needs to look around for a legitimate exception; he discloses everything far more clearly than the universal itself. The legitimate exception is reconciled in the universal. . . . If heaven loves one sinner more than ninety-nine who are righteous, the sinner, of course, does not know this from the beginning" (Søren Kierkegaard, *Fear and Trembling/Repetition*, ed. and trans. Edna Hong and Howard Hong [Princeton: Princeton University Press, 1983], 227).

25. Donald J. Trump (@realDonaldTrump), "At the request of many, and even though I expect it to be a very boring two hours, I will be covering the Democrat Debate live on twitter!," October 13, 2015, 2:43 A.M. Tweet.

26. Schmitt, *Political Theology*, 36–37.

27. Ibid., 64.

28. Ibid., 66.

29. Keller, *Face of the Deep*, esp. 74–75.

30. Ibid., esp. 12, 87.

31. Alfred N. Whitehead, *Process and Reality: An Essay in Cosmology*, ed. David R. Griffin and Donald W. Sherburne, corr. ed. (New York: Free Press, 1978), 50.

32. For a fresh rendition of the political temporality of kairos, see Rowan Tepper, "A Political Post-History of the Concept of Time," http://www.academia.edu/1468890/Kairos__A_Political_PostHistory_of_the_Concept_of_Time.

33. Eusebius of Caesaria, "From a Speech for the Thirtieth Anniversary of Constantine's Accession," in *From Irenaeus to Grotius: A Sourcebook in Christian Political Thought*, ed. Oliver O'Donovan and Joan Lockwood O'Donovan (Grand Rapids, Mich.: Eerdmans, 1999), 60. See also Eusebius, "From a Speech on the Dedication of the Holy Sepulchre Church," in *From Irenaeus to Grotius*, 60: "And thus by the express appointment of the same God, two roots of blessing, the Roman empire and the doctrine of Christian piety,

sprang up together for the benefit of men. For before this time the various countries of the world, as Syria, Asia, Macedonia, Egypt and Arabia, had been severally subject to different rulers. The Jewish people, again, had established their dominion in the land of Palestine. And these nations, in every village, city and district, actuated by some insane spirit, were engaged in incessant and murderous war and conflict. But two mighty powers starting from the same point, the Roman empire which henceforth was swayed by a single sovereign, and the Christian religion, subdued and reconciled these contending elements. Our Savior's mighty power destroyed at once the many governments and the many gods of the powers of darkness, and proclaimed to all men, both rude and civilized, to the extremities of the earth, the sole sovereignty of God himself."

34. Kelly Brown Douglas, *Stand Your Ground: Black Bodies and the Justice of God* (Maryknoll, N.Y.: Orbis Books, 2015), 7.

35. Ibid., 8–9.

36. Ibid., 15.

37. J. Kameron Carter, *Race: A Theological Account* (Oxford: Oxford University Press, 2008).

38. Agamben, *Time That Remains*, 6–7.

39. Ibid., 87.

40. Ibid., 6.

41. Quinta Jurecic, "Donald Trump's State of Exception," *Lawfare Blog*, December 14, 2016, https://lawfareblog.com/donaldtrumps stateexception.

42. "A certain quality of an individual personality, by virtue of which he is set apart from ordinary men and treated as endowed with supernatural, superhuman, or at least specifically exceptional powers or qualities. These are such as are not accessible to the ordinary person, but are regarded as of divine origin or as exemplary, and on the basis of them the individual concerned is treated as a leader. . . . How the quality in question would be ultimately judged from an ethical, aesthetic, or other such point of view is naturally indifferent for the purpose of definition" (Max Weber, "Charismatic Authority," in *The Theory of Social and Economic Organization*,

trans. A. R. Anderson and Talcott Parsons [New York: Free Press, 1964], 358–63).

43. Walter Benjamin, "Theses on the Philosophy of History," in *Illuminations: Essays and Reflections*, ed. Hannah Arendt (New York: Shocken Books, 2007), 254; emphasis original.

44. For a rich analysis of the divine "passion" as an *eros* that in "groans and birth-pangs" at once suffers and enjoys the cosmos, see the decolonial theology of Elaine Padilla, *Divine Enjoyment: A Theology of Passion and Exuberance* (New York: Fordham University Press, 2015).

45. I am thinking here of "Crucifixation" by Occam's Laser, first song on the band's album of the same name, with its six tracks of dark, demonic, retro-futuristic sounds: https://occamslaser.bandcamp.com/album /crucifixation.

46. Whitehead, *Process and Reality*, 342.

47. Ibid., 343.

48. Ibid., 215.

49. Naomi Klein, *No Is Not Enough: Resisting Trump's Shock Politics and Winning the World We Need* (Chicago: Haymarket Books, 2017).

50. See Karen Bray's concept of "queer art failure" in her dissertation "Unredeemed: A Political Theology of Affect, Time, and Worth" (PhD diss., Drew University, 2016).

51. Bloch's influence on early Moltmann forms one messianic pathway for political theology, and his influence on José Esteban Muñoz in *Cruising Utopia: The Then and There of Queer Futurity* (New York: New York University Press, 2009) forms quite another, with its own subversive hope. Indeed, without a queer multiplicity of love strategies, resisting the normativity of potestas—which Jasbir Puar calls in another context a sexual exceptionalism—what hope for an amorous agonism can there be? For a more extended discussion of Muñoz and Puar in the context of a theologically informed queer hope, see my recent *Intercarnations: Exercises in Theological Possibility* (New York: Fordham University Press, 2017), especially the essay "The Queer Multiplicity of Becoming."

52. Catherine Keller, *Apocalypse Now and Then: A Feminist Guide to the End of the World* (Boston: Beacon Press, 1996), 122.

53. The resonances between the writings of the Marxist Bloch and the process-relational vocabulary of Whitehead are not accidental. My student Winfield Goodwin has in a recent essay, "Messianic Materialism, Mundane Hope," begun to explore directly the influence of Whitehead's speculative cosmology on Bloch's *Principle of Hope*, in the context of the latter's more recent reception in the queer temporality of José Muñoz. For an account more generally of the relationship between Marxism and Whiteheadian metaphysics, see Anne Fairchild Pomeroy, *Marx and Whitehead: Process, Dialectics, and the Critique of Capitalism* (Albany: State University of New York Press, 2004).

54. See Catherine Keller, "Talking Dirty: Ground Is Not Foundation," in *Ecospirit: Religions and Philosophies for the Earth*, ed. Laurel Kearns and Catherine Keller, Transdisciplinary Theological Colloquium Series (New York: Fordham University Press, 2007), 63–76.

55. Whitehead, *Process and Reality*, 65.

56. Keller, *Apocalypse Now and Then*, 122.

57. Rebecca Solnit, *Hope in the Dark: Untold Histories, Wild Possibilities*, 3rd ed. (Chicago: Haymarket Books, 2016).

58. Benjamin, "Theses," 261.

59. Ibid., 264.

60. Ibid., 263. Rendered here also as an "enormous" abridgment.

61. In a political climate in which women's right to choose is in dire danger again, I am aware of the treacherousness of any metaphors of miscarriage, abortion, or, indeed, birth. But then the religiopolitical right must not be allowed to thus control our language.

62. Shelley Dennis, "Edible Entanglements: Toward a Political Theology of Food" (PhD diss., Drew University, 2017).

63. Martin Luther King Jr., "Beyond Vietnam," an address delivered to the Clergy and Laymen Concerned About Vietnam, Riverside Church, New York City, April 4, 1967.

HOW WE BECOME

Crystal Tennille Irby

Favorite cartoons:
  -Superfriends
  -Heman
  -Shera
  -Thunder Cats
  -Smurfs
Saturdays before noon:
  -Sister by my side
  -Cereal at six
  -Breakfast at nine
  -In PJs til ten
  -Smurfette escapes Gargamel's torcher chamber
  -Yelling drowns out the sound of her escape
I thought everybody
Fought/kicked/screamed/cursed
Violence was normal
All Mom's had black eyes
Everybody always got everything they wanted for Christmas
We would always live in a house
Surrounded by land
Stretching further than my imagination
Red clay dirt roads would always be a part of my journey home

42

Violence, would not spoil my vision of the world
Violence did.
Violence, consistently crawled out of insecurity
Tip-toed into my mother's mate's psyche
My father, welcomed her fear/her smallness
Violence, eventually interrupted all Satur-
day morning cartoons/school night sleeps
Shifting shape of someone we loved, into some-
one we recognized but did not know

I understand your passiveness
How violence tricks
Encircles with the illusion of security
Tells us,
        "It's normal for humans to mutate into crea-
tures who prey on weakness."
We believe the lie
Only men who wait in bushes/hide in parking lots late nights
Can't comprehend the word no
Suits/ties/money/he can have any girl he wants
Never seek power where it is refused
If you hide it/didn't scream/have no visible scars/never protest
Violence is not present
But silence,
Plus internal wounds do not equal absence of pain

Violence hides
Behind:
        -fear
        -shame
        -no access to 6 o'clock sound bites
        -no one cares if it's not happening to them
Violence,
Excuses executions
With excerpts of Bible verses
Confident,
We'll never read the whole chapter/check the context
Violence,
Convinces us it is inevitable

Tells us,

    "Truth/escape/freedom

    Will never be free/priceless

    Blood usually of color

    Always marginalized

    Will forever be the cost

    Peace/relinquishing power

    Will never come before the attempt to annihilate/take

    Dignity/faith/children

    Whatever clings us to life."

We believe the lie

Sit idly by

We don't disturb violence

We don't disturb rape/abuse/genocide

In:

    -hotel rooms she willingly went to

    -our neighbors' houses

    -churches

    -Rwanda

    -Sudan

    -anywhere in Africa

    -any inner city

    -draped in uniform/easy access to gun/

only one side the story left to tell

    -any place profit can be pickpocketed/people left for dead

We don't disturb violence

Until it kicks down our door

Like drugs infiltrating the suburbs

Like 9/11

Like the kids at Columbine/the guy in Colo-

rado/Sandy Hook/Charleston

    Note: How quickly we forget the names of people

Acting as though we're the first

As if we hurt the most

Because:

    -poor people are prone to use drugs

    -Black kids killing Black kids is expected

    -terrorism has nothing to do with America

So we have the right to unleash wrath

Deciding:
>   -whose life matters most
>   -whose pain matters least
>   -whose dignity should be sacrificed

While the cycle continues
While violence laughs
While we:
>   -count martyrs
>   -pretend to protect peace
>   -play heroes
>   -declare wars won
>   -occupy
>   -drop drones there
>   -pummel protestors here

While children like I once was
Sit on Saturday mornings:
Watching superheroes save the world
Watching violence parade around their house
In the shape of parents
Around the world
In the shape of patriotism
Watching their households imitate the world
Thinking,
>   "Violence is normal."

WHAT IF?

A Spoken Word Poem

Sapient Soul

I have been wishing I could write the poem that makes everyone stop in their paths of expertise and ask, "What if there is more that I should know?"

What if racism is all about whiteness and whiteness was developed for white people not to see it and for black people to believe that they can see it all so clearly?

What if my blackness is perceived to be a threat and I begin to believe the same? What if?

What if oppression is in the air that we breathe and I've been breathing it in since birth? Do my lungs have filters for oppression because I'm black or is it possible that patriarchy and white supremacy can come out of me, too?

What if I have internalized the image of savage so I can't see the beauty in my different hair, wide hips, and round ass?

What if I believe that white people are inherently evil and I miss the fact that whiteness and white people are two very different things?

What if I consider our humanity while evaluating the evil that has come of it? What if I could see the God of you waiting to be affirmed by the God of me?

What if race is all about power and it has birthed bias in each one of us, so whiteness gets filtered as oppressor and blackness gets filtered as inferior, what if?

What if I realized that it takes hard work and commitment for me to see you clearly?

What if #BlackLivesMatter gets filtered through the lens of whiteness, will it look like the Black Panther Party or Malcolm X being portrayed in 2016 as vigilante instead of valor?

What if I'm a conscious black man that sees Beyoncé dance in clothes that she chose, will I criticize her or send solidarity?

What if I was Latino or Asian or Indian or Arab or Indigenous or lesbian or gay or transgender or bisexual or queer, would I even belong in this Crayola box that whiteness has constructed?

What if protest is revolutionary and so is intellect and mothering and healing and living and loving and dreaming, what if?

What if US presidential politics is a distraction and your civic engagement beyond the polls is where your true work is?

What if policy often mutates into new forms of oppression, like slavery to Jim Crow to the War on Drugs to mass incarceration?

What if the 13th amendment abolished slavery but did not have an exception clause?

What if I believe that cash rules everything around me—*CREAM get the money, dolla dolla bill yall*—and I believe that money has more power than I could ever have?

What if my black friends and I become the black elite and racism does not cease to exist, what if?

What if the oppressed become the oppressor, will there still be a movement for lives to matter? Will we say all lives matter? Will we all of sudden become free of the oppression buried deep within our lungs?

Will we know how to love and live and heal and share and be whole? Will we realize that there is so much more to know?

Will we know that the human beings all around us might know something that we don't?

What if we have breathed in air complete with *false hotep* ideology, confederate flags, and *HIS- story* books from grades K–12?

What if Howard Zinn and Hidden Colors taught my god-daughter history?

What if my two-year-old nephew wears dreadlocks and rocks baggy clothes, his parents work full-time and his mother is pursuing her doctorate, will you see a baby boy or a baby thug?

What if every person with a confederate flag is not racist but it still hurts to see one? What if my vantage point is only 30% of the full picture at best?

What if nationalism comes out of racism and we have not even begun to know how truly dangerous exclusion and power is?

What if we just stop it?

What if we stop assuming that we have all of the answers?

What if we realize that critical race theory is only theory and there is nothing theoretical about people dying, whether it is a police officer killing an unarmed black person or white on white crime or black on black crime?

What if we stop defending ourselves long enough to be vulnerable with whatever *the other* is? What if we realized that the bias we carry kills real human people,

not simply thugs or criminals or racists, but actual living and loving people?

What if we stopped and listened?

What if there is more that you should know?

JEZEBEL AND INDO-WESTERN WOMEN

*Nation, Nationalism, and the Ecologies of
Sexual Violence in Revelation 2:20–25*

Sharon Jacob

> To stop rapes, ban celebrations like Valentine's Day and kiss
> of love campaigns. This is all blind imitation of the West
> and doesn't at all suit the Indian culture. In their stead,
> festivals like Bhai Dooj, Raksha Bandhan and Mata Pita Ki
> Puja (an event to worship one's mother and father) should be
> celebrated across the country on a grand scale to inculcate
> cultural values in today's youth.
>
> —A. P. SINGH, DEFENSE LAWYER[1]

"Indo-Western," a term first introduced by the Indian fashion industry describes a style that fuses Indian and Western designs to create a multicultural statement.[2] Participating in Eastern and Western cultures and behaviors, the urban Indian woman articulates a cultural hybridity within the nation. The Indo-Western woman shuttling between cultures embodies a materiality articulating a difference that threatens the homogenized image of the nation.[3] As a result, cultures and traditions of the past are glorified within the national imagination through the conscious and deliberate suppression of the West, which is constructed as an external threat to the nation.[4] Imagined as fragile and limited, the nation requires protection from both external and internal contagions that threaten its essentialist subjectivity. As a result, hybridity brought about either externally through globalization or internally through the willing participation of citizens in foreign cultural practices poses a risk to the nation. This essay focuses on the internal hybridity of a nation specifically; the attention will be on the cultural hybridity articulated by women, their relationship with the nation, and the ecologies of sexual violence generated by nationalistic and patriarchal systems.

The relationship between women and the nation is a symbiotic one, as women's bodies, fetishized into cultural objects of purity, become symbols of the nation. Simply put, the cultural purity of a nation is intimately connected to a woman's physical, emotional, and spiritual ability to protect, preserve, and keep alive the image of the puritanical nation. Culturally hybrid women, then, lead to hybrid nations. Women's bodies become an important part of the nationalist agenda as issues of nationalism and cultural purity are negotiated directly on their bodies. It is for this reason that women participating in foreign cultures and behaviors need to be reined in and oftentimes are threatened with sexual violence to stay within the boundaries of the nation. At the same time, sexual violence used as a deterrent to control and restrict the behaviors of culturally hybrid women is justified on the grounds of a regressive rhetoric of nationalism. The desire to restrict and control the bodies of women lays the groundwork for the development of a rape culture.

Emilie Buchwald, Pamela R. Fletcher, and Martha Roth define rape culture as follows: "A rape culture condones physical and emotional terrorism against women and presents it as the norm."[5] Although sexual violence is part and parcel of an Indian woman's daily existence,[6] the sexual violence targeted at Indo-Western women living in urban India is condoned under a regressive rhetoric of nationalism that systematizes and normalizes the sexual assault of women in the nation. Rape culture, then, contextualized in the postcolonial Indian context, uses the rhetoric of nation, national culture, and nationalism to justify and condone the sexual assault of Indo-Western women.[7] The transgression of cultures by women threatening the culture of a nation depicts boundaries as permeable, boundaries that can be easily violated by foreign elements. Drawing on the work of Mel Y. Chen, who argues that "ecology" serves as a marker for "an imagined system," a system "with interrelations between types,"[8] my essay employs the phrase "ecologies of sexual violence" to depict the enmeshed relationship between women, nation, and hybridity. I argue that ecologies of sexual violence bring to light the permeability between women, nation, and cultural hybridity. Hybridity threatening the purity of a woman and the nation is no longer a marker of globalization/urbanization, nor is it a positive marker of cultural fusion between the local and the global. Rather, it violates and ruptures the homogenous identity of the nation. In other words, the transformation of women and nation into cultural objects of purity are disrupted by cultural hybridity brought about through the deliberate fusion between East and West cultures. Unfortunately, the use of sexual violence directed toward culturally hybrid women as a deterrent under the false guise of a regressive patriarchal nationalist agenda is not new or unique to the contemporary context and, in fact, has been part of our ancient texts.

The character of Jezebel in Revelation 2:20–25 is also a culturally hybrid woman who is punished by John of Patmos because she assimilates with another culture.[9] Although Jezebel in Revelation 2:20–25 and the Indo-Western women are different in that the former is a textual character while the latter are real-life women, they, nevertheless, are connected in their willingness to assimilate with the empire. In assimilating with imperial cultures, Jezebel and Indo-Western women transform into culturally hybrid women whose sexual assault is condoned under the guise of preserving nation and national culture. Drawing on the ecologies of sexual violence that interpret rape culture through the lens of nation and nationalism, this essay attempts to read Revelation 2:20–25 through the contextual experiences of the urban Indo-Western woman. The use of ecology as an interlocking system that brings to light the connection between cultural hybridity, women, and nation helps to illustrate the ways in which sexual violence, seeping through these three groups, creates a nationalized rhetoric of rape culture that enforces a patriarchal and regressive vision of a limited and fragile nation. I argue that the rhetoric of a "nationalized rape culture" condones the sexual violence of women under a regressive and often tribalistic form of nationalism. Such a form of nationalism envisions a nation in which the white man is no longer in charge of saving the brown woman from the brown man; now brown women need to be rescued and deterred from assimilating with the white man and his culture by brown men. In short, the propaganda of nationalization of rape culture to justify sexual violence prescribes to the larger grand narrative of brown men saving brown women from white culture.

Imagining a Nation

In his book *Imagined Communities: Reflections on the Origin and Spread of Nationalism*, Benedict Anderson proposes the following definition of the nation: "It is an imagined political community—and imagined as both inherently limited and sovereign. It is imagined because the members of even the smallest nation will never know most of their fellow-members, meet them, or even hear of them, yet in the minds of each lives the image of their communion."[10] One cannot underestimate the importance of visions in the text of Revelation. The Greek word Ἀποκάλυψις, commonly translated in English as "apocalypse," refers to a dream or a vision that needs to be interpreted by a divine being.[11] The author of Revelation, John of Patmos, banished on the island of Patmos, is repeatedly shown visions about the new world that will replace the old world.[12] Although there are some stark differences between John of Patmos and the native intellectual, both employ a similar strategy that summons the nation or new world into existence through imagination. The visions in the text of Revelation, while highly symbolic and extremely violent in nature, visualize this new world as peaceful, spiritually and culturally superior to the present age.[13] The construction of New Jerusalem invokes the past by glorifying its purity and cultural superiority and presenting it over against the present world.[14] Cultural purity inscribed directly upon women's bodies renders them national symbols, thereby invoking and reinscribing memories of a glorious precolonial past.

Imaginings of nation purposefully summon traditions of the past to undermine the cultural mores of the present. Caribbean psychiatrist, philosopher, and revolutionary writer Frantz Fanon illustrates this urgency, writing: "Because they [the native intellectuals] realize they are in danger of losing their lives, and thus becoming lost to their people, these men, hot-headed and with anger in their hearts, relentlessly determine to renew contact once more with the oldest and most precolonial springs of life of their people."[15] Making a similar move in the text of Revelation, John of Patmos, like the native intellectual, reverts back to his past. Biblical scholar Jorunn Økland in her essay "Why Can't the Heavenly Miss Jerusalem Just Shut Up?" points out that the new waters of life and the tree of life in the book of Revelation, which are associated with John's vision of a New Jerusalem, evoke images from the Garden of Eden.[16] Similar to the native intellectual returning to the precolonial springs of life of his people, John of Patmos, drawing on the waters in Genesis, quenches his thirst for a precolonial past of his people, that is, the Christian community.[17] Therefore, the New Jerusalem envisioned by John of Patmos both idealizes and idolizes traditions of the precolonial past. The precolonialized embodiment of the New Jerusalem while strange and new is also familiar and old. And yet, the new and at once familiar new world imagined by John of Patmos needs to be protected from the cultural contamination brought about by assimilation with other cultures.

The Nationalization of Rape Culture

My interpretation of Revelation 2:20–25 is contextual and draws on the real-life experiences of Indo-Western urban women living in postcolonial India. Making these contemporary connections is pertinent to my interpretation because it illustrates the ways in which women's bodies have played and continue to play a role in the production of a new world / nation. I begin this section by relaying a real-life incident that took place in Bengaluru on December 31, 2016. Reading Revelation 2:20–25 alongside this incident demonstrates the ways sexual assault of culturally hybrid women is justified under a regressive ideology of nation and national culture, creating an ecology of sexual violence that leads to sustaining a nationalized culture of rape within the new world / nation. I move between the real-life experiences of Indo-Western urban women and the textual character of Jezebel in the text of Revelation.

The 2016 New Year's Eve celebration in Bengaluru quickly turned into a night of horror, as women coming out of pubs and restaurants after the celebration were descended upon by a mob of men who groped and grabbed them. This incident took place in the most commercial and well-known part of town, called Mahatma Gandhi Road, fondly known as M. G. Road. Although the police were present, they were rendered helpless given the sheer volume of the mob.[18] This incident left many shaken, angry, and frustrated at the growing incidents of sexual assault and rape of Indian women, especially in public spaces. In addition to this, Bengaluru has always been described as a far more Westernized city within southern India. In fact, it has often been referred to as the "pub capital of India." And in terms of music, along with traditional Carnatic music, Bengaluru is also known as the rock/metal capital of India. There is no other way to describe this city but as a true culturally hybrid urban center that takes pride into its ability to fuse Indian and Western cultures within its city limits.

While postcolonial biblical scholars have spoken about hybridity in Revelation[19] and some feminist scholars have spoken, though marginally, about the language of purity in this text, a direct link between the envisioned new world and cultural hybridity to issues of nation and nationalism has yet to be made.[20] Feminists have grappled with what they must do with the text of Revelation. While some have found ways to reclaim the text for themselves, others have rejected this text.[21] Women hold a special place in the book of Revelation.[22] Female characters occur a total of four times, and yet readers never hear their voices.[23] The closest we come to hearing a woman's voice is a maternal scream let out by the woman clothed in the sun in Revelation 12.[24] Among the four women, Jezebel (Revelation 2:20–25) and the Whore of Babylon (Revelation 17 and 18) share a special connection. This is because both are powerful women who are punished with sexual violence for their sexual transgressions.[25] At the same time, the misbehaviors performed by both these women are remarkably different. Homi K. Bhabha observes, "The problem is not simply the 'self-hood' of the nation as opposed to the otherness of other nations. We are confronted with the nation split within itself, articulating the heterogeneity of its population."[26] Thus, while Babylon threatens to dismantle the vision of John of Patmos from the outside, the cultural hybridity of Jezebel signifies an internalized corruption.[27] The character of Jezebel, then, willingly participating in the Roman imperial cult performative of a cultural hybridity, symbolizes cultural difference in the book of Revelation. As a result, myriad ways of violence are used to control and rein in women's behavior in globalized contexts.

Women's bodies constructed to resemble food items that can be voraciously and violently devoured by men if not properly protected is used as a tactic to control, sexualize, fetishize, and, most importantly, demonize women appearing in public spaces. Samajwadi Party leader Abu Azmi, commenting on the mass molestation incident that took place in Bengaluru on December 31, 2016, noted that "women are like sugar who will attract ants."[28] Explicit connections between women's bodies and food enable a culture of sexual violence that sustains and systematizes the sexual assault and rape of women by placing the blame on victims, thereby reifying rape culture within a nation's consciousness.

The relationship between women, food, and fornication is not new and can be found in cultures, both ancient and modern.[29] Revelation 2:20 reads, "But I have this against you: you tolerate that woman Jezebel, who calls herself a prophet and is teaching and beguiling my servants to practice fornication and to eat food sacrificed to idols." Scholars agree that the practice of fornication in Revelation is not about the act of fornication, per se, but rather about participating in the imperial cult. Warren Carter notes, "The verb translated 'commit fornication' (*porneuō*, 2:14, 20) can be taken literally as a reference to sexual immorality (1 Corinthians 6:18; 10:8). But it is also used figuratively. In this capacity, it condemns God's people who forsake their covenant commitments and participate in the ways of Gentile cultures, including idolatry."[30] Though the context of postcolonial India and Thyatira are vastly different, the threat to contaminate the nation / new world performed through the assimilation of both Jezebel and the Indo-Western urban woman loom large in the imagination of the native intellectual and John of Patmos. Interestingly, culturally hybrid women in both narratives are simultaneously transformed into both victims and perpetrators by the men in their societies. Language that was once used to segregate humans and nonhuman inanimate objects became porous as women and food permeate into each other. For examples, women's bodies described as "mouthwatering delicacies" are waiting to be devoured violently by men, while nations, taking on a female subjectivity when depleted of their national reserves, are often described as being raped or assaulted. In that, the rape and sexual assault of women bleeding into the national narrative also becomes the rape and assault of the nation.

Turning back to the biblical text, Revelation 2:21 reads: "I gave her time to repent, but she refuses to repent of her fornication." Abu Azmi notes, "Partying late night in half attire, blindly following western culture, has never been our culture. Ladies hailing from well-to-do families, be it from Maharashtra, Gujarat, Rajasthan or UP, they come out in decent attire and mostly with their family members."[31] A false sense of culture defined by John of Patmos and leaders like Azmi is used to advocate the repression of all women under the guise of a patriarchal nationalism. Here we see the complicities marking ecologies of sexual violence. One can argue that the call for repentance in Revelation 2:21 is also a call for reformation, urging Jezebel and her followers to take an antiassimilationist stance against the Roman Empire and revert back to a more authentic and separatist form of Judaism.[32] Val Plumwood writes, "Progress is the progressive overcoming, or control of, this 'barbarian' non-human or semi-human sphere by the rational sphere of European culture and 'modernity.'"[33] The depiction of culturally hybrid women as strayed women who need to be included within the vision of the nation / new world either through repentance or through the threat of sexual violence becomes the way through which national culture is progressed in a nation. The image of the strayed woman reflecting back imagines the nation as strayed. The nation envisioned as a culturally hybrid, strayed woman must be saved from its willingness to collude with imperial powers through repentance and reverting back to antiassimilationist and, therefore, more nationalist ways.

John of Patmos was directed to write to seven churches that were in seven different cities, namely, Ephesus, Smyrna, Pergamum, Thyatira, Sardis, Philadelphia, and Laodicea.[34] These churches, while part of the Roman Empire, did not consider themselves to be subjugated by Rome.[35] The imperial strategy of the Roman Empire to urbanize cities was an effort to co-opt resistance by promoting their civilization.[36] Roman colonization through civilization was done in two ways: the first being through urbanization, which was illustrated through the construction of theatres, gymnasiums, baths, and schools,[37] and the second was through the promotion of education.[38] Abu Azmi notes, "In these modern times, the more women are naked, the more fashionable, modern and educated they are considered. And this is increasing in the country. This is a blot on our culture."[39] Jezebel, in the book of Revelation, is described as a local prophet, meaning that she was not only a leader in her community but may have also had formal education. Deniz Kandiyoti writes, "There is a wealth of evidence to suggest that, for women, the 'modern' is always perilously close to the 'alien,' particularly when contemplated codes of behavior can be identified as an outright betrayal of expectations of their own communities."[40] Jezebel ensuring the safety of her people, allowing for the participation in the imperial cult, is condemned by John of Patmos, who sees this act as a betrayal of his separatist Christian values.[41] While the globalization of nation is deemed to be an important economic development, the notion of its women being globalized remains a threat. It is interesting to note that while a woman's cultural hybridity is accused of contaminating the purity of a nation, the globalized subjectivity of a nation is restricted from seeping and bleeding into the local subjectivity of the Indian woman. This is similar to the book of Revelation, where John of Patmos accuses Jezebel of assimilating with the empire and corrupting his vision of the kingdom; he himself fashions his visions of the new kingdom in the image of the Roman Empire.[42] Thus, while hybrid women can lead to hybrid nations, the idea of hybrid nations leading to hybrid women is never encouraged within the nationalist imagination.

Shifting our gaze to the contemporary postcolonial context of India, one of the shrillest voices, commenting on the mass molestation incident in Bangalore, was that of Karnataka deputy chief G. Parameshwara. He said, "On days like New Year's Eve, a large number of youngsters gather on Brigade Road, Commercial Street and M. G. Road. These youngsters, who are almost like Westerners, try to copy the westerners not only in the mindset, but even the dressing."[43] Though Parameshwara does not explicitly state the negative stereotypes of Western women and Western culture, the racialized and sexualized bias is apparent in his words. Stereotypes of foreign women as overtly sexual figures endangering the cultural identity of a nation are not new.[44] The name Jezebel also carries with it the sexual connotations of a foreign woman who is the Other.[45] Scholars have pointed out that the name Jezebel is symbolic for the author.[46] The rhetorical move to name the local prophetess Jezebel is also an attempt to sexualize her as the sexual history of this woman is summoned in the mind of the reader.[47] Plumwood writes, "Hyper-separation means defining the dominant identity emphatically against, or in opposition to, the subordinated identity, by exclusion of their real or supposed qualities. The function of hyper-separation is to mark out the Other for separate and inferior treatment."[48] For both Jezebel and the Indo-Western woman, the dominant identity presented as Roman or Western hyperseparated to sexualize their bodies is used to condone their sexual assault within their environments, used to create and sustain ecologies of sexual violence.

Revelation 2:23 reads: "So I will cast her on a bed of suffering, and I will make those who commit adultery with her suffer intensely, unless they repent of her ways." Jezebel disappears from the narrative. Pooja, one of the victims of the mass molestation in Bengaluru, relates the tales of the horrific night inside the pub: "In the pub too, groping was happening. When we pay 6,000–7,000 rupees ($88; £72) to go to a pub to get entry to celebrate, you expect people to be of a certain class. At least, that they wouldn't do such things. These people weren't illiterate or uneducated. They don't know what effect it has on a girl's life. It has an everlasting impact."[49] While the character of Jezebel is never groped, her being thrown on a bed without her consent is indicative of her sexual assault. Kandiyoti writes, "Wherever women continue to serve as boundary markers between different national, ethnic, and religious collectivities, their emergence as full-fledged citizens will be jeopardized, and whatever rights they may have achieved during one stage of nation-building may be sacrificed on the altar of identity politics during another."[50] It is interesting to note that unlike Pooja, Jezebel is familiar with her assailant.[51] The sexually violated bodies of Pooja and Jezebel become the foundations upon which imaginings of nations and the new world are visualized.

Conclusion

The rise of a fundamentalist and regressive view of nation/community and what constitutes national / new world culture perpetuates a culture and ecology of violence against women. Limiting women's bodies by rendering them primarily national and cultural symbols rather than real persons overshadows their subjectivity and their ability to rise as full-fledged citizens within the boundaries of the nation. Women participating in cultures other than their own are punished through explicit sexual violence in the name of nation, nationalism, and national culture. In this new context, the white man no longer saves the brown woman from the brown man, as he once did in the colonized contexts,[52] but rather the imagining of the nation through the eyes of patriarchy advocates a new kind of saving, one in which the brown man controlling the brown woman through sexual violence attempts to save her from participating in the culture of the white man. In other words, the "nationalization of rape culture" within the nation / new world sustains, systematizes, and normalizes the sexual violence of brown men attempting to rescue brown women from accommodating white culture. Thus, rescuing culturally hybrid women becomes a patriotic endeavor fervently adopted by the men of the nation. So the very act of rescuing, protecting, and preserving women and nations bolsters ecologies of sexual violence, thereby creating and sustaining systems of patriarchy and misogyny within the ecological imagination of a nation.

Notes

1. Harish V. Nair, "Gang-Rape Lawyer Singh Says 'Banning Valentine's Day Will Prevent Rape' as He Faces Loss of License for 'Shocking' Interview," *Mail Online India*, March 7, 2015, http://www.dailymail.co.uk /indiahome/indianews/article2984376/Rapists slawyerSinghfacessackclaimingbanningValen tinesDaypreventrape.html. AP Singh is the defense attorney for two of the four men accused of the brutal gang rape and murder of Jyothi Singh, the twenty-three-year-old physiotherapy student, that took place in Delhi, the nation's capital, on the night of December 16, 2012.

2. Jennifer Craig, *The Face of Fashion: Cultural Studies in Fashion* (New York: Routledge, 1993), 38.

3. Homi K. Bhabha, "Cultural Diversity and Cultural Differences," in *The Post-colonial Studies Reader*, ed. Bill Ashcroft, Gareth

Griffiths, and Helen Tiffin (New York: Routledge, 1995), 156.

4. Amil Cabral, "National Liberation and Culture," in *Colonial Discourse and Postcolonial Theory: A Reader*, ed. Patrick Williams and Laura Chrisman (New York: Columbia University Press, 1994), 56.

5. Kate Harding, *Asking For It: The Alarming Rise of Rape Culture—And What We Can Do About It* (Boston: Perseus Books Group, 2015), 2. See also Emilie Buchwald, Pamela R. Fletcher, and Martha Roth, eds., *Transforming a Rape Culture*, rev. ed. (Minneapolis, Minn.: Milkweed Editions, 2005), xiv.

6. Thomas Reuters Foundation, "The World's Five Most Dangerous Countries for Women," at http://hyperakt.com/items /archived/theworldsfivemostdangerouscoun triesforwomen. According to a TrustLaw Women Poll, India featured as the fourth most dangerous country for women alongside

57

Afghanistan, Congo, Pakistan, and Somalia. The poll noted that women in these countries faced perils such as lack of education and access to health care, rape, and violence.

7. Chandra Talpade Mohanty, "Under Western Eyes: Feminist Scholarship and Colonial Discourses," boundary 2, 12, no. 3, and 13, no. 1 (Spring–Autumn 1984): 339.

8. Mel Y. Chen, Animacies: Biopolitics, Racial Mattering, and Queer Affect (London: Duke University Press, 2012), 89.

9. Stephen Moore, Untold Tales from the Book of Revelation: Sex and Gender, Empire and Ecology (Atlanta: Society of Biblical Literature Press, 2014), 32. See also David Aune, Revelation 1–5, World Biblical Commentary 52A (Dallas, Tex.: Word, 1997), 148–49; Paul B. Duff, Who Rides the Beast? Prophetic Rivalry and the Rhetoric of Crisis in the Churches of the Apocalypse (Oxford: Oxford University Press, 2001), 36–47, 55–58; and Leonard L. Thompson, The Book of Revelation: Apocalypse and Empire (Oxford: Oxford University Press, 1990), 121–24.

10. Benedict Anderson, "Imagined Communities," in Ashcroft, Griffiths, and Tiffin, Post-colonial Studies Reader, 125.

11. Wes Howard-Brook and Anthony Gwyther, Unveiling Empire: Reading Revelation Then and Now (Maryknoll, N.Y.: Orbis Books, 1999), 4.

12. Susan R. Garrett, "Revelation," in Women's Bible Commentary, ed. Carol A. Newsom and Sharon H. Ringe, exp. ed. (Louisville, Ky.: Westminster John Knox Press, 1998), 469.

13. Howard-Brook and Gwyther, Unveiling Empire, 159.

14. Jorunn Økland, "Why Can't the Heavenly Miss Jerusalem Just Shut Up," in A Feminist Companion to the Apocalypse of John, ed. Amy Jill Levine and Maria Mayo Robbins (New York: T&T Clark, 2009), 100.

15. Frantz Fanon, "On National Culture," in Ashcroft, Griffiths, and Tiffin, Post-colonial Studies Reader, 119.

16. Okland draws on the work of Tina Pippin, "Peering into the Abyss: A Postmodern Reading of the Biblical Bottomless Pit," in The New Literary Criticism and the New Testament, ed. E. S. Malbon and E. V. McKnight (Sheffield: Sheffield Academic Press, 1994), 251–67.

17. Howard-Brook and Gwyther, Unveiling Empire, 42. Other scholars include Thompson, Book of Revelation, and Harry O. Maier, Apocalypse Recalled: The Book of Revelation After Christendom (Minneapolis, Minn.: Fortress Press, 2002).

18. Imran Qureshi, "Bangalore New Year: 'People Were Grabbing, Groping,'" BBC News, January 4, 2017, http://www.bbc.com /news/worldasiaindia38504186. As one victim explained, "I felt helpless. Although I have hands and legs and I could abuse and slap them, I could not do anything. I didn't know who was touching me and groping me."

19. In addition to the work of Moore, see Thompson, Book of Revelation, 121–24; Aune, Revelation 1–5, 148–49; and Paul B. Duff, Who Rides the Beast? Prophetic Rivalry and the Rhetoric of Crises in the Churches of the Apocalypse (Oxford: Oxford University Press, 2001), 36–47.

20. Several feminist biblical scholars have offered some insights on purity and the purity language in the book of Revelation. Hanna Stenstrom, "They Have Not Defiled Themselves with Women: Christian Identity According to the Book of Revelation," in Levine and Robbins, Feminist Companion to the Apocalypse, 32; Adela Yarbro Collins, Crisis and Catharsis: The Power of the Apocalypse (Louisville, Ky.: Westminster Press, 1984), 159–61; Garrett, "Revelation," 382; and Tina Pippin, Death and Desire (Louisville, Ky.: Westminster John Knox Press, 1992), 50. It is important to note that Stenstrom, while highlighting the issue of purity in the text of Revelation, still fails to make a connection back to conversations about nation and nationalism, or in the case of John of Patmos to his new vision of empire that is based in a limited sense of nation.

21. Amy-Jill Levine, introduction to Levine and Robbins, Feminist Companion to the Apocalypse, 1. See also Elisabeth Schüssler Fiorenza, Revelation: Vision of a Just World (Minneapolis, Minn.: Fortress Press, 1991), 133, and Antoinette Clark Wire, The Corinthian Women Prophets: A Reconstruction Through Paul's Rhetoric (Minneapolis, Minn.:

Fortress Press, 1990), 105. For a counterargument, see Tina Pippin, "The Heroine and the Whore: Fantasy and Female in the Apocalypse of John," *Semeia* 60 (1992): 78. Other works include Collins, *Crisis and Catharsis*, and Tina Pippin, "Revelation/Apocalypse of John," in *The Women's Bible Commentary*, ed. Carol A. Newsome and Sharon H. Ringe (Louisville, Ky.: Westminster John Knox Press, 1992), 627–32.

22. Tina Pippin, "'And I Will Strike Her Children Dead': Death and the Deconstruction of Social Location," in *Reading from This Place*, ed. Fernando F. Segovia and Mary Ann Tolbert (Minneapolis, Minn.: Fortress Press, 1995), 1:191–98. Similar to Pippin, my essay focuses on the cultural impact of the text of Revelation rather than focusing on the veracity of the events that really happened in this text. Some scholars who have noted that there is no external evidence of persecution around the time that Revelation was written are Schüssler Fiorenza, *Vision of a Just World*, 124–29; Thompson, *Book of Revelation*, 171–201; and Collins, *Crisis and Catharsis*, 84–110.

23. Women in the book of Revelation appear in chapters 2, 12, 17, 18, and 21.

24. Revelation 12:1–2 says, "A great portent appeared in heaven: a woman clothed with the sun, with the moon under her feet, and on her head a crown of twelve stars. She was pregnant and was *crying out* in birth pangs, in the agony of giving birth" (emphasis added). Tina Pippin, in her article "The Heroine and the Whore," argues that "the female in fantasy literature is also an image; in the Apocalypse this image is blurred or stereotyped when present or absent altogether. Women are either on 'the edge of time' (to borrow from Marge Piercy) or completely displaced from time" (67).

25. Tina Pippin, *Apocalyptic Bodies: The Biblical End of the World in Text and Image* (New York: Routledge, 1999), 110.

26. Homi K. Bhabha, *The Location of Culture* (New York: Routledge, 1990), 212.

27. Moore, *Untold Tales*, 34.

28. Divyanshu Dutta Roy, "Bengaluru Molestation: On New Year's Eve Horror, Politician Abu Azmi's 'Naked Women' Shocker,"

http://www.ndtv.com/indianews/onbengaluru newyearsevehorrorpoliticianabuazmisnaked womenshocker1644496.

29. When speaking about the Whore of Babylon, John of Patmos fantasizes her flesh being devoured and eaten by her own followers. For instance, Revelation 17:16 says: "The beast and the ten horns you saw will hate the prostitute. They will bring her to ruin and leave her naked; they will eat her flesh and burn her with fire. See also Abhinav Gargi, "Defence Lawyers Blame Nirbhaya for Rape," *Times of India*, March 4, 2015, http://timesof india.indiatimes.com/india/Defencelawyers blameNirbhayaforrape/articleshow/46451407 .cms. Similarly, advocate M. L. Sharma, one of the lawyers defending the young men accused of raping and murdering the twenty-three-year-old physiotherapist student Jyoti Singh Pandey in a moving bus in Delhi, the nation's capital, said: "If you keep sweets on the street then dogs will come and eat them."

30. Warren Carter, "Accommodating 'Jezebel' and Withdrawing John: Negotiating Empire in Revelation Then and Now," *Interpretation* 63, no. 1 (January 2009): 35.

31. "Partying Late Night Not in Indian Culture: Abu Azmi," *Hindustan Times*, January 3, 2017, http://www.hindustantimes .com/mumbainews/partyinglatenightin halfattirehasneverbeenourcultureabuazmi/ storycAbohmUx66q5ykUWgKEeMO.html. Azmi notes, "Partying late night in half attire, blindly following western culture, has never been our culture. Ladies hailing from well-to-do families, be it from Maharashtra, Gujarat, Rajasthan or UP, they come out in decent attire and mostly with their family members."

32. Moore, *Untold Tales*, 33. John W. Marshall, "Gender and Empire: Sexualized Violence in John's Anti-Imperial Apocalypse," in Levine and Robbins, *Feminist Companion to the Apocalypse*, 25.

33. Val Plumwood, "Decolonizing Relationships with Nature," in Ashcroft, Griffiths, and Tiffin, *Post-colonial Studies Reader*, 503.

34. Howard-Brook and Gwyther, *Unveiling Revelation*, 89.

35. Ibid., 91.

36. Ibid., 95–96.

37. Ibid., 95.

38. Ibid., 96. Howard-Brook and Gwyther also wrote: "The Romans also knew that the local elite could be successfully controlled through 'education'" (89).

39. "Women 'Straying Away' from Indian Culture Reason for Bengaluru Mass Molestation, Says Abu Azmi," *Indian Express*, September 6, 2018, http://indianexpress.com /article/india/womenstrayingawayfromindian culturereasonofbengalurumassmolestation abuazmi4456974. Abu Azmi notes, "In these modern times, the more women are naked, the more fashionable, modern and educated they are considered. And this is increasing in the country. This is a blot on our culture."

40. Deniz Kandiyoti, "Identity and Its Discontents: Women and the Nation," in Williams and Chrisman, *Colonial Discourse and Postcolonial Theory*, 382.

41. Mary Ann Beavis, "Jezebel Speaks," in Levine and Robbins, *Feminist Companion to the Apocalypse*, 132.

42. Moore, *Untold Tales from the Book of Revelation*, 15–16.

43. "Bengaluru Molestation: G. Parameshwara Blames 'Western Ways' of Youngsters," *Deccan Chronicle*, January 3, 2017, http://www .deccanchronicle.com/nation/currentaffairs /030117/bengalurumolestationparameshwar blameswesternwaysofyoungsters.html.

44. Kandiyoti, "Identity and Its Discontents," 380.

45. Tina Pippin, *Apocalyptic Bodies*, 33. See also Pamela Thimmes, "'Teaching and Beguiling My Servants': The Letter to Thyatira (Rev 2:18–29)," in Levine and Robbins, *Feminist Companion to the Apocalypse*, 79.

46. Pippin, "'And I Will Strike Her Children Dead,'" 193. Similarly, Stephen Moore argues that the names Balaam and Jezebel are symbolic in the text of Revelation (*Untold Tales*, 32). See also Collin J. Hemer, *The Letters to the Seven Churches of Asia in Their Setting* (Sheffield: Journal for the Study of the Old Testament, 1986), 123.

47. Pippin, *Apocalyptic Bodies*, 42.

48. Plumwood, "Decolonizing Relationships with Nature," 504.

49. Qureshi, "Bangalore New Year."

50. Kandiyoti, "Identity and Its Discontents," 382.

51. Moore, *Untold Tales*, 32.

52. Gayatri Chakravorty Spivak, *A Critique of Postcolonial Reason: Toward a History of the Vanishing Present* (Cambridge, Mass.: Harvard University Press, 1999), 287. In the colonial context of India, the ritual of sati, a practice where Hindu widows ascended the pyres of their dead husbands and immolated themselves, was abolished by the British. Spivak explains the abolition of this ritual in the colonial context as a case of "white men saving brown women from brown men."

CLIMATE CHANGE AS RACE DEBT, CLASS DEBT, AND CLIMATE COLONIALISM

Moral Conundrums, Vision, and Agency

Cynthia Moe-Lobeda

The consequences of differentials in privilege and power based on how difference is constructed and abused are lifted to a new plane by climate change and the new world conditions into which it has propelled us. I propose a new category of difference that depends upon race, class, and gender. This category could have moral and material impacts too vast to face without the courage to hold horror and hope in one breath. It is the category of climate privileged and climate condemned. Who causes climate change in relationship to who dies from it is a foremost moral issue of the early twenty-first century.[1]

The race and class dimensions of the dilemma are stark. *Climate change may be the most far-reaching manifestation of white privilege and class privilege yet to face humankind.* Caused overwhelmingly by the world's high-consuming people, climate change is wreaking death and destruction first and foremost on impoverished people, who also are disproportionately people of color. The island nations that will be rendered unsuitable for human habitation by rising sea levels, subsistence farmers whose crops are undermined by climate change, and coastal peoples without resources to protect against and recover from the fury of climate-related weather disaster are not the people largely responsible for greenhouse gas emissions. Nor are they, for the most part, white.[2] Many voices of the Global South recognize this as climate debt or climate colonialism and situate it as a continuation of the colonialism that enabled the Global North to enrich itself for five centuries at the expense of Africa, Latin America, Indigenous North America, and parts of Asia.[3]

62   The moral problem has three layers. First, the people most vulnerable to the ravages of climate change are—in general—not those most responsible for it. Second, climate-privileged societies and sectors may respond to climate change with policies and practices that enable them to survive with some degree of well being under the limited conditions imposed by the planet's warming while relegating others—the most "climate vulnerable"—to death or devastation as a result of those conditions.[4] The third layer is less widely recognized and perhaps most ominous from a moral perspective. Measures to reduce carbon emissions designed by privileged sectors may further endanger climate-vulnerable sectors. A team of Indian scholars points out that "poor and marginalized communities in the developing countries often suffer more from . . . climate mitigation schemes than from the impacts of actual physical changes in the climate."[5]

Within the United States, too, economically marginalized people—who are also disproportionately people of color—will remain most vulnerable to ongoing suffering from the extreme storms, as well as the respiratory illness, food insecurity, and disease brought on by climate change.[6] Environmental racism and white privilege strike again in climate change. This is not to suggest that some people are exempt from climate change impacts, but rather that some are vastly more vulnerable than others.[7]

My fervent hope is that people of good will in climate-privileged sectors will help forge paths away from this scenario of climate injustice and toward a more just and humane future, what some call "climate justice." "What," I ask, "are the ethical implications of climate change for those of us who are the material beneficiaries of the overconsumption and the colonial heritage that now culminate in climate change as climate injustice?" The larger project of which this is a part involves an interdisciplinary team and considers what changes may be called for at the levels of lifestyle, corporate policy and practice, public policy, and consciousness/worldview, and it considers also the motivational and political aspects of realizing those changes.

This chapter's focus is more limited. It first posits climate change as a compelling moral matter of race- and class-based climate debt and Global North climate debt. The second part of the chapter draws on the descriptive and transformative tasks of Christian ethics to face the problems of moral oblivion and moral inertia. A third section proposes a subversive liberative resource for building moral vision and agency. And the final part looks more practically at that resource. Along the way, I propose the concepts of "climate privilege," "climate violence," and "blinders of climate privilege" as tools for demystifying our situation; "climate reparations" as a dimension of a moral response; and "climate citizenship" as a form of moral identity.   63

Climate Change as Climate Debt and Climate Colonialism

Climate debt is a term coming from the Global South to describe the imbalance between nations and communities likely to suffer first and worst from climate change and those contributing most to it.[8] More specifically, climate debt refers to the disproportionate per capita use of the atmospheric space for carbon sinks by industrialized countries in the past and present. Climate debt theory posits that the costs of adapting to climate change and of mitigating it are the responsibility of the countries that created the crisis, the industrialized world. Said differently, "The polluter pays." Article 3(1) of the 1992 United Nations Framework Convention on Climate Change addresses this responsibility by obligating the Global North to take the lead on efforts to combat climate change.

Climate debt theory derives from the more established body of theory pertaining to ecological debt, which posits three kinds of ecological debt: intragenerational, intergenerational, and interspecies.[9] Mirroring this formulation, climate debt also has these forms.[10] The first, intragenerational, refers to the "debt" owed by countries of the Global North to people of the Global South as a result of their historical and current overemissions of greenhouse gases and thus overconsumption of atmospheric space. The World Council of Churches uses intragenerational debt with additional reference to "the debt owed by economically and politically powerful national elites to marginalized citizens." I share this additional use of the term, although this use is not common in the literature of climate politics or international environmental law.[11] Climate debt, in its second sense— intergenerational—refers to the debt owed by current generations to future generations due to climate change, ocean acidification, loss of biodiversity, and other implications of our overconsumption on Earth's atmosphere. Climate debt in the third sense is the debt owed by humankind to otherkind for the ecological damage wrought now and in centuries to come by climate change.[12] In this essay, we deal only with the first form of climate debt, intragenerational.

Intragenerational climate debt has three interdependent means of repayment, and they will be discussed shortly. Suffice it here to note that voices from the Global North have joined others of the Global South in arguing that climate debt must figure centrally in climate negotiations, international trade and investment treaties, and development policy.[13] Indeed, in environmental law, development economics, environmental planning, and theological ethics, climate debt is becoming recognized as a critical factor in climate policy.[14] The concept also has appeared substantively in the natural sciences.[15]

The obstacles to operationalizing the concept of climate debt in public policy, international climate negotiations, corporate policy, and individual lifestyles are significant. One is the vagueness of the terms involved (e.g., exactly what constitutes "disproportionate appropriation?"). Another is the difficulty of measuring atmospheric space use, and yet another is the porous and changing boundaries between different groups of people (i.e., previously unindustrialized nations, such as China, becoming some of the highest emissions producers). Nevertheless, the concept marks profound historic and current inequity and is crucial for negotiating the different responsibilities of various nations and sectors. Moreover, efforts to operationalize it are under way. One example is the effort in Belgium to calculate a part of that country's ecological debt.[16]

Why Look at Climate Change as Climate Debt?

Why look at climate change as climate debt? I offer three reasons. First, what constitutes the morally right response to a moral dilemma depends on what the problem is understood to be. Inadequate analysis leads to inadequate diagnosis and remedies. To illustrate, when asked in the mid-1940s about the "Negro problem" in America, Richard Wright responded: "There isn't any Negro problem; there is only a white problem."[17] The history of racism in the United States in housing, health care, law, education, exposure to toxic land use, and more would have been dramatically different had we recognized and addressed race as a "white problem" rather than as a black problem.

Response to the perilous reality of climate change is frequently framed around the principle of sustainability. Climate change as a matter of sustainability calls for reducing carbon emission through technological advances, energy efficiency, and energy conservation, and replacing fossil fuels with renewable energy sources. The moves are crucial, to be applauded and supported. If climate change were not connected, historically and contemporarily, to the power imbalances that have rendered climate debt, then this response—together with assistance to the victims of climate change—would be ethically adequate. It is, however, an inadequate and deceptive moral response for affluent societies and sectors if we: (1) are disproportionately responsible for climate change, (2) could choose sustainability measures that have adverse impact on impoverished people and peoples, (3) are material beneficiaries of the fossil fuel economies that generated the climate crisis, and (4) have produced economic orders that impoverished vulnerable peoples, thus rendering them less able to survive disaster related to climate change.

A response organized around sustainability alone allows the world's high-consuming societies and people to address climate change in ways that do not take moral responsibility for these factors and for the disproportionate impact that climate change and efforts to mitigate it have on people of color and economically impoverished people. In this case, the world's high-consuming and affluent minority could continue to

- respond to climate change in ways that reduce our carbon footprint and protect the more racially and economically privileged members of our society from the worst of the disastrous impact, at least for a time;
- assume that all nations have *equal* obligations to reduce carbon emissions;
- respond primarily with charitable assistance to the disastrous impacts of climate change on vulnerable people of the Global South;
- implement mitigation efforts that endanger vulnerable communities; and
- fail to take on compensation for climate debt.

The probable consequences are sinister. To illustrate: When yields of the world's staples diminish due to rising temperatures, neoliberal international trade and investment mechanisms would enable corporate agribusiness and the finance industry to raise prices to maximize profit. In the process, those of us with investments in those industries would gain financially, while impoverished people would be priced out. That is, once again, starvation would happen as a result of economic policy.[18] The flood of climate refugees includes not only those fleeing flooding waters but also those fleeing climate change–induced famine.[19] The numbers of predicted refugees are staggering. The Pentagon names it a national security issue.

If climate change—on the other hand—is seen not only as a problem of ecological sustainability but also of climate debt, damage done by one group to another, or human rights abused, then more is required in response. Debt owed by the wealthy to the impoverished calls for compensation. Damage done or rights abused may call for reparations. If climate change is seen also as a matter of race- and class-based climate privilege, then a moral response includes acknowledging and challenging that privilege. This essay examines the moral implications of climate change understood in these terms.

Before framing a moral response, a word about the "who" of this inquiry is in order. This essay grapples with the moral dilemma of a particular people of whom I am one. I speak of this people as "we," referring to the set of United States citizens who are white and are economically privileged.[20] The boundaries of this "we" are ambiguous. In some senses, many U.S. citizens are economically privileged while also being exploited through inadequate wages, nonexistent or sparse benefits, poor working conditions, wage theft, regressive taxation, exorbitant health care costs, and more. As a result, many live in poverty that may have life-threatening consequences or maintain a constant struggle to avoid it. These people are not the "we" of whom I speak, although much of what I say herein may pertain to them.

A second reason for seeing climate change as climate debt is theological. It pertains to repentance. Christians profess that freedom from sin begins with repentance. Where we do not repent, we remain in bondage to sin. Repentance, however, is possible only where sin is acknowledged. Climate violence is a powerful form of structural sin. If we do not see it, we cannot repent of it.[21] Failing to repent, we remain captive to it.

A third reason, also theological in nature, is the transformative potential of lament. In a powerful sermon on the book of Joel, Christian womanist ethicist Emilie Townes claims that social healing begins with communal lament. Communal lament, she explains, is the assembly crying out in distress to the God in whom it trusts. It is a cry of sorrow by the people gathered, a cry of grief and repentance, and a plea for help in the midst of social affliction. Deep and sincere "communal lament . . . names problems, seeks justice, and hopes for God's deliverance." "When Israel used lament as rite and worship on a regular basis, it kept the question of justice visible and legitimate."[22] Perhaps for us, too, lament is integral to social restoration. Lament, like repentance, is not possible if we fail to see that for which we are called to lament.

If repentance and lament are doorways to social healing, and if they depend on seeing the wrong that is done, then climate-privileged sectors and societies must open their eyes to the reality of climate debt and the catastrophic devastation and suffering that it will continue increasingly to spawn. These, then, are three reasons for seeing climate change as a moral matter of climate debt.

Ethics Capable of Moral Response to Climate Debt

For any who value justice or compassion, soul-shaking, mind-numbing, gut-wrenching questions surge forth. I have been trying in recent years to name them and pursue them. Consider one: What approach to ethics for climate-privileged people is capable of meeting the raging moral problem of climate debt? That is the concern of my book *Resisting Structural Evil: Love as Ecological-Economic Vocation.*[23]

In it, I suggest three understandings of ethics. We focus here on one articulated by Paul Tillich: The "meaning of ethics" he writes, is "to express the ways in which love embodies itself and life is maintained and saved."[24] What is the meaning and embodiment of love for people whose lives are destroying the conditions for life on Earth and condemning millions to devastation or death? The book elaborates a framework for an ethic of love as an ecological-economic vocation rather than only an interpersonal vocation.

Two foci of that ethic are morally empowering seeing and moral agency. Explore with me these two facets of morality. Ethics commonly is seen as a normative discipline, responding to the question of what we ought to do and be. Two dynamics of the climate crisis—the *"blinders of climate privilege"*[25] and the ease of moral inertia—render the normative task alone inadequate, calling forth a descriptive task and what I refer to as a transformative task of ethics. That is, in addition to its normative function, ethics must also:

- enable seeing reality for what it is in order to take moral responsibility for it, in particular, demystifying what is hidden from view by the blinders of privilege (descriptive task);
- ignite and sustain moral agency and hope for radical change toward a more socially just and ecologically sustainable future (transformative task).

I cannot overstate the crucial nature of both. The survival of civilization in a relatively humane form may depend on them. The two must be held together because the former (seeing climate change clearly) is a fast and sure way to disable the latter (moral agency and hope). We need, then, an ethics for climate justice that is capable of naming reality for what it is and—in spite of that—instilling hope and moral agency. This is a charge to ethics and to all people of good will at this point in human history.

Only by unearthing why we fail to "see" clearly what is going on in climate change can we transform that oblivion into courageous moral vision. In previous work, I have dissected moral oblivion, naming eight ingredients of it, and possible paths to overcoming it.[26] Here we note six other barriers to seeing what it is that we are doing as we carry on with public policies, corporate and institutional practices, and lifestyles that spew deadly amounts of greenhouse gases into the air.[27] Then we explore some territory in response to the last of these barriers.

I refer to these barriers as "blinders of climate privilege."

- For those of us who are white, whiteness feeds moral oblivion regarding climate change and its consequences. The links are many. As David Gushee notes, white privilege can lead white people to assume subconsciously that things will work out for us. Many structures of Euro-Western society for at least five centuries have been set up to benefit white people while endangering others (e.g., the criminal "injustice" system, housing codes, hiring and firing norms). Enculturation from birth by white supremacy provides a second link between whiteness and climate oblivion. White people are shaped by a deeply engrained but utterly denied societal presupposition that white lives matter more than other lives. And the lives of moneyed people matter more than the lives of economically destitute people. North American and European societies would respond far differently to climate disaster if we were experiencing that disaster as it is now experienced by Africans bearing the drought or the Maldives preparing to be submerged by rising seas. Privileged white folks in the United States would respond differently to the fossil fuel orgy if we were living the horrors of Shell Oil in the Niger Delta or Cancer Alley in the United States. We would not deem a 1.9-degree climate increase acceptable if it would have the impact on us that it will have on sub-Saharan Africa, Southeast Asia, and South Asia—death by starvation and water shortage.[28]
- Seeing would mandate radical changes in how we live, changes that bear economic cost. "Confronting climate change requires swearing off something that has been an extraordinary boon to humankind: cheap energy from fossil fuels."[29]

- A privatized sense of morality obscures the moral dimension of our roles in social systems and obscures the importance of engagement in social movements. All too easily we assume that being moral in interpersonal relationships and in individual or household lifestyles is adequate for moral being. That is, if I treat others with care, recycle, drive a hybrid or ride a bike, and take other steps to reduce my carbon footprint, I am morally good. Yet this does nothing to acknowledge that I continue as a player in economic systems that exploit Earth and others to assure my ongoing mode of living.[30]

- The moral dimensions of climate change are monumentally complex. For example, the harm has been done over centuries and generations, by people unaware of it, and by people who may be both victims and perpetrators of the harm done. Some of the harm is done through participation in systems from which many people arguably cannot disentangle themselves without doing immediate harm to themselves or dependents. The harm is difficult to quantify.

- We do not have a picture of the good that we need. It is not clear what it means to be a moral person or to lead a good life in the context of climate debt. The current human population living sustainably on the planet with relative environmental equity between and within societies is an unprecedented state of being involving changes not yet conceptualized.[31]

- We flee from the shame, guilt, and sense of impotence that seeing would evoke. The consequences of climate change as experienced by millions of people today are dire, and projected consequences—unless emissions are reduced much more rapidly than called for by current climate negotiations—are catastrophic, unthinkable. Moreover, the warming that has been set in motion cannot be undone. The reality that our way of life is destroying Earth's capacity to sustain life is too terrible to face; we flee into the comfort of ignorance, pretending that life can go on as it is. We cannot bear for long the idea that we have generated so much horrific suffering and death that we are undoing Earth's life-generating capacities. We cannot bear to see ourselves as so "bad." For some, the specter of unredeemability haunts. Will we face ultimate judgment by God or by karma or by the universe for having so cravenly destroyed so much?[32] A sense of powerlessness joins shame and guilt when we dare to acknowledge the power of the fossil fuel industry to influence public policy and the extent to which every action of daily life depends in some way on petroleum.

These are some of the attitudinal and perspectival reasons that we fail to see climate violence clearly or, if seeing it, why we are easily sucked into moral defeat.[33] The limitations of a single essay preclude addressing all of these barriers. Thus, we turn now to address only one of them, the last in this list.

A Subversive Liberative Resource in Christian Traditions: Incarnation

What would disarm the power of shame, guilt, and powerlessness to immobilize? What would enable facing the reality of "what we are doing" while also sowing moral agency and hope? To where should we turn for the crucial power to hold together fierce honesty about the destruction that our lives cause and fierce hope about our power for good?

Perhaps this is a responsibility of the world's religious traditions. Religion at its best has long been a wellspring of hope and moral power for overcoming seemingly insurmountable odds and for acknowledging both the evil and the good that seem to inhere in the human condition. Precisely here in the crucible of good and evil, the paradox of bondage to sin and freedom from it, religions are called to search their depths for potent seeds of hope and moral power for the work of ecological healing. All fields of human knowledge are called upon today to bring their resources to the great panhuman task of forging sustainable Earth–human relations marked by justice. Religion is one of those fields. If the people faithful to particular religious traditions do not uncover and draw upon the resources offered by their tradition, then those lifesaving and life-sustaining resources remain dormant. Tremendous gifts of power for life and for resisting structural violence go untapped.

In this essay, the religion considered is Christianity. Before moving on, a word is in order about the use of theological discourse to address public moral matters. Forms of theological discourse are many. The one used here is to interpret central Christian symbols (crucifixion, resurrection, and incarnation), suggesting that this interpretation holds morally empowering "truth." Four presuppositions regarding my use of religious truth claims undergird this move. First, in noting the power of Christian claims to serve the common good, I presuppose that other religious traditions also have that power; I make no claim that Christianity holds moral wisdom superior to that of other religious or spiritual traditions.[34] Second, I presuppose that spiritual and moral wisdom within religious traditions can benefit and enlighten people who do not identify with that tradition or share its belief systems. That is, I hold that religions exist not only for the benefit of their adherents but also for the benefit of the world. Third, I hold that the wisdom of each religious tradition is not adequate on its own and requires the supplemental insights of other religions. Finally, while my interpretation of Christian symbols and story is solidly grounded in biblical and theological scholarship, it is not the only valid interpretation. Valid interpretation of crucifixion, resurrection, and incarnation are multiple and have been since the earliest days following Jesus's death. The multiplicity of valid interpretations does not make any solid interpretation less valid any more than the differences between the four biblical accounts of Jesus's life are less valid because they differ. This is, in part, because Christianity has been, since the outset, a contextually based movement; the God revealed in Jesus "speaks" differently to people in different situations. These four presuppositions are crucial to what follows in this chapter, and I ask the reader to bear them in mind.

Christian traditions bring profound resources to the quest for morally empowering vision and agency. They span liturgical resources, hermeneutical approaches, theological claims, institutional networks, historical guides, value systems and moral norms, spiritual practices, and more.

One resource is an incarnation perception. It is a way of seeing all of reality as embraced and imbued by the great mystery that some call God. Christian traditions know that transcendent and incarnate presence as love, a love that is, according to the biblical witness, life-generating, justice-seeking, and Earth-treasuring.

Incarnate love is the breathtaking centerpiece of Christian faith. According to the story of love incarnate, creation unfolds embraced by a love that can be deterred by no force in heaven or earth. This love "will not cease in all the endless ages to come."[35] It is a love both intimately personal—for everyone without exception, embracing our very being—and expanding vastly beyond the person to envelop creation as a whole.

But that is not all. Christian traditions hold that this Spirit of love—the creating, liberating, healing, sustaining Source—is at play in and *within* the world, breathing life into it. It is present within, among, and beyond Earth's creatures and elements, luring us and all of creation toward the reign of God, a world in which justice and compassion are lived in their fullness by all and in which all of creation flourishes in the light of God.

We human creatures are created and called to recognize this gracious and indomitable love, to receive it, to relish it, and to trust it. More astounding yet, after receiving God's love—being claimed by it—humans are then to embody it in the world. We are beckoned to be the body of God's Earth-relishing, justice-making love working through us, in us, and among us to bring healing from all that would thwart God's gift of abundant life for all.

And here we arrive at the terrible truth. We human earthlings embody this love with a moral capacity unique to the human. It is the capacity to recognize the brutal and deceptive forces lined up against this love and to comply with, organize, and nourish these forces. This is the blessing and terrible burden of being human—our trifold moral identity. We are at once beloved beyond measure, the body of a love that surmounts all else, and broken by the magnetic pull to ignore, defy, and blatantly transgress that love.

Let us return for a moment to the particular nature of this love as manifest in the life of Jesus and the quest of his people, the ancient Hebrews, to know God. Thus revealed:

- This love created and is creating paradise on Earth.
- This love treasures the Earth and calls humans to serve and preserve it.
- This love has justice-making at its core.
- This love is so subversive of humanly constructed systemic domination that it took on fleshly form as a dark-skinned Palestinian Jew, born on the underbelly of imperial power and privilege.
- This love persisted in challenging the domination and exclusion institutionalized by imperial power, even at the cost of execution on a stake.

What Would It Mean to Practice Incarnation in the Face of Climate Debt?

What, then, does it mean to practice love incarnate in the face of climate debt? What would it mean to trust that we are claimed by and embody this kind of love, not only in individual life as interpersonal vocation but also as a vocation shaping us as bodies politic?[36] What love is and requires is the great moral question permeating Christian history. For two millennia, people who follow Jesus have struggled to grasp what it means to claim that God's love takes on fleshly form in the human creature and beyond in Earth's other creatures and elements. Just as the Great Spirit is both intimately knowable and infinitely beyond our knowing, so, too, is love; the nature of neighbor-love flowing from divine love is beyond full comprehension.

What can be said is that the love of God—as known in the tradition 73 of the Hebrew Bible and Jesus—seeks to address suffering and to undo oppression and exploitation that cause suffering. Love, therefore, is contextual and asks different things of people based on their situations. Jesus bids us ask: "What does it mean *in our here and now* to love neighbor as God loves us?" This contextuality is fitting, for the Holy One revealed in Jesus is a living God, a God in process, dynamically and actively engaged in the world, not a God of timeless concrete rules implemented in the same way for all people in every situation. Process theologian Daniel Day Williams says it well: "Love . . . changes form and brings new forms into being. . . . God in his creativity and freedom reforms the modes of love's expression."[37]

Therefore, we must ask what it means for climate-privileged peoples to practice incarnate love in the face of climate debt: What is love's bidding for those of us who are disproportionately responsible for climate change and owe our material wealth to the fossil fuel economies that generated the climate crisis? What is love's bidding for white economically privileged U.S. citizens in the early twenty-first century? This is the question I put before us. I suggest three partial responses.

Resistance and Rebuilding

Love for the climate privileged calls for a wedding of resistance and rebuilding. That is, it seeks to dismantle the power structures and ways of life that undergird climate change[38] while also rebuilding alternatives that are both ecologically sustainable and socially equitable. Resistance and rebuilding are intertwining streams in the movement toward climate justice. One alone cannot begin to free us from our bondage to climate-catastrophic ways of living. This duo is anchored in Christian theology as *denouncing* that which thwarts the in-breaking reign of God and *announcing* that which furthers it.

"Resistance" means refusing to participate in aspects of the global economic system that are quickly destroying Earth's atmosphere and countless communities and lives. Boycotting, divesting in fossil fuels, and withdrawing money from large corporate banks are examples. "Rebuilding" signifies supporting more socially just and ecologically healthy alternatives that are accountable to a "triple bottom line" (social, ecological, and financial). These alternatives pertain to all levels of social being: household/individual, corporate, institutions of civil society, and public policy.

Examples include small-scale and local or regional business and banking, local sustainable agriculture, and investing in renewable energy. Resistance and rebuilding are meant as a "way of life," not merely as incidents in the midst of it.

Resistance and rebuilding—as an expression of love known in Jesus and his scriptures—will be practiced in a mode of being that is vastly foreign to the consciousness of contemporary U.S. society, formed as it is by the individualism of modernity and the privatization of neoliberalism. Incarnation as resistance and rebuilding will take fruitful form in a communal and ancestral mode. I make no claim to understand fully what this entails. My aim is more humble—to offer them as pointers to be tested and explored as we forge our way into a future that we do not yet know.

Communal

To explain "communal," the wrong question is helpful. "What does it mean for me to live as if I am risen from the dead, and to live as if the Spirit of God is incarnate in my body, as if that Spirit has made Her home in my being?" This is the wrong question. Resurrection and incarnation in Christian tradition are not primarily a matter of *I* and *me*. Rather, resurrection and incarnation are communal realities.

We rise from and against death-dealing ways of life, and we embody God not primarily as individuals. Rather, we do this as woven into a body, a web, a communion, a mystery beyond our ken. After his crucifixion, when Jesus appears to his disciples, who were still living in terror, he addressed them with a plural "you." For example, in John's story (chapter 14), set in the upper chamber, when individual disciples address Jesus, he responds in the plural. The verse "Let not your hearts be troubled" (John 14:1) refers to the community's heart. The "your" is plural. When the Spirit comes at Pentecost, She comes to a body of people.

God—abiding within us—is calling forth a communion. It is a reality that even the disciples did not yet perceive. Nor do we—except in glimpses. In the imagery of Irenaeus of Lyons, it is a union and communion among those who hear God, and between them and Godself. In our communities of resistance and rebuilding, we begin to enact the communion that already exists, but that we only glimpse dimly. This communion that we are called to embody in faithful resistance and rebuilding is our home.

Practicing incarnation means discovering ever more fully what it means to live into this already-given union and communion with divine love that ultimately will overcome all forms of death and destruction, including the climate injustice that threatens to undo us, destroying the very people whom we are called to love and the garden that we are called to tend. This communion is not a present reality alone—it is a past, present, and future reality. It includes those who will come after us and those who came before, the ancestors. On a very practical level, it means creating communities of extraordinary ordinary life. What they look like is a key question before faith communities now and in the years to come. Explore it!

Ancestral

Christians and others who seek justice in the face of exploitation and domination stand in a heritage of resistance and rebuilding. The early church told stories and believed that the community was shaped by an epic story in which they were players.[39] They deemed it vital that the church perceive itself as situated within a heritage of resistance to whatever powers-that-be demanded them to defy God's ways and will. Today, that includes resistance to lifestyles, public policies, and economic practices that generate climate change, enable some to accumulate wealth at great cost to others and to Earth, reinscribe white privilege, or justify any other form of structural sin.

Faith communities embodying love by seeking climate justice and garden Earth's renewal will highlight that heritage of resistance in sermon, song, and sacrament. We will tell this sacred story in art and education, in prayer and celebration. What kinds of moral power will emerge if the practices of Christian communities teach our children that they walk in the footsteps of fiercely faithful, loving, Spirit-filled resisters whose words and deeds said no to ways of life that transgressed God's call to justice-making, Earth-serving love? This is the heritage of the Hebrew prophets; Jesus, who refused to comply with the ways of empire; parts of the early church, whose declaration that "Jesus is Lord" defied imperial Rome; the abolitionists; the "righteous gentiles," who defied Hitler's death machine; the Huguenots in the village of Le Chambon-sur-Lignon, whose quiet resistance saved four thousand Jews even while occupied by fascist forces; the civil rights movement; and more. What if our youth learned that this is "the people" into whom they were baptized? What if our children frequently heard sermons such as that preached by one of my pastors: "I could empathize with Paul in prison," she declared, "because last time I was in prison, I too was in solitary confinement." She had been jailed many times for protesting the Trident nuclear submarines stationed near Seattle.

Contemporary Christians and others who long for climate justice and Earth's healing will be more apt in the arts of resistance and rebuilding if we locate ourselves in this rich heritage of resistance to dominant powers that demand people to transgress ways of God's love. This ancestry is at the heart of Christian and Hebrew scriptures. Knowing it breeds courage and wisdom. Where we honor it as our ancestral home, present in our present, we will be more fertile ground for incarnate love that resists climate violence and rebuilds Earth-honoring, neighbor-loving ways of living.

In Closing

When we harness for God the energies of love, declared the great mystic Teillard de Chardin, we will for the second time in the history of the world have discovered fire. It is time to rediscover fire.

Toward that end, we have suggested a new category of difference in the entanglement. It is the category of climate privilege. After posing climate change as climate debt and climate colonialism, we noted the danger of moral oblivion and moral inertia, explored a radical incarnational perspective as one ingredient of moral vision and agency, and then asked what it would mean to practice incarnation. I now welcome, invite, and hunger for your collaborative, creative, questing wisdom to probe these musings, strengthen them, find problems in them, or springboard from them onto other paths toward ecological civilization.

Notes

1. The introductory paragraphs as well as the first part of this chapter draw heavily on my article "Climate Change as Climate Debt: Forging a Just Future," *Journal of the Society of Christian Ethics* 36, no. 1 (Spring/Summer 2016): 27–49, reproduced with permission.

2. Another example: the 40 percent of the world's population whose lives depend on water from the seven rivers fed by diminishing Himalayan glaciers are largely not white people.

3. The National Council of Churches in India declares: "Climate change and global warming are caused by the colonization of the atmospheric commons. The subaltern communities are denied of their right to atmospheric commons and the powerful nations and the powerful within the developing nations continue to extract from the atmospheric common disproportionately. In that process they have emitted and continue to emit greenhouse gases beyond the capacity of the planet to withstand. However, the subaltern communities with almost zero footprint are forced to bear the brunt of the consequences of global warming."

4. "Climate vulnerable" refers to nations and sectors that are particularly vulnerable

to the impacts of climate change, including drought, fierce storms, rising sea levels, disease, food shortage, and more. As defined by the IPCC, *vulnerability* refers to "the degree to which a system is susceptible to, or unable to cope with, adverse effects of climate change." *Third Assessment Report, Annex B: Glossary of Terms*, IPCC Working Group 2, 2001. I use *climate privilege* to indicate nations and sectors most able to adapt to or prevent those impacts, or to be less vulnerable to them.

5. Soumya Dutta, Soumitra Ghosh, Shankar Gopalakrishnan, C. R. Bijoy, and Hadida Yasmin, *Climate Change and India* (New Delhi, India: Daanish Books, 2013), 12. This study notes that climate change has "two sets of impacts" on vulnerable sectors. One is the actual impact of climate change. The "second set of impacts originates from actions that our governments and corporate/industrial bodies undertake in the name of mitigating climate change. This includes large-scale agro-fuel and energy plantations in the name of green fuel . . . extremely risky genetically modified plants (in the name of both mitigation and adaptation to climate change), more big dams for 'carbon-free' electricity," and more. Law professor Maxine Burkett articulates legal and governance dimensions of the moral problem: Those who "suffer most acutely [from climate change] are also those who are least responsible for the crisis to date. That irony introduces a great ethical dilemma, one that our systems of law and governance are ill-equipped to accommodate. Indeed, attempts to right this imbalance between fault and consequence have resulted in a cacophony of political negotiation and legal action between and amongst various political scales that have yielded insufficient remedies" (Burkett, "Climate Reparations," *Melbourne Journal of International Law* 10 [2009]: 2).

6. The report (Nia Robinson and J. Andrew Hoerner, *A Climate of Change: African Americans, Global Warming, and a Just Climate Policy for the U.S.* [Environmental Justice and Climate Change Initiative, 2008]) shows that "global warming amplifies nearly all existing inequalities" (1), "African Americans are disproportionately affected by climate change" (2), and some approaches to reducing greenhouse gas emissions have disproportionately adverse impacts on African Americans.

7. As early as 2001, the Third Annual Report of the IPCC alerts that "the impacts of climate change will fall disproportionately upon developing countries and the poor persons within all countries, and thereby exacerbate inequities in health status and access to adequate food, clean water, and other resources." https://www.ipcc.ch/report/ar3/syr.

8. The term *climate debt* was introduced into the international discourse at the 1992 UN Conference at Rio by Latin American nongovernmental organizations. Some refer to climate debt as "carbon debt." It is seen as one form of ecological debt.

9. For more on ecological debt, see Athena L. Peralta, ed., *Ecological Debt: The Peoples of the South Are Creditors, Cases from Ecuador, Mozambique, Brazil and India* (Quezon City: World Council of Churches, 2004); Andrew Simms, *Ecological Debt: The Health of the Planet and the Wealth of Nations* (Chicago: Pluto Press, 2005); and WCC Central Committee, "Statement on Eco-justice and Ecological Debt," September 2, 2009, http://www.oikoumene.org/en/resources/documents/central committee/2009/reportonpublicissues/state mentonecojusticeandecologicaldebt. An excellent theorizing of the concept and its application to national energy and climate policy is in Gert Goeminne, Erik Paredis, and Wouter Vanhove, *The Concept of Ecological Debt: Its Meaning and Applicability in Applicability in International Policy* (New York: Academia, 2008). See also websites of: Southern People's Ecological Debt Creditor Alliance (SPEDCA), European Network for the Recognition of Ecological Debt (ENRED), Ecuador's *Accion Ecologica*, England's Christian Aid, Friends of the Earth International, and WCC.

10. Cynthia Moe-Lobeda, *Resisting Structural Evil: Love as Ecological-Economic Vocation* (Minneapolis, Minn.: Fortress Press, 2013), 208–9.

11. WCC, "Statement on Eco-justice and Ecological Debt."

12. "Ecological debt" and "climate debt" are used also to signify the debt owed by specific corporations rather than nations. This raises another set of moral considerations not addressed in this essay. Finally, climate debt may be contextualized chronologically as a form of ecological debt appearing third. First, colonialism and neo-liberalism produced vastly unequal access to Earth's natural goods. This misdistribution of access was an initial form of ecological debt. To it was added a second: the corporate practice of transferring ecologically dangerous production plants to countries of the Global South in order to avoid environmental regulations and gain corporate tax breaks. "Pollution havens" joined tax havens. "Pollution haven," according to Matthew Clarke and Philip Lawn, refers to "any instance involving the relocation of capital induced by cost savings arising from disparate [environmental] regulations between countries." Matthew Clarke, "The End of Economic Growth?," *Ecological Economics* 69 (2010): 2219. Climate debt is a third form of ecological debt.

13. See WCC, SPEDA, ENRED, and *Accion Ecologica*.

14. For the first three fields, respectively, see, for example: Karen Mickelson, "Leading Towards a Level Playing Field, Repaying Ecological Debt, or Making Environmental Space," *Osgoode Hall Law Journal* 43, nos. 1–2 (2005): 137–70, and the law professors cited in this essay; Duncan McLaren, "Environmental Space, Equity and the Ecological Debt," in *Just Sustainabilities: Development in an Unequal World*, ed. Robert D. Bullard, Julian Agyeman, and Bob Evans (London: Routledge, 2003), 19–37; and T. Buhrs, "Sharing Environmental Space: The Role of Law, Economics and Politics," *Journal of Environmental Planning and Management* 47 (2004): 429–47.

15. A study led by University of California scientists and published in the *Proceedings of the National Academy of Sciences* found that "climate change and ozone depletion impacts predicted for low-income nations have been overwhelmingly driven by emissions from [high-income and middle-income nations]. . . . Indeed, through disproportionate emissions of greenhouse gases alone, the rich group may have imposed climate damages on the poor group greater than the latter's current foreign debt" (U. Thara Srinivasan, Susan P. Carey, Eric Hallstein, Paul A. T. Higgins, Amber C. Kerr, Laura E. Koteen, Adam B. Smith, Reg Watson, John Harte, and Richard B. Norgaard, "The Debt of Nations and the Distribution of Ecological Impacts from Human Activities," *Proceedings of the National Academy of Science* 105, no. 5 [2008]: 1768–73). Coauthor Richard B. Norgaard, a UC Berkeley professor of energy and resources, notes: "At least to some extent, the rich nations have developed at the expense of the poor and, in effect, there is a debt to the poor. . . . That, perhaps, is one reason that they are poor. You don't see it until you do the kind of accounting that we do here" (UC Press Release, *Rich Nations' Environmental Footprint Falls on Poor*, http://www.berkeley.edu/news/media/releases/2008/01/22_ecosystem.shtml).

16. The study proposes "an emission rights system that embodies compensation for the historical carbon debt. In this proposal debtors compensate creditors by realizing extra emission reductions and thus giving creditors extra emission rights. In this way industrialized countries would take the lead in combating climate change" (Paredis et al., *Concept of Ecological Debt*, xiii). The study was a response to the inclusion of "ecological debt" in Belgium *Federal Plan for Sustainable Development* 2001–4. Paragraph 582 of the plan states: "Belgium will study the concept of ecological debt and its practical applicability in policy" (xvii). I am aware of no other such efforts by northern nations.

17. Raphael Tardon, "Richard Wright Tells Us: The White Problem in the United States," *Action*, October 24, 1946, as cited in George Lipsitz, "The Possessive Investment in Whiteness: Racialized Social Democracy in the White Problem in American Studies," *American Quarterly* 47, no. 3 (1995): 369–87.

18. Mike Davis, *Late Victorian Holocausts: El Niño Famines and the Making of the Third World. (London: Verso, 2001).*

19. The term *climate refugees* is not used by the United Nations, which does not recognize as refugees people who are environmentally displaced, referring to them instead as displaced persons or migrants and thus not entitled to the political rights of refugees.

20. By "economically privileged," I connote people whose economic lives might be described in the following terms: Their income is not totally dependent on wages or salaries. They have backup resources (e.g., family support, possibility of buying a less expensive home, investments). A severe recession probably would not place them in a position of having no home, inadequate food, or no access to health care, transportation, or other necessities. Perhaps more significant to this project, the economically privileged have enough economic resources that, without jeopardizing the basic ingredients of life for themselves and their dependents, they *could* make economic choices (pertaining to consumption, investment, employment, etc.) that would serve the cause of climate justice *even if those choices were to diminish their own financial bottom line.* They could choose, for example, to buy local, divest from fossil fuels and reinvest in renewable energy, purchase a hybrid car or commuter bike, boycott products even if they are less expensive than the alternative, or take time away from income-earning work and dedicate that time to efforts for social change. This category of "economically privileged" is porous. The terms involved are fluid, and the people fitting this description of economic privilege occupy wide-ranging economic strata. Nevertheless, the intent is to signify the large body of U.S. citizens whose economic status bears these characteristics.

21. For an account of climate violence as structural sin, see Moe-Lobeda, *Resisting Structural Evil*, chapter 3.

22. Emilie M. Townes, *Breaking the Fine Rain of Death* (New York: Continuum, 2001), 24.

23. Moe-Lobeda, *Resisting Structural Evil.*

24. Paul Tillich and James Luther Adams, *The Protestant Era* (Chicago: University of Chicago Press, 1948).

25. By "blinders," I mean factors that enable those most responsible for climate change to ignore it and our responsibility for it (emphasis original).

26. Moe-Lobeda, *Resisting Structural Evil,* chapters 4, 5, and 6.

27. See "From Climate Debt to Climate Justice: God's Love Embodied in Garden Earth," in *The Wiley-Blackwell Companion to Religion and Ecology,* ed. John Hart (Hoboken, N.J.: Blackwell, 2017), 203–19. In previous publications, I explore more deeply the ingredients of moral vision and of hope and moral agency.

28. See the 2013 World Bank report at http://www.worldbank.org/en/news/feature /2013/06/19/whatclimatechangemeansafrica asiacoastalpoor.

29. I would change "humankind" to "parts of humankind." Charles C. Mann, "How to Talk About Climate Change So People Will Listen," *Atlantic,* August 13, 2014, http://www .theatlantic.com/magazine/archive/2014/09 /howtotalkaboutclimatechangesopeoplewill listen/375067.

30. For elaboration of this idea, see Moe-Lobeda, *Resisting Structural Evil,* 88–90 and 117–30.

31. See Jonathan Lear, *Radical Hope: Ethics in the Face of Cultural Devastation* (Cambridge, Mass.: Harvard University Press, 2006). According to Lear, there is a "radical hope" required to look toward "a future goodness that transcends the current ability to understand what it is" (104).

32. See the most recent report (2014) of the Intergovernmental Panel on Climate Change for an account of what has been and will be destroyed by climate change: http://www.ipcc .ch/report/ar5/index.shtml.

33. These factors are joined by other factors of a social structural nature. I examine one such factor—corporate investment in maintaining public moral oblivion—in *Resisting Structural Evil,* 98–100. Another factor— the subordination of political power to economic power—is the subject of Cynthia Moe-Lobeda, *Healing a Broken World: Globalization and God* (Minneapolis, Minn.: Augsburg Fortress Press, 2002), chapter 2.

34. While I do not see Christianity as holding superior moral wisdom for the work of Earth-healing, I do believe that it bears a unique burden. Christianity, inseparably wound up in the philosophical, ideological, and cosmological assumptions of modernity, has contributed immeasurably to the Earth crisis. Scholars and activists have analyzed those contributions endlessly. Doing so is essential—for only by recognizing them can we rethink and reconstruct. Rehashing that story is not my aim here. I assume the damage done by Christian beliefs and practices undergirding human dominion and oppression. I assume also that, having played this historic role, Christianity bears a tremendous responsibility to offer its resources to the panhuman task of rebuilding Earth's health. Yet I write out of a sister assumption, a conviction that the damage wrought by Christianity is matched and surpassed by the potential within Christianity for helping to build new ways of being human marked by equity among people and mutually enhancing Earth–human relations.

35. See Hadewijch and Columba Hart, *Hadewijch: The Complete Works* (New York: Paulist Press, 1980).

36. In *Resisting Structural Evil* and elsewhere, I have tried to flesh out what this would mean.

37. Daniel Day Williams, *The Spirit and the Forms of Love* (New York: Harper and Row, 1968), 4–5, 9.

38. Implications for specific public policy changes are in Cynthia Moe-Lobeda, "Climate Debt, White Privilege and Christian Ethics as Political Theology," in *Common Good(s): Economy, Ecology, Political Theology*, ed. Catherine Keller, Melanie Johnson-DeBaufre, and Elias Ortega-Aponte (New York: Fordham University Press, 2015), 286–306, and in Moe-Lobeda, "Climate Change as Climate Debt." For more extensive accounts of policy implications, see Maxine Burkett, "Climate Refugees," and Carmen G. Gonzalez, "Environmental Justice and International Environmental Law," in *Routledge Handbook of International Environmental Law*, ed. Shawkat Alam, Jahid Hossain Bhuiyan, Tareq M. R. Chowdhury, and Erika Techara (New York: Routledge, 2012), 77–98 and 717–30, respectively.

39. Wayne Meeks, *The Origins of Christian Morality: The First Two Centuries* (New Haven: Yale University Press, 1993), 189–210.

THE MYSTERY OF LOVE IN
THE *VIA COLLECTIVA*

Gail Worcelo, SGM, and Marg Kehoe, PBVM

> Love alone is capable of uniting living beings in such a way as
> to complete and fulfill them, for it alone takes them and joins
> them by what is deepest in themselves.[1]

—PIERRE TEILHARD DE CHARDIN

On a recent visit to New York City, we took the subway to the Upper West
Side of Manhattan and found ourselves walking into the magnificent space
of the Episcopal Cathedral of St. John the Divine.

To our surprise, Edwina Sandys's sculpture *Christa* was hanging over
the altar of a side chapel as part of an art exhibit hosted by the cathedral
titled *The Christa Project: Manifesting Divine Bodies*.

You may recall that during the Easter season in 1984, Sandy's controversial *Christa* was displayed in the cathedral as part of a small exhibition
on the feminine divine.

The current exhibition, featuring the work of twenty-one female artists,
includes a new sculpture by Edwina Sandys, which caught our attention.
The piece is titled *Freedom Circle* and depicts female forms emerging from
the stone that once bound them. This piece playfully reimages Stonehenge
in southern England—with female forms arising from the historic landscape. Freed from the weighty stone, the figures remain part of it, suggesting

a kind of liberation, one that remains connected to context while moving beyond.

New Frontiers of Being

Freedom Circle speaks to us of a new momentum in our time, a collective emergence out of the stone from which we have been hewn into "New Frontiers of Being."

Many women mystics throughout the ages have explored the spiritual life by plunging into the vast space of the interior alone, giving voice to what they discovered through writings, paintings, poetry, and art.

St. Teresa of Ávila, for example, gifted us with the *Interior Castle*, and St. Hildegard of Bingen created complex mandalas, both mapping the spiritual architecture of inner space during their lifetimes.

These women were scientists of the spirit, and through their sustained discipline and dedication presented us with templates that have advanced consciousness, offering humanity a stepping stone into deeper union with the Divine.

Freedom Circle points to a new emergence, perhaps a more intricate expression of our spiritual lives as we step into the vast space of the interior together, a shared space that does not exist within us but between us.

In speaking about "the space between us," we are referring to a shared interior experience of the Divine, represented spatially as "between us" rather than inside or outside us.

Pioneers in physics and related areas of scientific research are investigating and speaking about this same interior space, telling us that what we often think of as empty space, or "the space inside ourselves," is actually a vast relational field, mysterious, alluring, inviting.

In probing this mysterious space, they have come up with names such as *quantum field, pure vacuum, unseen ocean of potential*, and *plenum*, describing this space as a realm of generative potentiality, a fecund ground, an empty fullness.[2]

Insights from the time/space model of the quantum world give us fresh language to describe what we, the authors, mean by our "collective plunge into the heart of the Mystery."

We could just as easily speak in scientific terms and say that we are plunging into "the Unified Field of Infinite Possibility, an invisible field of information, unpredictability, and energy that unifies, organizes, and connects."[3]

As we come into alignment with this field of Divine Love, we become greater expressions of wholeness, coherence, and communion.

The Mystery of Love in the *Via Collectiva*

Let us reflect on Edwina Sandys's sculpture again, placing our attention on the collective emergence of the women into the open space, remembering that this space is not empty but seething with infinite possibility and the energy of Divine allurement.

Freedom Circle reminds us that we are at a new stage of evolutionary transformation: we are emerging collectively from the solid stone in which we have been embedded for centuries and are unfolding a new, fluid space in consciousness together.

The solo journey into the heart of the Divine is giving way to the *Via Collectiva*, a phrase we came up with to describe our collective journey into Love.[4]

Several months ago, we asked ourselves the question, "What would it be like to plunge into the waters of Divine Love together?"

We wanted to access this question by going beyond the narrow bandwidth of logic and reason, and began by simply sitting on either side of a piece of paper with colored paints, allowing the Mystery to express itself in the "space between."

Over a period of several months, twenty-five paintings emerged, portals into the Divine. In sitting with each painting, names were revealed: *Ever Steady Presence, Boundless Nature, Contraction and Infinite Possibility, Coherence, and the Fiery Spine of the Godhead.*

Upon completion of the first twenty-five paintings, we asked the question again: "What would it be like to plunge into the waters of Divine Love together?"

In April 2016, we sent a simple email invitation to forty women from around the world, laywomen and sisters we knew from various religious congregations, asking them to "join us for a four-month collective journey into the Divine Heart in a shared Field of Awakening."

To our surprise, thirty-nine of the forty women, from countries spanning the globe—Chile, India, Peru, Zambia, the United States, Ireland, New Zealand, Australia, Holland, Ecuador, Indonesia, Philippines, Jamaica, and France—accepted our invitation!

We called the gathering Continual Blossoming[5] because of its beautiful, poetic imagery and because we recognized it as an actual and already-existing dimension of our shared field, a fresh place to discover ever more expanded dimensions of ourselves in the Mystery.

In the invitation, we were clear that Continual Blossoming was not a course, program, retreat, or workshop but rather an emergence, the coming-to-be of something entirely new.

We also shared our sentiment that changing the world from the inside out, through collective engagement at the level of the interior, is a form of activism equal in potency to our direct, hands-on work in the world.

Our first gathering took place using Zoom technology,[6] and it was a thrill to see forty-one of us arrive together on the screen, instantly experiencing the dissolution of any boundaries of separation across distance and time zones.

We began by introducing our first four paintings and activating them in our shared field:

Dive In

Go Beyond the Known

Lift and Take Flight

Discover the Space Between Us

The directives coming from the paintings were simple and clear:

Dive!

Abandon all reference points.

Leave ego density and lift higher.

Indwell.

In the Field of Continual Blossoming, we are discovering that the deep interior is a space that exists not only within us but between us, and unlike current contemplative practices of sitting together in a shared space with our eyes closed, our eyes are open as we discover the Mystery present in the "space between."

This is a huge shift and is somewhat mind-boggling. It is like saying that the space inside the atom is 99.9999999999996 percent empty space! Or like exclaiming, "The reign of God is not so much within but between!"

In plunging into the waters of Divine Love together, we are not losing ourselves in oneness but rather finding ourselves inside the relatedness of the godhead.

The Mystery reveals itself in and through the collective in ways not possible inside solitary practice. Through monthly *holon* gatherings (five or six women), for example, we use simple inquiry to explore the "space between" with questions such as "What is present?" or "What are we experiencing now?"

Here are some email notes we have received from the women participating in Continual Blossoming:

- "We are entering a new country and learning a new language together."
- "This is what I have been longing for."
- "All sense of separation is dissolving."
- "Set your life on fire, seek those who can fan your flame."
- "Diving in together, flying as a flock. . . . Here's to the unfolding of the unfolding."
- "How zesty and invigorating to collectively lean into what has never been before; we are entering into the numinous together, the not yet known."

Creative Union

"Great steps occur," said Teilhard de Chardin, "when cosmic organization goes to another level of complexity, uniting elements into new creative unions."

These new "creative unions" bring into being something that never existed before. A new being emerges from the deep connections and interactions, constituting greater depth and levels of oneness and wholeness.[7]

The elements that compose the new being exchange a certain degree of individual autonomy for a new level of collective capacity and depth. We see this process occurring throughout the entire universe story. Atoms unite to form molecules, molecules unite to form cells, and so on.

As structural complexity increases, so does consciousness. The more highly organized the physical form, the greater its capacity for manifesting deeper being.

Since evolution is still unfolding, and the pattern holds true, it is our turn as a new humanity to become the next creative union by linking and sharing what is deepest in ourselves.[8]

We are already entering this new space of creative union as we step out of the weighty stone edifice from which we have been hewn and open together to the possibilities before us.

As we awaken the energies of love together, humanity will make its next contribution to the evolutionary process by forming a new being, an inter-Christic field[9] that will bring about a more coherent, flourishing, and divinized world.

figure 1 Gail Worcelo, SGM, and Marg
Kehoe, PBVM, *Creative Union*. Painting
by hand, 24 × 24 inches. Used with kind
permission by the artist. Photo: Amelia
Hendani.

figure 2 Gail Worcelo, SGM and Marg
Kehoe, PBVM, *Lift and Take Flight*. Painting
by hand, 24 × 24 inches. Used with kind
permission by the artist. Photo: Amelia
Hendani.

Notes

88

1. Pierre Teilhard de Chardin, *The Human Phenomenon*, ed. Sarah Appleton-Weber (Chicago: Sussex Academic Press, 2015), 189.

2. Barbara Fiand, *Awe-Filled Wonder: The Interface of Science and Spirituality*, Madeleva Lecture in Spirituality (Mahwah, N.J.: Paulist Press, 2008), 16.

3. Joe Dispenza, *Becoming Supernatural: How Common People Are Doing the Uncommon* (Carlsbad, Calif.: Hay House, 2017), 235.

4. *Via Collectiva* is a phrase we came up with to describe our next emergence on the spiritual path.

5. *Continual Blossoming* is an ongoing emergence that we began in May 2016. At the time of this writing, we are in our second session (October 2016–June 2019), with forty women from around the world.

6. ZOOM is a user-friendly web and video conferencing technology that enables participants to see each other, break into groups, and record sessions.

7. Kathleen Duffy, SSJ, *Teilhard's Mysticism: Seeing the Inner Face of Evolution* (Maryknoll, N.Y.: Orbis Books, 2014), 60–61.

8. Beatrice Bruteau, *The Grand Option: Personal Transformation and a New Creation* (Notre Dame: University of Notre Dame Press), 2001, 49–63, and Beatrice Bruteau, "A Song That Goes on Singing," *EnlightenNext Magazine*, interview by Amy Edelstien and Ellen Daly (July 13, 2013). https://amyedelstein.com/evolutionaryspiritualitybeatricebruteau. This is a wonderful interview on "Creative Union" and has been a source of deep inspiration for us.

9. The *Inter-Christic Field* is a term coined by Gail Worcelo in reference to our next lived expression of the Christ Life. It is beyond the scope of this essay to develop.

DEEP SOLIDARITY

Dealing with Oppression and Exploitation
Beyond Charity and Advocacy

Joerg Rieger

Charity and Advocacy

Charity is one way in which people of faith seek to address problems of exploitation and oppression. Providing relief, charitable giving and charitable acts can ameliorate suffering to some degree and sometimes even save lives. Most people of faith seem to assume that charity is the most faithful response to the suffering of others because they remember some of the things that Jesus said.

Charity, however, does not address the causes that exploit and subjugate people and that lead to suffering. If it treats symptoms without regard for the underlying problems, it can make people complacent and support systems of exploitation and oppression. Those who provide charity for others often end up feeling good about themselves and their benevolence, and those who receive charity might conclude that the system is not so bad after all and that there is no need to change it. What if failure to address the underlying causes of exploitation and oppression amounts to covering them up and worse?

Charity takes on a different quality when it does not remain a one-way street. When the eyes of those who engage in charity are opened to the causes of the problems they are trying to address, things change. That this step is a move in the right direction is evidenced by pushback. As Bishop Dom Hélder Câmara once put it: "When I give food to the poor, they call me a saint. When I ask why they are poor, they call me a communist."[1] Pushback, no matter how harsh, sometimes tells us that we are on the right track.

For religious communities and for theologians, it is, of course, better to participate in acts of charity than to remain locked up in their ecclesial or academic ivory towers. At best, however, this is only a first step, and we always need to keep in mind the temptations. Too often charity amounts to applying bandages and justifying the structures of oppression and exploitation; if some are taking care of the exploited, and if some of the exploited are making it back into the system, things are possibly not so bad after all.

Charity that is tied to a deeper understanding of oppression and exploitation often leads to advocacy, which means speaking out against the injustices at the root of our problems. Practices of advocacy include prophetic statements, protest, lobbying, organizing, and marching in the streets.

In more progressive religious circles, advocacy is often understood as an alternative to charity. This is a good move for two reasons. First, advocacy is indeed a significant improvement over charity. Unlike charity, advocacy is concerned with the causes of the problems that people experience. To use an image: at a dangerous traffic intersection where many people get hurt, proponents of charity might build a hospital, promoting healing for those injured people. Proponents of advocacy, on the other hand, might lobby for a traffic light in order to address the dangerous situation at its roots.

Second, and contrary to a commonly held belief, advocacy is more deeply rooted in many faith traditions than charity. Many of the prophets of the Hebrew Bible, also recognized in Christianity and with some resonances in Islam, speak out against the injustices that oppress the poor and other marginalized groups, such as widows, orphans, and strangers.

Like other prophets, Amos condemns those who "trample on the poor and take from them levies of grain" (Amos 5:11). In Christianity, Jesus speaks out against oppressive customs that put pressure on the poor, women, children, and those who are sick and thus excluded from the community. Jesus preaches good news to the poor, not charity: receiving handouts is not good news to the poor; being no longer poor is (Matthew 11:5; Luke 4:18).

When dealing with poverty, for instance, advocates are not blaming the poor for their misery, and neither are they simply trying to provide services to poor people; rather, advocates seek to address and bring to an end the conditions that cause poverty. Instead of blaming low-wage workers for their inability to make ends meet, for instance, advocates speak out for the need to raise the minimum wage and to establish a living wage that allows workers and their families to make ends meet. The same is true for ecological and environmental problems. Advocates are not merely trying to clean up the air or the water. Advocates seek to address the causes and sources, which often means "speaking truth to power."

Deep Solidarity

Solidarity, and deep solidarity in particular, pushes us one more step beyond advocacy and helps us address exploitation and oppression at a deeper level yet. Advocacy reaches its limits when advocates fail to understand their deep connections with those for whom they are advocating. Too many advocates assume that they are somehow above or less affected by the problem, primarily seeking to help others—whether human or nonhuman—who are less fortunate. This pattern has been especially prevalent in religious communities.

Advocacy, while well-meaning and sincerely trying to help, creates several problems. One is that those who consider themselves privileged are calling the shots, acting as if they had the ability to fix the problems alone. This rarely works, because the problems are usually too big and because the privileged group is not able to understand what is going on without listening those who are most immediately affected. Another problem has to do with the fact that those who consider themselves privileged feel like they can walk away from solidarity whenever they have had enough because they fail to understand the deeper connections.

I have been using the term "deep solidarity" to tackle these problems.[2] Deep solidarity takes into account the solidarity of those who are under the gun in the current situation. It develops along the lines of class and describes a situation in which the 99 percent of us who have to work for a living realize that we are in the same boat. The question is not primarily how the church can support working people; the question is how faith communities can begin to understand that they are mostly made up of working people, that most of us are workers now, and that even the divine joins us in deep solidarity. The environment is part of this solidarity as well, as it, too, is put to work by capitalism and subject to exploitation by the same interests that exploit working people. To be sure, understanding our deep connections and relationships does not mean that our differences have to be covered up. Just the opposite: deep solidarity allows us to respect our differences and to put them to productive use.

Deep solidarity includes those who consider themselves middle class or somewhat privileged. As the fortunes of the 1 percent are growing, the middle class is less able to keep up, faced with increasing college costs for the next generation that may not even find jobs, reduction of benefits and job security, reduction of social security and ever more limited health care plans, and an increasingly obvious loss of political power. In terms of simple math, someone who earns $150,000 a year is closer to someone who earns $15,000 a year than to someone who earns $500,000 a year—the realm where membership in the 1 percent barely begins. Earnings are, of course, merely the tip of the iceberg. What matters is power. Even members of the middle class have surprisingly little power over their future: they cannot do much to push back when the corporation requires them to work harder and longer hours; they cannot do much to secure their personal investments, which are subject to ever greater market fluctuations from which mostly the insiders benefit; and they cannot do a whole lot to secure their future. Once again, this deep solidarity includes the environment, which is underappreciated under the conditions of capitalism.

The 99 percent increasingly find themselves in the same boat, as even the better jobs are becoming more and more precarious, with the potential of being cut at any time. Today, white-collar workers are often just as affected as blue-collar workers by corporate efforts to maximize profits at all costs; unlike workers, the environment often does not even show up in the calculation of the cost to do business. The proletariat of working people is turning into what some have called the "precariat," a diverse group of working people that includes a cross section of the 99 percent, who are forced to bear the brunt of increasing insecurity, risk, and pressure at work.[3] Whenever jobs are cut, the jobs that are coming back are designed for temp workers, workers without benefits, and those who are willing to work for less.

Unfortunately, what happens at the level of work and labor also happens in every other area of life. Like the members of the working-class majority (at 63 percent of the population), members of the middle class (at 35 percent of the population)[4] have less and less power in their communities, whereas the larger donors and philanthropists call the shots in cities and towns, as well as religious communities. Influencing elections at the regional, state, and national levels is completely out of the reach of individual members of the working and middle classes.

As the middle class finds itself closer to the working class and the poor than ever before, the question is not helping the underprivileged. Required is solidarity rather than advocacy, based on understanding what we have in common and the need to work together if we want to make a difference. For the 99 percent working majority, trying to replicate the power of the 1 percent is not an option. We will never be able to beat them at their game. Of course, there are differences within the top 1 percent as well. It is very hard to comprehend in financial terms that one family can own as much as 40 percent of all Americans combined; it is almost impossible to comprehend what that difference means in terms of power and influence.[5]

Not all is lost, however. To the contrary, these sharp differences can help us to develop an understanding of what the rest of us—both human and nonhuman—have in common, to resist oppression, and to reconnect that which belongs together. In the process, we can learn to develop different forms of power, which are not only more powerful than the power of the 1 percent but also longer-lasting.

Ancient Stories of Deep Solidarity

Deep solidarity is embodied by some of the key figures of our faith. Mary, the mother of Jesus, is often portrayed wearing the vestments of nobility and a crown. In real life, she was a common person—being ostracized as an unwed mother and later marrying a construction worker—and there is no indication that she ever joined the 1 percent. Mary is aware that by choosing her to be the mother of Jesus, God lifted up the lowly (Luke 1:48, 52). In the Bible, Mary also celebrates the fact that the God who lifts up the lowly pushes the powerful from their thrones and fills the hungry with good things while sending the rich away empty (Luke 1:52–53). Mary thus joins God in deep solidarity with those who are pushed to the ground. Who knows, the powerful who are being pushed from their thrones and the rich who are sent away empty might use this opportunity to join the emerging deep solidarity as well.

Another story of deep solidarity is the story of Moses, who was a descendant of the Hebrew slaves raised as an Egyptian prince in Pharaoh's court. Things change, however, when he sees the Hebrew slaves being mistreated in Egypt. According to the story, Moses overreacts and kills one of the Egyptian slave masters. This act certainly does not make him a leader, even in the eyes of the Hebrew slaves (Exodus 2:11–14). In exile, Moses learns to live the life of a worker, and it takes years before he moves to the next step, developing the skills of an organizer in collaboration with his brother Aaron and his sister Miriam (Exodus 15:20–21).

The ancient story of the Burning Bush resonates with the notion of deep solidarity. In this story, God speaks to Moses out of a bush that is burning but is not consumed. While this miracle is often noted and remembered, the speech is not. God said to Moses:

> I have observed the misery of my people who are in Egypt; I have heard their cry on account of their taskmasters. Indeed, I know their sufferings, and I have come down to deliver them from the Egyptians, and to bring them up out of that land to a good and broad land, a land flowing with milk and honey, to the country of the Canaanites, the Hittites, the Amorites, the Perizzites, the Hivites, and the Jebusites. The cry of the Israelites has now come to me; I have also seen how the Egyptians oppress them. So come, I will send you to Pharaoh to bring my people, the Israelites, out of Egypt. (Exodus 3:7–10).

Deep solidarity is expressed in this passage, first of all, in God's own actions. God speaks of seeing and hearing what is going on as the Egyptian slave masters wage class struggle against the Hebrews. What is more, God decides to join the struggle for liberation. Moses, the shepherd of his father-in-law's flock, having long abandoned his status as a prince in Egypt, now joins the struggles of his people in Egypt under the leadership of a God who is committed to taking sides. Both men and women collaborate in the movement, even though Miriam only gets short mention in the texts, which were probably written by men. Deep solidarity opens up a window on who God is in the Abrahamic religions. In the Exodus stories, God is not working from the outside, as the models of charity and advocacy often assume; rather, God is part of the struggle, and God takes sides.

The dominant powers who benefit from oppressing and exploiting others are not pushed aside here but called to conversion and repentance. Even Pharaoh gets several chances (Exodus 5:1, 7:16, 8:1, etc.; see also Qur'an 7:105). Even though this does not happen in the Exodus story, in some cases the 1 percent decide to join the 99 percent working majority.

Deep solidarity is also expressed in the life of Jesus of Nazareth. He grew up among construction workers who, in the Roman Empire, were often hired for large building projects. There, they experienced conditions that many construction workers experience today, including long working hours, lack of water and safety equipment, and no benefits. When the jobs were finished, many of them would be laid off, so it is very likely that Jesus experienced unemployment as well.

Jesus embodies deep solidarity not merely because he grew up as a worker but because he never made any efforts to move "up and out." To the contrary, he stayed in deep solidarity with working people his whole life. Many of his disciples were working people, four of whom (Peter, Andrew, James, and John) were fishermen. Jesus's parables are full of examples from everyday labor and work, telling the stories of shepherds, who usually were not the owners of their flocks; of working women; of workers in vineyards and in fields; of fishermen; and of service workers.

That one of Jesus's disciples, Matthew, reportedly was a tax collector further affirms what I mean by deep solidarity. If he was a member of the 99 percent, Matthew realized his deep connectedness to the common people who made up the Jesus movement. If he was a member of the 1 percent, Matthew shows that the 1 percent can indeed join the solidarity of the 99 percent and that true conversion is possible. In either case, what is very clear is that Matthew and other privileged people who were part of the Jesus movement did not convert Jesus to the 1 percent; the opposite is the case: he converted them to the 99 percent.

Several wealthy and prominent women who followed Jesus (Luke 8:1–3), as well as Zacchaeus, a prominent tax collector who may have been a 1 percenter (Luke 19:1–10), also embody this deep solidarity. When Zacchaeus, after his encounter with Jesus, turns over half of his wealth to the poor and makes fourfold restitution to those whom he defrauded, he is not merely engaging in charity but joins in deep solidarity with those who are trampled underfoot in the Roman Empire: working people, peasants, and the unemployed. It is not hard to imagine the consequences of this public stand of solidarity. The solidarity of the powerful, with whom Zacchaeus was connected before he met Jesus, is now no longer available to him. The same is most likely true for the wealthy women who joined Jesus. Imagine the consequences when Joanna, the wife of one of King Herod's officials, began supporting the Jesus movement (Luke 8:2)!

The Resilience of Deep Solidarity

Joining others in deep solidarity and taking a stand against oppression and exploitation have never been easy. According to the Gospel of Luke, Jesus's first proclamation of good news to the poor ended with an attempt by the faith community to throw him off a cliff (Luke 4:16–30). What seems to have enraged the community in particular was that Jesus claimed that he would be the one bringing the good news.

Had Jesus merely intended to be a heroic advocate for the oppressed and exploited, without working toward deep solidarity, his movement might have ended abruptly if they had managed to throw him off that cliff in Nazareth. Otherwise, it would have ended later, at the point of his crucifixion. However we interpret Jesus's story here, the reality of pushback highlights the limits of advocacy and the need for deep solidarity.

Two big drawbacks of advocacy are, first, that advocates often stifle the agency of those for whom they speak and, second, that advocates often overestimate their own power. The dominant powers benefit from both moves. Jesus would have scarcely been a threat to the Roman Empire of his times if he had acted alone or with a small group of radicals. And Jesus would not have been a threat had he assumed that he could do this work all by himself, like an ancient superhero. The same is true for individual organizations or groups of people who refuse to be in solidarity with other groups or broader movements, no matter how committed or radical they might be.

Working people, the 99 percent who work for a living, will not be able to make a difference if they assume that the support of a few advocates will do the trick. Elected officials, sympathetic 1 percenters, and a couple of nonprofit organizations can make some difference, but they will not be able to turn the tide. Deep solidarity requires us to think about the agency of all of us and what contributions we can make to the common good together. This includes thinking about the agency of nonhuman forces, a topic that goes beyond what can be addressed here.[6]

The second problem, that advocates tend to overestimate their own power, is equally significant. Rarely are the dominant powers challenged by a few prominent voices. This is why these dominant powers want us to believe that individuals like Martin Luther King Jr. or Rosa Parks acted singlehandedly. If Parks were merely a woman who at some point got tired of segregation in public transportation and sat down in the wrong section of a bus, her acts are heroic but not dangerous. If a pastor, however eloquent or prominent, preaches a good sermon, his act may be heroic, but it is hardly dangerous, either, without the support of an organized community.

White males who enjoy some privileges in particular often overestimate their own power. We tend to assume that people are actually listening to what we have to say, and that when we stand up and make demands or issue calls to action, things will change. Such advocacy is doomed to failure because the dominant system will not be impressed by a few dissidents, even if they band together in small groups.

Power that works in terms of the system cannot easily be transformed into alternative power. Harnessing dominant power for other purposes usually ends in failure. At the systemic level (whether in economics, politics, or religion), such efforts are quickly subsumed by the dominant powers. At the personal level, resignation and burnout result from too much reliance on dominant power. Examples can be given for both cases. Consider, for instance, the efforts of an (actual) regional organization of churches to "eradicate poverty" in two different zip codes. It is impossible to eradicate poverty without addressing what caused it in the first place; trying to harness the dominant powers to clean up the mess that they created will not very likely lead to success. Moreover, those who are charged with making it happen may be assigned blame that is easily internalized; burnout, unfortunately, is very common.

Deep solidarity is necessary to deal with these problems. Rosa Parks, for instance, in addition to being a person of great courage, was trained in the solidarity of the civil rights movement and prepared for the role that she would eventually play in the Montgomery bus boycott. By the same token, Martin Luther King Jr. acted in deep solidarity with many grassroots groups that emerged all over the country in diverse locations linked to diverse organizations. This is why the civil rights movement did not end with the shooting of King. Despite the shock and the deep depression King's murder caused, things continued to move ahead.

Deep solidarity helps us overcome roadblocks, including the divide-and-conquer efforts of the system that thrives on the back of others. Those of us who have to work for a living—the 99 percent working majority—find ourselves in the same boat, however, not because we are all alike and our differences do not matter; rather, we find ourselves in the same boat because of the dominant system and its efforts to use our labor for someone else's profit and gain. Once again, working people and the environment are subject to the same pressures.

The clearer we are about this, the more deep solidarity becomes an option. Belonging to the working majority is what connects us, up and down the various social ladders and scales that exist among the 99 percent.[7] Deep solidarity is built on the awareness that we are all working people now—including the underemployed and the unemployed, most of whom would much rather work than wait for handouts.

Valuing Diversity and Putting It to Use

98   Deep solidarity is anything but narrow. One of its most important traits is
that it does not require us to be alike or set our differences aside.[8] Just the
opposite: deep solidarity benefits from our differences, brought together
for the common good, and it develops power by putting our differences to
productive use while deconstructing their negative aspects. Moreover, as we
put our differences to use, we begin to realize that those who are forced to
endure the greatest pressures might have the most valuable lessons to teach.

Deep solidarity not only thrives on differences but also brings to light
otherwise hidden privileges and helps to deconstruct them. The world of
working people is one of the best places to start. As W. E. B. Du Bois has
observed: "Probably the greatest and most effective effort toward interra-
cial understanding among the working masses has come about through
the trade unions."[9]

The tensions of race and ethnicity may serve as our first example.
Becoming aware of deep solidarity as working people, white people begin
to understand that they may have more in common with so-called racial
and ethnic minorities than with white elites. The advantages that white
working people enjoy in comparison to their minority colleagues may be
significant, but they pale in comparison to the advantages that the white
elites enjoy over white workers. White employees may indeed have the ear
of white employers; receive slightly better salaries and benefits than African American, Hispanic, or Asian employees; and may have better chances
to get hired. Nevertheless, their whiteness does not put them on par with
their employers. White workers, like other workers, are hardly able to challenge and confront their superiors on matters of consequence.

In this situation, an awareness of deep solidarity can provide white
people with an opportunity to use whatever power they may have in the
fight against oppression and exploitation. White workers who have more
clout with their bosses can use it in alternative fashion, for instance, by
putting in a good word for others or by speaking up when nobody expects
it. White shoppers who are more valued have a choice either to conform
or to challenge the places they frequent. In the process, the power of the 99
percent is built when white working people begin to listen to other working people, who, due to the fact that they are forced to endure even greater
pressures, might be able to see more clearly not only the problems but also
the possibilities.

Employing one's limited privilege in the fight against oppression and exploitation may be the best way to deconstruct it. White power is deconstructed when white working people begin to question their ties with dominant white power and put whatever privilege they have in the service of deep solidarity with their fellow workers of racial and ethnic minorities. Feeling guilty about one's privilege, on the other hand (a common response when people become aware of it), prevents its productive use. While white working people should not overestimate their own power—the whiteness of a worker by itself will not win the battle—underestimating it would also be a mistake.

What about gender relationships? In 2013, white women were paid 78 cents for every dollar a white man earns doing the same work, Asian American women 90 cents, African American women 64 cents, American Indian (and Alaska Native) women 59 cents, and Latina women 54 cents.[10] In addition, women earn only 38 percent of what men earn during their prime working years, between ages twenty-six and fifty-nine. Deep solidarity for men, in this case, means to understand how their fate is actually connected more closely to women than to men of the elite groups. While a man in a heterosexual marriage may get some benefits out of being macho or a patriarch at home, he might benefit a good deal more if the work of his wife were valued equally and if solidarity led her to activate her own powers for the common good.

When relating to women in these new ways, men can learn how to use whatever power they have in a patriarchal world to challenge the dominant powers that oppress and exploit women. This is how patriarchal power is deconstructed. Some feminist theologians have made this argument about Jesus's ways of being a man: the fact that a man spoke out against patriarchal power and in support of women must have come as a surprise, as men are expected to support other men. The dominant system was certainly not anticipating this, and neither were some of Jesus's closest followers, but this is why it made a difference.[11] Of course, using male privilege against patriarchy means to lose it eventually, as the good old boys will not easily forgive and forget.

When race, ethnicity, gender, and sexuality come together, matters become more complex yet. Deep solidarity in these relationships can only be forged if it becomes clear how the work and labor of all of us are under pressure, although this is the case for the work of some more than others. When jobs are sent overseas, for instance, the racism and sexism that endorse treating nonwhites and particularly women in other countries less well also hurts white male workers in the United States. Likewise, sexism hurts men as well when, during the Great Recession, men were sometimes laid off before women because women earned less.

Deep solidarity in these cases can prevent us from blaming the victims, identify where energy and agency are found, and direct our agency to where it can make a difference. In organizing poultry workers in the south of the United States, for instance, African American workers were in a stronger position to speak out against unfair labor practices than immigrant workers from south of the border, making multiracial and ethnic dialogues essential.[12] While many white American men who belong to the 99 percent working majority still need to learn about the limits of their power, they can now employ this limited power in such a way that the community benefits rather than the elites.

Even for relatively privileged members of the middle class, things change when they become aware of deep solidarity. Now they can put some of their privileges to use so that they will actually make a difference in the fight against oppression and exploitation, reshaping their identity in the process. Instead of using their education to shore up the position of the 1 percent, college-educated people can now put their expertise to work for the well-being of the 99 percent. All areas and fields of study are useful: how do we assess the current political, financial, psychological, social, cultural, scientific, and religious situations?

Still, the middle class will not be able to do any of this without the input and guidance of those who experience greater oppression and exploitation. Deep solidarity should not make us forget that some are worse off than others. Those who feel the pressures of the system most acutely are the ones who have no reserves, who depend on their income from work with no safety nets, and who are therefore predisposed to see and feel more clearly what is going on. In this regard, we might also learn by taking a closer look at the superexploited environment.

For those of us who are part of the working majority, the 99 percent, the need to work for a living ties us into concerns of many of the popular movements, including the Occupy Wall Street movement, realizing the fundamental difference between the 1 percent and the 99 percent, and the Black Lives Matter movement, as black lives are destroyed in ways that include what is happening at work or as a result of a lack of work. Even human trafficking, perhaps one of the most heinous crimes of our time, is tied to work, as most human trafficking turns out to be labor trafficking.

Likewise, wage theft and the worst cases of wage depression are often tied to racism, ethnocentrism, and sexism. The burdens of environmental destruction, finally, also fall to those who are marginalized along the lines of race and class. Garbage dumps are more likely to be put in their neighborhoods, as are heavy polluters such as power plants and factories.

In this light, deep solidarity becomes a matter of life and death. Here is where we might find the power and the energy to make a difference and to preserve life. Work, due to the fact that we are spending too much time at it and that its pressures affect us more deeply than we ever imagined, welds us together at many levels. Minds, hearts, and bodies are all involved. As one of my graduate students, Ben Robinson, put it: "We may march together, we may work together, but we are not in solidarity until we *feel* together."[13]

Deep solidarity, to recap, helps us to take into account and make use of the fact that the 99 percent have more in common with each other than with the 1 percent. This allows for more effective action and collaboration without erasing differences.

Conclusion

While the 99 percent working majority are together in this fight against oppression and exploitation, not everybody will join us. In fact, because things are urgent, it would not be wise to waste too much time on those who are not yet ready. Instead, we need to connect with those growing numbers of people who are waking up every day to the fact that oppression and exploitation affect them to growing degrees. These people come from all walks of life; from various races, genders, sexualities; from farmworkers toiling in the hot sun all day to white-collar cubicle workers. For change to happen, certain critical mass is needed, but it will not take 99 percent of the 99 percent.

The best news is that deep solidarity does not have to be produced artificially. Unlike charity and advocacy, deep solidarity does not depend on moral exhortation: it is about finding common roots in our experiences with working people and with an exploited environment. As a result, the task at hand is helping people deepen their senses of what is going on and that we find ourselves in the same boat. Finding God at work there will further contribute to the growing energy and help us determine direction.

Notes

1. Zildo Rocha, *Helder, O Dom: Uma vida que marcou os rumos da Igreja no Brasil* (Sao Paulo: Editora Vozes, 2000), 53.

2. See Joerg Rieger and Kwok Pu-lan, *Occupy Religion: Theology of the Multitude*, Religion in the Modern World (Harrisburg, Pa.: Rowman and Littlefield, 2012), and Joerg Rieger and Rosemarie Henkel-Rieger, *Unified We Are a Force: Growing Deep Solidarity Between Religion and Labor* (St. Louis, Mo.: Chalice Press, 2016).

3. See Jan Rehmann, "Poverty and Poor People's Agency in High-Tech Capitalism," in *Religion, Theology, and Class: Fresh Engagements After Long Silence*, ed. Joerg Rieger (New York: Palgrave Macmillan, 2013), 147–52. See also Guy Standing, *The Precariat: The New Dangerous Class* (London: Bloomsbury Academic, 2011).

4. See Michael Zweig, *The Working Class Majority: America's Best Kept Secret*, 2nd ed. (Ithaca, N.Y.: ILR Press, 2012), 36.

5. In 2010, the combined fortunes of the six heirs of Sam Walton, the founder of Walmart, were as large as the worth of the bottom 40 percent of American families. "Walmart Heirs Worth Same Amount as Bottom 40 Percent of Americans in 2010: Analysis," *Huffington Post*, July 12, 2012, http://www.huffingtonpost.com/waltonsnet worth_n_1680642.html.

6. In this regard, the discussions of the so-called New Materialism are helpful. See, for instance, Clayton Crockett and Jeffrey Robbins, *Religion, Politics, and the Earth: The New Materialism* (New York: Palgrave Macmillan, 2012), and Joerg Rieger and Ed Waggoner, eds., *Religious Experience and the New Materialism: Movement Matters* (New York: Palgrave Macmillan, 2015).

7. There may be an advantage to talking about work rather than class. Unlike class, work cannot be misunderstood as a fixed identity: work is always dynamic, in process. On that issue, see Kathy Weeks, *The Problem with Work: Feminism, Marxism, Antiwork Politics, and Postwork Imaginaries* (Durham: Duke University Press, 2011), 17.

8. The same insight applies to class solidarity, which does not mean being identical (sameness) but having the ability to put one's differences to use. See Joerg Rieger, "Instigating Class Struggle? The Study of Class in Religion and Theology in the United States and Some Implications for Race and Gender," in Rieger, *Religion, Theology, and Class*, 189–211.

9. Du Bois, *Writings by W. E. B. Du Bois in Periodicals Edited by Others*, ed. Herbert Aptheker (Millwood, N.Y.: Kraus-Thomson Organization, 1982), 4:68. The comment praises the Congress of Industrial Organizations, founded in 1935.

10. American Association of University Women, "By the Numbers: A Look at the Gender Pay Gap," September 18, 2014, http://www.aauw.org/2014/09/18/genderpaygap.

11. Elizabeth A. Johnson, "Redeeming the Name of Christ," in *Freeing Theology: The Essentials of Theology in Feminist Perspective*, ed. Catherine Mowry LaCugna (San Francisco: HarperSanFrancisco, 1993), 126.

12. Helene Slessarev-Jamir, *Prophetic Activism: Progressive Religious Justice Movements in Contemporary America* (New York: New York University Press, 2011), 118.

13. Benjamin Robinson, "Can the Colonial Order be Redeemed: Fanon and the Politics of 'Burning It Down,'" term paper, Southern Methodist University, December 2014.

FROM LATIN AMERICA WITH LOVE

Practices Sustaining Us at This Time of Great Turning

Mary Judith Ress

Yes, the picture is bleak indeed. Yet, at a deep, barely conscious level, there seems to be a "groaning" to remember who we really are: stardust contemplating the stars. Here in Latin America, as elsewhere on the planet, we search for ways to roll back what seems to be an inevitable ecological collapse.

Some of us have found inspiration in ecofeminist thought and practice. This essay invites you to step briefly into the history and life-giving commitments of our Con-spirando movement: our early inspirations and practices, our encounter with the lights and shadows of strong female archetypes, our tussling with the Christian tradition, and our engagement with forgotten or neglected indigenous cosmologies. In all these engagements, we trust the knowledge offered by our bodies and our imaginations. We seek no easy answers but trust that both the shadows and the lights bear wisdom that can transform ourselves, our communities, and possibly the planet.

Latin American Ecofeminism: Roots

Ecofeminist theology in Latin America emerges in the "third stage" of feminist theology, which began in the 1990s.[1] Without exception, those of us working in this field in Latin America have been deeply influenced by the thought of Ivone Gebara, the region's foremost ecofeminist theologian. Gebara, always admitting that ecofeminism "is not a native flower of Latin America" but takes on the region's specific tonalities and contexts,[2] has been influenced by shifts in cosmology based on the new science as expressed by thinkers such as Teilhard de Chardin, Fritjof Capra, Thomas Berry, and Brian Swimme, and from feminist theologians such as Mary Daly, Rosemary Radford Ruether, Sallie McFague, and Dorothee Soelle.

Gebara's philosophical and theological roots are in liberation theology. For her, its major contribution is a more collective understanding of God as well as a sense of the social nature of sin. Whereas classical liberation theology had yet to challenge the patriarchal anthropology and cosmology upon which Christianity is based, Gebara posits a Christianity flexible enough to change the foundations of its anthropology and cosmology to respond to what she calls "holistic ecofeminism." For her, God becomes the God of life and of justice, who has a preferential love for the poor.

In *Longing for Running Water*, Gebara describes her "holistic ecofeminism" in this way:

> With ecofeminism I have begun to see more clearly how much our body—my body and the bodies of my neighbors—are affected not just by unemployment and economic hardship but also by the harmful effects the system of industrial exploitation imposes on them. ... I sense that ecofeminism is born of daily life, of day-to-day sharing among people, garbage in the streets, bad smells, the absence of sewers and safe drinking water, poor nutrition, and inadequate health care. The ecofeminist issue is born of the lack of municipal garbage collection, of the multiplication of rats, cockroaches and mosquitoes, and of the sores on children's skin. . . . This is no new ideology. Rather, it is a different perception of reality that starts right from the unjust system in which we find ourselves and seeks to overcome it in order to bring happiness to everyone and everything.[3]

Con-spirando

Con-spirando is a women's collective working in the areas of ecofeminism, theology, and spirituality. It began in 1991 in Santiago, Chile, and since then Gebara has served as one of its midwives. As early as the writing of *Longing for Running Water*, she had been collaborating in the rise of what she calls "the liveliest ecofeminist group in Latin America."[4] I, too, am a founding member of this collective.

From 1993 to 2009, Con-spirando published *sixty* issues of its journal, *Con-spirando: Revista latinoamericana de ecofeminismo, espiritualidad y teologia*. This journal explores themes as diverse as images of divinity (God, Mary, Jesus, the Pachamama) to violence against women, money, sexuality, sustainable communities, and the goddess traditions as related to archetypal patterns of behavior—to name a smattering. We are also rediscovering the richness in the teachings of our indigenous ancestors. We have held workshops, seminars, and an annual school on ecofeminist theology, spirituality, and ethics, and offer a yearly cycle of rituals.

In our journal's first issue, we set out our purpose, which more than twenty-five years later still very much defines what we are about. Because this original statement is so influential, I quote its full length:

> In the patriarchal culture in which we live, women's contributions are not taken seriously. This is particularly true in the area of theology. Our lives, our everyday religious practice and our spirituality are simply not present in current theological reflection. Absent too are our experiences of suffering, joy and solidarity—our experiences of the Sacred. Besides expressing our criticism of patriarchal culture, we also seek to contribute to the creation of a culture that allows theological reflection to flower from our bodies, our spirits—in short, our experiences as women.
>
> We seek theologies that take account of the differences of class, race and gender that so mark Latin America. We hope to open new spaces where women can dig deeply into our own life experiences without fear. These experiences are often negative, even traumatic, in terms of the religious formation we have received. We seek spaces where women can experience new ways of being in community; where we can celebrate our faith more authentically and creatively; where we can rediscover and value our roots, our history and our traditions—in short, to engage in an interreligious dialogue that helps us to recover the essential task of theology, which is to search out and raise the questions of ultimate meaning.
>
> We are convinced that, to bring about relationships marked by justice and equality, we must celebrate our differences and work toward a greater pluralism worldwide. To this end, we need theologies that unmask the hierarchies in which we live, theologies that,

rather than seeking to mediate Mystery, celebrate and explore the Holy without reductionisms or universalisms. We call for theologies that question anthropocentrism and that promote the transformation of relationships based on dominance of one race, nationality, gender or age group over another and of the human over other forms of life. Such theologies will have profound political consequences.

Such a feminist perspective based on our diversity of class, race, age and culture must also take up our love as well as our anguish for all life on the planet that we feel is so threatened today. We call this posture ecofeminism. It is within this perspective that we seek a spirituality that will both heal and liberate, that will nourish our Christian tradition as well as take up the long-repressed roots of the native peoples of this continent. We want to explore the liberating dimensions of our experience and imagination of the Holy. To do this, we *"con-spirar juntas."*[5]

Over the years, we have contributed to Latin America's theological thinking through our publications. This corpus of published material also represents our work in embodied methodology and in the creation of ritual, through which we celebrate what we continue to accomplish on behalf of women's liberation.

School of Ecofeminist Spirituality (2000–2006): Myths and Their Power over Us

Besides our publications, Con-spirando has influenced the region through its annual School of Ecofeminist Spirituality (Escuela de Espiritualidad Ecofeminista). The school, which brought together around forty activist women leaders from Latin America, fleshed out our evolving understanding of ecofeminism. Many school participants had been involved in the political struggles of their countries from an intentional faith perspective—they were from *comunidades de base* (base communities) or *casas de la mujer* (women households). Some were academics.

This initiative grew out of an earlier project called the Shared Garden (1996–98), co-coordinated by the Women's Alliance for Theology, Ethics, and Ritual in Washington, DC; Ivone Gebara in Recife, Brazil; and Conspirando in Santiago, Chile. It was in the Shared Garden gatherings that the theme of myths and their power over us first emerged. Participants enacted and then analyzed the creation story of Adam and Eve found in Genesis 2, the foundational myth undergirding our current patriarchal Christian culture. We began to realize how much we had internalized this myth, which sustains both our cultures and our cosmologies, and continues to operate within us at a very deep, although frequently unconscious, level.

Con-spirando members felt the need to delve more deeply into how myths originate and how they operate to uphold patriarchy as "normal" or "God-given." This led to Con-spirando's commitment to hold an annual school that would offer a contained space where women could ask their theological questions without fear. It would be a "safe space," allowing participants to search together for more life-giving theologies, cosmologies, and ways to celebrate their emerging spiritualties. It would be a space for Latin American women engaged in the religious debates of our region to search together and to formulate a body of thought, study, and reflection.

We were convinced that it was key for women in Latin America to deepen their analysis and theoretical deconstruction of the Genesis myth, and myths in general, in order to see how they act in us subconsciously and how they affect the way we relate to one another. At the same time, we recognized the need to build new practices and power relations in order to sustain ourselves as we searched for new constructs of meaning individually and communally. In the end, we felt the need for new stories of meaning, new myths, and new rituals.

The first school, in January 2000, chose the theme of "Myths and Their Power over Us" and began with the important process of deconstruction. Participants developed understandings of myth based on their own experiences, examining in particular those myths that deal with women's bodies, how myths evolve in the human psyche, and how they develop in an individual woman's life cycle. The analysis included the cultural and psychological need for myths and how they can be transformed from using their power over us to myths that empower us. We identified four basic archetypes that shape us as women—Mother/Life-giver, Lover/Companion, Amazon/Warrior, and Wise Woman / Medium—and saw these archetypes reflected in the many goddesses who have appeared throughout the ages.

Because both the participants and the facilitators found these themes so gripping, we decided that the second school, in January 2001, would continue this same theme, building on the previous year. The second session concentrated on the four feminine archetypes as developed by Toni Wolff, a close collaborator of Carl Jung. The Mother/Life-giver archetype helped us trace the lineage of women in our lives, and it honored those who gave us life, whether physically, intellectually, or spiritually. We discovered the strength of the overriding image of the Virgin Mary, Mother of God, throughout Latin America. We began to look behind the image of Mary to older, more indigenous images of the Mother. This, we recognized, was a major area for further research.[6]

In the Companion/Lover archetype, we looked at the evolution of sexual pleasure and puzzled over how the separation, or even opposition, between pleasure/eroticism and spirituality came about.

The Amazon/Warrior archetype brought participants face to face with the whole issue of power: how women's power has been symbolized in different periods of history and in different cultures and how, from a gender analysis, "man" and "woman" are social constructs. The discussion also looked at how power might be used in new ways. These reworkings of power sought to move beyond stereotypes from the past in which women "warriors" sacrifice their lives for their people.

Finally, the Wise Woman / Medium archetype invited us to meet our shadow side—that part of us we often repress or ignore. It became evident that what has been kept in the shadows or repressed can become a deep source of wisdom for us.

Based on evaluations of the participants and facilitators, the Conspirando team pursued this theme in its third year. Although it concentrated on explorations of the shadow side of each of the archetypes, the third school also examined how ethical norms that relate to women and their bodies developed over time as patriarchy became more entrenched.

With regard to the shadow side, the Mother/Life-giver archetype presentation asked participants to look at their own history of being contained—by mother, church, political party, and various movements—to determine how they were nurtured as well as "devoured." Specific attention was given to the Virgin Mary in Latin America and how she might be a domesticated form of earlier, more sexual "dark" goddesses.

The shadow side of the Companion/Lover archetype surfaced in the patriarchal need to control eroticism, placing it safely within the confines of marriage or the "bad woman," or prostitute. To tap into our erotic powers and feelings, two women from the feminist collective Newen Kuche in Concepción, Chile, gave a workshop on belly dancing, a dance among women to the goddess and often a dance to help women at the time of childbirth, to demonstrate that sensual movement can be liberating.

To connect with the shadow side of the Amazon/Warrior archetype, participants selected to be a certain animal and enacted a battle for territory.

Most participants did not choose to attack but were always aroused to defend their territory. It is worth noting that most participants recognized that they were indeed "warriors" (i.e., leaders within their different communities), and that they were "tired" of always having to "lead the charge" to fight for their rights. Many participants discovered that they had overdeveloped their Amazon/Warrior energies at the expense of their erotic and Wise Woman / Medium energy fields.

The group concluded that the Wise Woman / Medium archetype has been relegated to the shadow side by patriarchy. Although elderly women appear to be invisible and irrelevant in modern society, it is precisely in times of crisis that the vision of the Wise Woman / Medium would be useful.

Ritual has been a key ingredient of the school. One of the most powerful rituals is the reenactment of part of the Sumerian myth of Inanna, the queen who descends to the underworld to meet her "dark sister," Ereshkigal. On the descent to the underworld, each participant, dressed as Inanna, leaves a sign of her power at each of seven gates marking the descent.[7] Once below, each saw her essence, now stripped of all powers, reflected back as she gazed into a mirror; behind her appeared her dark sister, a masked figure clothed in black. The task of the participants was to integrate this dark sister into their psyche. After taking time in the underworld, participants began their ascent, donning again the seven powers, now transformed by contact with Ereshkigal. This ritual had a powerful effect on everyone.

Another powerful ritual is walking the labyrinth, an ancient practice that has been rediscovered in recent times. The invitation is to walk slowly in silence to the center, which symbolizes journeying to one's own center. This is an exercise in integration that formally concludes the school. At the end, participants and leaders form a circle to thank the spirits who have accompanied us during our time together.

What did we take away from the school experience? First, we were able to see the Christian myth within the broader sweep of our evolution as a species and gain a much larger sense of the history of the universe and of the antiquity of our roots. Part of this process has been to rediscover the feminine image of the divinity. When the feminine is not present, honored in ritual or in a culture's sacred image of the divine, the entire social fabric is affected, and violence against women becomes commonplace.

A word of caution here is fitting. We at Con-spirando do not want to return to some ancient past. We are not interested in resurrecting the goddess. But we *are* interested in seeing how our images of the divine evolved from the Great Mother to one male god, father almighty. Ecofeminist women are concerned with synthesizing and moving toward a postpatriarchal future.

110 It takes courage to look critically at the Christian myth and reinterpret it, knowing full well that others may look askance at our efforts, even go so far as to label them heretical. Experiences like the school require "safe spaces" in which to do the work of deconstruction. Participants are committed to embracing diversity, accepting differences, remaining flexible, and refusing rigid postures. We take seriously our responsibility to continue educating ourselves as we work to build sisterhood and compassion as a learning community journeying together toward wholeness. Empowering one another is part of the process.

Con-spirando team members have taken the school experience to Ecuador, Venezuela, and the United States. In the first school, our guest lecturer was Madonna Kolbenschlag. Madonna died suddenly after the school ended. The next year, Rachel Fitzgerald joined us as our guest facilitator. Both Madonna and Rachel have been influenced by Jungian thinking, especially as developed by Toni Wolff. Rachel continues to mentor us. Currently, we are forming a study group to dig into the myth of Tiamat and how her dismemberment by Marduk has shaped our collective psyche through the ages to the present.

Ritual and Spiritual Practices

The starting point of ecofeminist methodology is listening to our bodies. This includes staying profoundly connected to dreams, intuitions, emotions, sensations, and the wisdom found in women's rituals. We espouse an embodied theology, holding up women's bodies as "sacred text." Many women in Con-spirando's network have been trained in the *concientizacion* methodology of Brazilian educator Paulo Freire, by which oppressed groups, concentrating on their own experience, engage in social analysis for change (*praxis*).[8] We have learned that our women's bodies are social and cultural constructs, that our history of violence and pain and of joy and pleasure is stored in our body's memory. The body, then, becomes our theological starting point to counteract the patriarchal mind-set that a woman's body is the source of evil. We strive to heal the dualistic split between body and spirit, and to learn to love our bodies as embodied "temples" of the Holy. "My bed is large and I know many possible and unrepeatable ways to love. I go about the land reform in the soil of my body and my bed," writes Brazilian theologian Nancy Cardoso.[9]

Much of Con-spirando's work involves healing. Workshops introduce simple practices such as Tai Chi, deep breathing exercises, and a variety of massage techniques, including Reiki. We have seen real transformation take place. Participants tell of feeling loved, cared for, safe, and protected. We also encourage returning to some of the age-old healing practices of our indigenous ancestors, who did not separate physical and psychological illness, and whose concept of health was based on a power to heal that comes from within.

This methodology has opened our eyes to the intrinsic connection between our bodies and our spirituality. Since our beginnings, we have celebrated the link between wholeness and holiness, and we have developed rituals to pray through body movement, dance, and chant.

The Con-spirando team feels that naming and reflecting on one's own experience of the Holy is essential in the process of speaking one's own theological word. Offering new images of the Sacred—out of which evolve both new ethical demands as well as new spiritual practices—has been part of Con-spirando's work since its beginning. In our workshops and rituals, we try to empower women to rename the Sacred according to their own experience and insights. New images that have surfaced include, among others, a pregnant woman giving birth, a great uterus as the body of God, a nest, a tree, a mountain, a flowing river, the ocean, a gentle breeze and a wild wind, a web, a hungry child, an elderly invalid, a circle of laughing children, and the sunset. Con-spirando workshops encourage women to draw, mold, and dance their sense of the Sacred.

Every year, Con-spirando holds a series of rituals open to the public, coinciding with the changing seasons. We also hold a vigil on October 31 to commemorate the many women burned or ostracized as witches. Facilitators align the seasonal rituals to the cycles of our own lives. In March (Southern Hemisphere), we celebrate the harvest, take note of the earth's changes, colors deepening, leaves falling. We prepare for winter. We form a circle around the outside altar, decked with the fruit of the season, grapes and apples. What have we harvested this year? Each participant will have the chance to mention her harvest. . . . There are various moments to each ritual, which can include circle dancing, chanting, or movements such as Tai Chi or Chi Kung. In late June, we celebrate the winter solstice, which is also the Mapuche and Aymara New Year. The fire is key here, as we gather to wait for the moment when the sun begins its return journey to our hemisphere. Since it is cold, we often huddle together and drink warm wine and eat sopaipillas and tell stories. We prepare ourselves for the season of hibernation. "When the earth rests, the people of the Earth must rest, too," say the Mapuche. In September, we celebrate the arrival of spring and the earth's and our new life! Here in Chile, in September we celebrate our national independence day. But we also recall September 11, 1973, when Chile's democratic government was overthrown by a military coup and a bloody dictatorship that lasted seventeen years. Finally, in December, at Christmastime, we celebrate the fullness of life, the fruits and flowers, and the passion of summertime!

Each of these rituals is well attended. While the majority of us are women, we do not exclude men. We celebrate life, our sisterhood, and the joys and lessons the earth teaches us at each turn of the wheel. Over the years, Con-spirando has developed a wide variety of rituals. Each issue of our journal offers an example.

A recent Good Friday ritual brought seventeen of us together to knit mandalas. In the age-old custom of women's sewing circles, we gathered to weave together as an act of healing on a day when we acknowledge the long history of suffering and unrequited death we, as a species, have meted out on one another.

Indigenous Cosmology

The recent discoveries of the new science offer confirmation of what the original peoples of the earth have long known: that the earth is a living "mother" and all creatures, great and small, are her children. Therefore, we are all related. The variety and richness of indigenous cosmologies are once again being studied and embraced, now not as mere folklore but as extraordinarily creative ways in which humanity has told its "story." Furthermore, their traditional love and care for the earth can now lead the rest of us to a deeper understanding of the land and its ecosystems. As Thomas Berry points out: "One of the significant historical roles of the primal people of the world is not simply to sustain their own traditions, but to call the entire civilized world back to a more authentic mode of being. Our only hope is in a renewal of those primordial experiences out of which the shaping of our more sublime human qualities could take place."[10] "[These people] seek to survive within a cosmic harmony and wisdom. Such human groups are at the far edges of the modern world. They feel the sacred in their entire existence; they interact intensively with their ancestors and with benign and evil spirits; they see woman as a socializing and spiritual center; and they have devised warm rituals and mythical accounts having to do with life and death. . . . In doing so, they implicitly question a modernity that plunders nature and splits persons."[11]

Notes

1. For more on the three stages of feminist theology in Latin America, see Mary Judith Ress, *Ecofeminism in Latina America* (Maryknoll, N.Y.: Orbis Books, 2006). See also our recent work on the fourth stage in Mary Judith Ress, *Un ovillo de lana de muchos colores* (Santiago, Chile: http://www.conspirando.cl [2014]).

2. Mary Judith Ress, "Interview with Ivone Gebara," *Feminist Theology* 3, no. 8 (January 1995): 208.

3. Ivone Gebara, *Longing for Running Water: Ecofeminism and Liberation* (Minneapolis, Minn.: Fortress Press, 1999), 2.

4. Gebara, *Longing for Running Water*, 14.

5. *Con-spirando: Revista latinoamericana de ecofeminismo, espiritualidad y teología*, no. 1 (March 1992): 2–5. The publications of the journal of Con-spirando can also be accessed through this website: http://www.conspirando.cl.

6. Throughout 2003 ten grassroots teams in Latin America researched the Marian feasts in their region and discovered images hidden behind the Virgin Mary. See *Vírgenes y diosas en América Latina: La resignificación de lo sagrado*, ed. Veronica Cordero, Graciela Pujol, Mary Judith Ress, and Coca Trillini (Santiago: Colectivo Con-spirando, 2004).

7. The seven gates are linked to the seven chakras.

8. Paolo Freire, *Pedagogy of the Oppressed* (New York: Herder & Herder, 1970).

9. *Revista Con-spirando*, no. 30 (March 1999): 42.

10. Thomas Berry, *The Dream of the Earth* (San Francisco, Calif.: Sierra Club, 1988), 4.

11. Diego Irarrázaval, *Inculturation: New Dawn of the Church in Latin America* (Maryknoll, N.Y.: Orbis Books, 2000), 20.

painting 2 José Ernesto Padilla, *TitoArt 8*. Oil on canvas, 21½ × 18 inches. Private collection. Used with kind permission by Gladys Soto.

SPOOKY LOVE

Dwelling in the Face of Ecosystemic Annihilation

Elaine Padilla

> Love is the pain of being one alone
> And not two (two in a union).
> A hand in my hand which is not my hand . . .
> . . . the mouth that is not your mouth.
> I am scouring the universe for a lover.

—ERNESTO CARDENAL, CANTIGA 42, "A CERTAIN SOMETHING THAT THEY STILL"[1]

Looking through a glass window, one might perceive worlds at a distance, admire the dark brilliance of sky and stars along with a planetary existence whose capacity to transfigure our interiority cannot be readily perceived. We merely look through the window. Perhaps its glass seems to separate the "you" from the "me," the other species from the human, the living from the dead, and to collapse temporalities of past and future in the present. All of these separations appear as geometries that limit our imaginations. Yet looking through the window might also entice us to cross these boundaries and encounter the raw reality that appears external and feels romantic. As we feel the world out there differently, an entire universe and planetary life of crepuscular and darkened bodies converge inwardly. We make a conscious effort to feel the intimate touch of each cosmos and collaborate in creating an exuberant world.

As relational beings, we long for these affective forms of proximity in the intimately concrete experience in which we dwell. Hence, we might imagine how a home with no glassed boundary lines but instead with open windows could help us to experience the kind of cosmic love that Ernesto Cardenal describes. The pluriverse that embraces all beckons us to resist alienation, to risk vulnerability, to reach like a lover toward one another. Hence, windows and other borders, real or imagined, also expose the cavities of our hearts to the worlds on the other side of their frames. Even ghost-like realities can haunt the cavernous depths of our beings. The magnificent relationality of the dark universe beyond is not unlike the plenitude of the microcosm that is within or the bodies that we long to hold and kiss, including dark-skinned bodies often demonized in our societies. The materiality of the spaces that are yonder and near, the inner and outer geometries, share in the same elemental particles that make pulsating life intimate.

But how to speak of cosmic love when dealing with issues of planetary devastation? Might it seem trivial in such instances to ponder this principle of love when the ghosts of the many dead and decimated populations and species point to the darkening of our future? Perhaps we also fear roman-ticizing the quotidian components of worldly existence, not hearing the cry of a child as her tiny body is ravaged by war, not touching the dying glacier, not smelling the polluted waters, not seeing the migrants dying at sea or in the desert, and not tasting the honey of the many bees whose colonies have collapsed. The darkened geometries of our spatial realities (human and other-than-human) can quicken "the pathema of the soul"—the desire that unnerves the very core of intimate being.[2] So it can be true: amid practical questions and solutions to our present dilemma, cosmic love cannot lift us into a world of fantasy to escape from the earthly tremors of ecological devastation that are shaking the very foundations of our plan-etary coexistence.[3] Yet I find no alternative but to reflect on how cosmic affect is an adequate response to the distress call emanating from the over-lapping realities of near and far.

This essay argues for the kind of love that "spooks"—a pejorative term that often refers to dark bodies. It suggests that spooky love—awakening our inner cosmos through the embodied darkness that may seem to be far and distant but with which we are intimately connected—can stir the kind of affect capable of overcoming the attitudes and behaviors annihilat-ing planetary life. With a universe that like a cosmic lover embraces and is embraced by us, as each living thing makes manifest its livingness. Thanks to affective entanglements even at the subatomic level, we can respond with love rather than *fright*. By listening to nature, by bringing to consciousness what we feel, by experiencing anew seemingly remote geometries, we can

wage a *fight* of love in order to dwell together in love.

Becoming a Dwelling

Being is dwelling.[4] To be means to dwell in the imaginatively undulating time and elongating space that links all things and to restore the interior capacity to open its windows. A passion for shared life can awaken us to the vibrancy of dwelling in common with the starry and dark that is seemingly above us as well as the natural and the urban that inescapably grounds us here. So perhaps the way to explain a loving model of our geometrical realities is by exploring how we might face the *pain* of "being alone" and "not two (two in union)" of which Cardenal speaks in the epigraph at the start of this essay.

I believe this parenthetical embrace that reflects the longing of becoming joined with another is an aspect to which the reflections on St. Francis of Assisi point in the encyclical *Laudato Si'.* Joining St. Francis in calling the moon and the sun and all of creation our "brother" and "sister," Pope Francis turns our sense of alienation into "joyful mystery."[5] His encyclical takes a cosmic tone of intimacy as he appeals to our human "ability to work together in building our common home."[6] This "joyful mystery" grounded in what is imaginatively common can be defined by the incalculability of being human in community. This incalculability lies in how it is measured in the present, the lived experience of moment by moment, and open-endedly, as in an abiding consciousness of the particles of a future hope being made manifest in the now.[7] Even further, dwelling according to the incalculability of love can mean that home can take on the contours of an interiority and habitation that far extends its interior spaces so that the distant can become filial.

Such a loving form of dwelling shifts the shape of our geometrical imaginations as lines intersect spaces. This transformation of shape is like a seashell spiraling outward as the immensity of ocean life surges into the intimacy of its abode, shaping its sonorous depths of color patterns. Gaston Bachelard describes the interior walls of shells being sturdy yet so diaphanous that vapors can slip through to recombine with its internal odors.[8] This dwelling contains the blueprints of love. Mobile in its settlement, extensible in its geometry, dwelling in love: all these crack open its interior tunnels so that each of its crevices and corners can inch out into the immensity of the universe. As with Emmanuel Levinas, interiority is contoured as an inhabitation that *faces* an-other while having its "footsteps reverberate the secret depths of being."[9]

In that sense, dwelling is love "in the making," with the inner and outer movements and an elongating organicity that shapes it. Building our common home then means imaginatively dwelling in the likes of an embracing elasticity that draws us outside our inner windows as if *yearning* for another like a lover. While exuding dwelling from within, the embrace also draws in the outside and *shrinks* it into space. Cardenal describes it as the act of embracing and being embraced by a female cosmic lover that for him is like the Night (*la noche* is a feminine noun in Spanish), which in its imperceptibility unites "in some manner two in one, two pleasures in one."[10]

Apart from the economy of possession—for yearning like a lover wants nothing and is penetrated by Nothing[11]—to dwell lovingly in common, therefore, would occur as one faces an-other in being enlarged and shrunk by passion, by passionately *feeling* space with each fiber of one's being. Worlds in magnitude and in miniature become liberated from dimensions of time and space as an interior in diastole breathes in cosmicity and in systole relaxes it out into small spaces.[12] The awareness of geometric shifts, hence the imaginative becoming of dwelling-space, can thus do away with strict oppositions of outer and inner, resurrect fossilized membranes, and energize our shell life. Vastness and voluptuousness embrace inwardly, expanding our windowlike horizons and making us humans become conscious of our ability to love even beyond humanity itself.

Reenchanting Our Inner Chambers

The windowless or shut-in existence that creates an "us" versus "them" is an apt descriptor of a unidimensional manner of viewing reality. When geometries appear on a flat level, their lines and angles seem inert and immobile, as if lacking elasticity. This tendency illustrates a limited perspective. At the heart level, it can imply an interior that is unresponsive, resulting in patterns of behavior that negate life. Today, such a familiar behavior would be our environmental racism, which denies to the vulnerable rights to a livable space. For the one who chooses to flatten its view, and thus to enclose and close off its dwelling, the risk might seem minimal, except for the wound of an-other's pain being still latently oozing within our deepest membranes. The injury might not seem visible enough to appear pervasive, and perhaps it can be ignored for a while. But by failing to respond, the ghosts of those injured by our present overconsumption and wasteful practices will continue to haunt us. The *landless* of countless species at the brink of extinction who presently embody our *dark planet* that *spooks* us plead with us: "Be in union with me! *Love me!*"

A passionate response of care, by contrast, would begin with an acknowledgment that we seldom notice those who dwell far away, for we do not hear or see them. An example is the Uru-Murato people, the longest-surviving indigenous population of the remote areas of Lake Poopó in Llapallapani, Bolivia. The once-teeming lake known as the "mother and father" of this indigenous community has become a flat surface of salt, its water diverted and plundered upstream to farm the quinoa suddenly popular here in the United States. No water means that the lake is silting up, creating the sediment useful for mining salt. Worsened by El Niño effects of less precipitation and higher temperatures, the precarious conditions of this erstwhile rural society once dedicated to fishing Lake Poopó have forced the Uru-Murato to work at mills where unrefined salt is being ground, heaped into a pile, and then placed in small packages for twenty-five cents each. Though they survived the Inca and the Spanish, the Uru-Murato have fallen prey to our neocolonization, our present capitalistic system, and our capitalistic habits that have dried up their lake, depriving them of their daily sustenance and livelihood.[13]

Many populations are likewise being displaced from their farming communities. Some are far closer to us geographically than the Uru-Murato. I refer to the U.S. southern borderlands not too far "beyond" our interior walls. With free-trade zones or export-processing zones and their *maquiladoras*, which have been on the rise since the 1940s, have come violations of environmental laws, of child labor laws, and of basic workers' rights and fair compensation. In addition, because free-trade zones cannot sustain the increase in population, they create slum-like conditions and what Juan Gonzalez describes as a "public health nightmare of industrial pollution, untreated human waste, and disease."[14] Then there is the boom in the amphetamine business that free-trade deals like NAFTA (North American Free Trade Agreement) create. For a consequence of limiting the possibilities for traditional farming is that growers are lured into the illicit-drug agribusiness through economic necessity. This results in rapidly depleting natural resources and causing social instability as farmlands become monocultures and as drug cartels wreak mental and physical havoc on both sides of our borders.

Perhaps we could still be at ease if the yonder of our windows would merely depict a picture of a world out there that is unable to escape the vampirizing ghosts of the colonial era. Yet, given the repercussions that every event and every decision causes, the whole of the geometrical spectrum becomes our ubiquitous environment *here*. Ultimately, we cannot conceal the facts. For what appears to be an environment *out there* merely exposes the heartbeat of our racial and sexist attitudes—not to mention our environmental greed—confronting us through the effects being wreaked here.

We can define love by how we perceive planets, worlds, or territories intersecting. The macrocosmic ill entangles all its components so that we perceive and feel intimately the pain of its maladies. So unlimitedly and at such rapid pace does the planet appear to be deteriorating that, with Timothy Morton, one could describe the future before earth as a *dark planetary ecology*. Morton asks, "What does one do with 'the leakiness of the world?'" as he reflects on the accidental and nonaccidental release of the poisonous plutonium.[15] The human "I" quakes as it faces its own fragility and responsibility over its demise, as it recognizes that *we are this dark environment!* We mourn as we admit we are responsible for becoming the ghosts of our colonizing past. For far too long, we humans have been what Morton calls "a viral supplement to an organic whole."[16] To recognize this involvement could be to glimpse the end of an epoch through the eyes of those *darkened*, not just made opaque or deemed insignificant in history as humans and other-than-humans. But it could also be a reminder of the many ghosts of autonomized mechanisms that vampirize, suppress, repress, and in the end impoverish, uproot, and crush the living.

Why do we continue to ignore these cosmic entanglements? Dare we not be attuned to these ecological murmurs of our common home? Why can we not listen to the plight of the Latin American and Caribbean lakes, rivers, rain forests, wetlands, coral reefs, oceans, fauna, and dying species together with the already impoverished who depend on them for their health and natural wealth? At first glance, their *matter* might appear to hold no relevance, hence we allow its soil to become disenchanted, a site of indifference. As Eduardo Kohn argues, phantom-like qualities of semiosis normally appear to be unidentifiable. Since these are iconic,[17] according to a Peircean order of signs, we seldom distinguish them as different.[18] And following a Marxian logic of disenchantment, matter, being no longer magical and becoming void of its mystery and transcendence, can only be rendered transparent and predictable, a thing for use ruled by the calculus and precision of natural laws.

Yet disruptions, such as the dry and now-salinated lake(bed) of the Uru-Murato, disappearing birds and dead fish, and the mass impoverishment of populations living in slum-like conditions neighboring our borders, are indices of a crying difference—an unnatural order of things that is no longer sustainable. We can grasp, at least in part, this planet's hauntings because all living beings communicate by means of codified entanglements. As anthropologist Kohn showed us by spending four years doing fieldwork in the Amazon rain forest with the Runa tribe, even as animals and plants represent themselves beyond human understanding, they manifest their *sentir* or livingness through vast and complex ecosystems. They make themselves felt via assembled ecologies that mutually affect and organize beings.[19]

This manner of "listening" in the sense of *sentir* or of feeling nature refers to giving back the world its quality of reenchantment. In that regard, the landless at the brink of extinction can spook us, and their geometrical dwelling can intersect ours because nature, being enchanted, is an inhabited space where the other-than-human represents the future that is now affecting the present across our sociopolitical limits. For Kohn, the "absent histories" of nature come to be mediated in the present by means of survival. This is particularly so with organisms whose concealment has allowed them to escape the clutches of the predator and ensured their survival. But it is no longer concealed; it is no longer a secret that in just one year in the Amazon, deforestation "rose nearly two million additional acres from August 2015 to July 2016."[20] Likewise, in the surrounding areas of Llapallapani in Bolivia and the southern borderlands of the United States, the enchantment of nature might best refer to the calamitous ghost lands now arising from concealment to human consciousness. What can we grasp as we feel entire ecosystems whose "absent histories" are becoming the very opposite of survival, hence an irreplaceable "now" on the verge of extinction?

Would not enchantment make us attentive to the sounds of life that are striving to survive the calamitous future? By living multidimensionally, by perceiving geometries as organically extending far and wide, we can become attuned to the vast networks of meanings being shared beyond the common mechanisms of mere exchange of sociocultural data and bare facts. Also with lives, or with whole ecologies as loci of enchantment,[21] we can encounter each particularity, including the other-than-human, as an "I" in its uniqueness, a self with a unique point of view, what Kohn describes as "soul-possessing," as open to the conscious flow of intersubjective relations.[22] To be indifferent to the *sentir* of other particularities is to suffer from "soul blindness" or an inability to be aware. It is to experience an "isolating state of monadic solipsism" that flattens reality, shuts the windows of the soul, and encapsulates an individual or the human collective in itself as if devoid of attachments and interconnections.[23]

Loving Sentience

Intimate hauntings can transform our *sentir* and our consciousness because the universe is a continuum of relatedness that embraces and is embraced by us. According to Alfred N. Whitehead, we can "feel" unconsciously and consciously that which is particular within the universe because the universe contains a dynamically binding quality known for its process of *sentiri* or *sentire*.[24] This means that the universe has a character of solidarity that is immanent to each entity. As Brian Greene has observed, physical reality is nonlocal, composed of vibrating and electrodynamic particle-types that as Einstein would argue "spook" at a distance.[25] In response, we can bring into consciousness what we feel intimately because vast ecologies are bound by original links of particles. These particles, even when pulled apart in opposite directions, Catherine Keller explains, will "remain immediately responsive to one another—*no matter what the distance*. They remain 'entangled.'"[26] Like actualizations of a dark cloud of enmeshment, both objects—the one *over there* and the one *over here*—show "care" for each other, a randomness that for Keller "can be linked across space . . . instantly at any distance."[27]

So how would cosmic particles quicken a loving sense of common home? In a similar manner to how dark matter and dark energy pull together, all visible matter can expand the horizons of spatial orbits. Cardenal describes it poetically as a cosmic lover who acts as "the principle of union for all beings," for Eros passes "through all things," causing the union of all "cosmic forces."[28]

The Eros of the Universe,[29] or the divine incarnation of the primordial aim, or that which initially entices us to advance creatively, embraces the whole for the purposes of elongating geometries transfigured by "care" for one another. The capacity to "feel" that for Whitehead is the result of pure potentialities (also known as eternal objects) materializing as events (clusters of interconnections) emerges out of a continuum or "the universe as solidarity."[30] This organic universe in which we dwell and that inhabits us, as with seashells, is shaped by the "felt" or absorbed subatomic stratum by which an entity actualizes itself. Because the universe embraces it, each entity subsequently includes the universe by reason of its attitude toward every element in the universe.[31] This is what Whitehead calls "the principle of relativity."[32] With each "feeling," particles transition from indetermination to determination. And while difference is being constituted at each novel determination, the universe entangles itself in concrete reality through this process. This entanglement enables creative advance.[33] Without this organic process of love, there would be only a monist and static universe.[34]

Perhaps this organic model of dwelling according to a *continuum* can be the product of the imaginative birth of what Sean Miller calls "the domestication of a wilderness-like space" produced by the very colonizing systems of exploration and conquest that we seek to challenge.[35] Here also the cosmos can resemble "a space of flows" or current systems of easy spread of information through networks, not too unlike the global integration of financial markets, segmented articulation of production, and proliferation of international trade.[36]

Given that these organic processes cannot extricate themselves from the negative impact of past and present deadly materializations of "space of flows," might such organic processes not also signal with their *infinite leaps* a potential for loving solidarities that are mutually constituted and can result in a planetary flourishing yet to be realized? The "spooky action at a distance" of quantum relatedness can be useful in reflecting on remote particles that can mobilize life toward fullness (a people, a land, a species) as these cross vast distances to enter into the windows of our souls. Like waves, subatomic particles darkly approximate or draw near, demonstrating their presence in the bodies transgressing the limits of this annihilating epoch and enabling solidarities to come into deep contact with one another for the purposes of caring transformation. And while the outcome of entangled particles is indeterminate, hence deemed "flaky" and less reliable in predicting optimum outcomes, the dark embodiments of these particles can still pose the *chance* for events to pull gravitationally toward recreative centers. The potential of the cosmic lover's enticements being rearranged in a flourishing manner might turn the tide against extinction.

From a process perspective, because of this similar ontological principle of "the universe as solidarity," whereby, according to Whitehead, "everything is positively somewhere in actuality, and in potency everywhere,"[37] I am suggesting that the pure potentialities of the darkest of ecologies both as negation and affirmation of life can be "felt" among subjects in a similarly caring manner as Kohn's notion of sentir. For the universe is solidarity itself, that is, an embraced and embracing universe. Also, consciously, because subjects determine themselves, self-create, or self-form by means of ingressing pure potentialities, they can turn an inexplicably evocative or powerful "blind feeling,"[38] which could be easily dismissed from relevance and thus become trivial (indifference), into a vision ripe with immediacy and purpose (difference).[39] Viewing geometries as parts of constellations, rather than as flattened and isolated, can result in shape-shifting matter, meaning in a social action that engages in a struggle for ecological renewal.

For instance, an initial emotion such as *fright*, caused by our dark ecology—as can occur when dark bodies cross our national and local borders, making manifest also a trace of the ecocide of millions of species—can lead to the kind of mourning that stirs a compassionate *fight* of love, rather than causing *flight* or shirking one's ability to respond—an example of the former in scholarly activism is exemplified in this book. Even as potentialities are neutral to any physical ingression "in any particular entity of the temporal world,"[40] we can be spooked or lured "for feeling" love just as much as "horror, disgust, and indignation."[41] The spooky livingness or feeling at the sight of these dark or opaque embodiments entering the realm of one's foresight or seeing can otherwise shift from mere "propositional potentiality" to a "realized fact" of care. For instance, the private quality of a "feeling" can lead to loving solidarities capable of creatively transfiguring spaces and their geometrical demarcations that have become alienated and bound by despair. What is "enjoyed" or "suffered" privately by means of entangled vibrations and pure potentialities can surface publicly[42] through our enactments of love—our fight or struggle.

We can engage in this fight, and we can dwell in solidarity, since we, because of the cosmic love at our sub-micro levels, can create anew even amid massive destructions. As Salvator Cannavo describes quantum physics, our collectivity can act as "a turbulent discontinuous sea of spontaneous creation [occurring along] abrupt annihilation."[43] The subatomic potential of matter is such that life can rearrange itself by means of borrowing what's needed from its surrounding environment. The most destructive of ecologies is not only entropic;[44] it resists lifelessness, can transition toward new orders, and can reshape itself geometrically. Through the entangled interactions of living organisms that cooperate with the forces of love in the cosmos, we can self-create out of near extinction. New options for how to dwell arise, for potentialities become relevant when we bring our entanglements into consciousness and give them meaning.[45] The fight of love for mutual forms of flourishing becomes possible when we "feel" the ravaged ecologies and deplorable living conditions. We mourn and respond actively with care in solidarity, for this spooky story of the planet that embraces and is embracing has yet to be closed.

Open Embraces

In any initial public act of defiantly becoming the mutually constituted *we*, the entangled *we*, or the *we-in-solidarity* that arises from one's most subatomic level, the first risk taken can be toward an affective solidarity for the purposes of countering *geo*, *eco*, *homi*, and *femicidal* impulses. A conscious and public act of flourishing entanglement can bring about positive change by means of rebuilding a world whose goal is exuberance even amid social destruction.

That is why the challenge that *Laudato Si'* raises is fitting. Modernity's tendencies to split affect from thinking and acting, "the twilight of the 'passion,'"[46] which results in the dichotomy between the "feeling" subject and its environment, has failed us. In the prevalent concept of "ecology" as that of building a dwelling in the sense of the earth endlessly bearing more fruit to sustain the whole human family, nature has been a holder of human ambition and has been at the service of humanity.[47] Its perfection has come by means of heartless development with the aid of technology.[48] This view of nature as extension and separation from one's soul and as the "canvas" of modern social and economic movements has long been challenged.[49]

Elongating the uncanny geometries of at-home likeness into the urban, suburban, and rural marketplaces of our ecosystems might aid humans to *sentir soulfully*, what Morton refers to as striving below the threshold of regular listening. The noise of obsolete forms of technology and development might be the cause for a pregnant pause (syncope), a silence saturated with tone and intensity auguring that the worst has already happened and that we are fully implicated.[50] Can we continue to be absolved from any wrongdoing, from ecogenocides and other crimes committed *out there* by our mega conglomerates?

Hence, we ponder how to respond to the "spooky" injunctions of countless humans and their other-than-human counterparts counted among our living dead (*animas*). How can we dwell receptive to their spectrality if not by thinking of the haunted realities of their dying ecologies that narrow the distance between us? For Antonio Negri, their sentir would announce the need to exorcise our phantasmagoric systems that vampirize resources and displace native inhabitants yet also, and paradoxically, the need to quicken "the pathema of the soul." Drawing from Spinoza, Negri explains that pathema arises from a state of confusion by which the mind acknowledges its bodily existence more so than before and resolutely determines to think differently. The pathema is an emotion with a spectral quality (what I call spookiness) of a "dual state of mind, which is between passivity and activity and lives in the present though it is prefabricated in memory, enduring the past while turned towards action."[51] It is that open moment that results in an ontological passage that grasps desire "beyond the (past) determinations of existence or the (present) external dialectic of sadness and joy."[52] Like a shadow of our consciousness, the fright that the specter causes can simultaneously compel us to dwell blatantly according to organic behaviors with which to counter the demarcations of geometries that appear to act in a ghost-like manner, independently of class domination and power relations of nations and parties.

The ghost-like existence of countless bodies lost in the Mediterranean Sea, drowned in the Rio Grande, powerless after hurricane devastations, or desiccated in the desert, and of dying and extinct ecologies would be among the most welcomed "illegitimate" and "clandestine" spirits to intersect our countervisions and transformational uprisings.[53] As Derrida puts it, "So well disguised, so perfectly encrypted, that they themselves never suspected that that's what they were!"[54] With these material ghosts occupying such spaces, would there be a glimmer of joy with which to confront what Negri calls "humanity's archghosts"? Perhaps the departed await an "event" that can make the past explode and also anticipate "a real coming-to-be,"[55] what *Laudato Si'* refers to as the "joyful mystery" of dwelling in common—to dwell in love. Would we be daring to love unless there is a collaborative effort to thwart the negation of existence, the blockade to inventions that dry out the only subterraneous veins capable of hydrating into life the brick-like soil?

Why a joyful mystery? Because in this era of disenchantment, we humans have given few signs of improving the environmental deterioration due to relaxed enforcement of, or total absence of, environmental laws, with wealthy nations using territories as extracting grounds to becoming even wealthier. So to dwell in soulful ways can defiantly combat the root causes of our capitalist dominion over nature; the "debt boomerang"; the high rates of famine, poverty, and illiteracy globally; the loss of jobs that results in the proliferation of drug production and trafficking; and mass migrations alongside the increase in greenhouse effects. Also because our conscious awareness of that space beyond our windows that can be indexed, because that *over there* of ecology that we can exploit entangles us in a web of love, and because of that we can experience a sentir that motivates us to gain insight "from the environment."[56] In that sense, the absent, the landscapes of ghosts reveal our flattened attitudes and disquiet us so that we collaborate with nature in cocreating the conditions for exuberant or thriving ecosystems. For without a conscious effort to dwell in a manner that can be "joyful" for the entire planet, the birth of an ecological society will indeed be a utopia.[57]

Joyfulness would present itself in the defiant act to embed oneself in this dark ecology at the most mundane level. Along with cobuilding deep solidarities, and as we become aware of our consumption habits and fair trade, for instance, we can question the source of the quinoa we eat. Similarly, through our electoral actions and representation we can contend with international laws that, on the one hand, seek to create peace across borders and, on the other, fail to denounce and enforce equity in the marketplace, such as the removal of "foreign debt."[58] For this also, we can seek comprehensive reforms that aid in planetary well-being, like an increase in the use of alternative forms of energy, cars that are less dependent on petroleum, and of new housing that is sustainable. For ecological destruction is a sign of crisis rather than of development, progress, and advancement.[59]

There have already been some well-intended efforts to adapt to the rhythms and patterns of nature and local populations.[60] Yet an unquestionable belief in the "samaritanism" of European and North American nations will fail us, as if all "good" will flow from their capitalist coffers. Such an agenda has created impoverished territories but allowed "little or no participation in the design of projects by those who would be affected by them," as John Sniegocki reminds us.[61] Development, Leonardo Boff points out, ostensibly has been "carried out for the people or with the people," yet without asking or listening to opinions of the people, as, for example, in Latin America and the Caribbean.[62] The indigenous, who are often the most exploited and the ones who have suffered the most from the internationalization of their or others' use of their land, are the least consulted.

This does not mean that all blame falls on capitalism to the exclusion of socialism. Particularly in Latin America, forms of socialism have likewise become top-down structures that allow for very little participation by the people in decision-making processes.[63] Socialism has disenchanted the earth, deemed it sheer matter, in order to use it. So both ecocapitalism and ecosocialism have reduced the land to capital: the former at the hands of those with capital and the latter at the hands of the state. Terms such as *ecocapitalism* and *ecodevelopment* can mask the perversity of the paradigms of growth and adaption for the purpose of domination.[64] According to Boff, "The worst has happened: human beings have become separated from the cosmic community and have forgotten the web of interdependencies and the synergy of all the cosmic elements that enabled them to emerge in the cosmic process."[65]

Engaging in a fight of love or building a common dwelling in love would require the kind of imaginary akin to open windows: it would contemplate sustainable planetary and cosmic possibilities, it would welcome the leadership and the contributions of disadvantaged populations, and it would be mindful of the local impact that our actions cause.

In summary: life as a whole contains a wealth of potentialities, with variegated shades of opportunities to cultivate a sustainable and exuberant coexistence in any context and environmental condition. Indeed, because our bodies are societies and events that welcome timely undulations and spatial elongations from near and far, the potential for conscious acts toward the proliferation of well-being remains a possibility despite the grim realities of our planet. For we are ensouled bodies with open windows who are embraced by a cosmic lover and can embrace each other. The *here* and the *yonder* of our horizons are but a fraction of a distance apart. As with every breath that is inhaled and then released, as seashells that long for the ocean's swell to recombine vapors within and shape their cavernous interiors, so, too, can we embody love in our daily living and reshape reality geometrically. From the molecular and the subconscious can surface the most imaginative and cocreative insights and love-attuned acts of enriching mutuality. This would be to dwell as love in the making.

Notes

I thank the Louisville Institute for awarding me a Sabbatical Research Grant that afforded me the time and space to conceive this essay.

1. Ernesto Cardenal, *Cosmic Canticle* (Willimantic, Conn.: Curbstone Books, 2002), 451.

2. Antonio Negri, "The Specter's Smile," in *Ghostly Demarcations: A Symposium on Jacques Derrida's Specters of Marx*, ed. Michael Sprinker (London: Verso, 1999), 12.

3. I am aware of the limitations that any "we," "our," and "us" in this essay can have, in

particular when writing as a Latinx scholar residing in the United States. Yet I speak from this place or locus in order to challenge the "out there" thinking that alienates and impoverishes the ecologies and populations below our southern borders. This "we" would be the "being-with" seeking to connote a bond of solidarity.

4. For a deeper understanding on dwelling poetically, see Martin Heidegger, "Building Dwelling Thinking," in *Poetry, Language, Thought* (New York: HarperCollins, 2001), 141–61.

5. Pope Francis, *Laudato Si'* (Vatican: La Santa Cede, 2015), 12.

6. Ibid., 13.

7. Heidegger, "Building Dwelling Thinking," 156. Unfortunately, as history has witnessed, the Heideggerian *homo economicus* might purposefully refuse to live up to its utmost potential in the sense of love for the stranger.

8. See Gaston Bachelard, *The Poetics of Space: The Classic Look at How We Experience Intimate Spaces*, new ed. (Boston: Beacon Press, 1992), esp. 140.

9. Emmanuel Levinas, *Totality and Infinity: An Essay on Exteriority* (Pittsburgh: Duquesne University Press, 1969), 156.

10. Cardenal, *Cosmic Canticle*, "Cantiga 42," 451.

11. Ibid.

12. Bachelard, *Poetics of Space*, 162.

13. See Nicholas Casey, "Climate Change Claims a Lake and an Identity," *New York Times*, July 7, 2016, https://www.nytimes.com /interactive/2016/07/07/world/americas/ boliviaclimatechangelakepoopo.html?_r=0.

14. Juan Gonzalez, *Harvest of Empire: A History of Latinos in America* (New York: Penguin Books, 2011), 252.

15. Timothy Morton, *Ecology Without Nature: Rethinking Environmental Aesthetics* (Cambridge, Mass.: Harvard University Press, 2009), 159.

16. Ibid., 195.

17. For C. S. Peirce, the icon is the simplest type of sign, revealing reality as is without adding any meaning to it. See, for instance,

Peirce, *Philosophical Writings of Pierce* (New York: Dover Publications, 1955), 104–7.

18. Eduardo Kohn, *How Forests Think: Toward an Anthropology Beyond the Human* (Berkeley: University of California Press, 2013), esp. 49–62.

19. Ibid., 5.

20. Hiroko Tabuchi, Claire Rigby, and Jeremy Whitefeb, "Amazon Deforestation, Once Tamed, Comes Roaring Back," *New York Times*, February 24, 2017, https://www .nytimes.com/2017/02/24/business/energy environment/deforestationbrazilboliviasouth america.html?_r=0.

21. Kohn, *How Forests Think*, 90.

22. Ibid., 106–7 and 117.

23. Ibid., 117.

24. Alfred N. Whitehead, *Process and Reality: An Essay in Cosmology*, ed. David Ray Griffin and Donald W. Sherburne, corr. ed. (New York: Free Press, 1978), 220 and 41.

25. See Brian Greene, *The Elegant Universe* (New York: W. W. Norton, 1999).

26. Catherine Keller, *Cloud of the Impossible: Negative Theology and Planetary Entanglement* (New York: Columbia University Press, 2015), 147; emphasis original.

27. Ibid., 147–48.

28. Cardenal, *Cosmic Canticle*, 458.

29. Alfred N. Whitehead, *Adventures of Ideas* (New York: Free Press, 1967), 253, 201, and 274.

30. Whitehead, *Process and Reality*, 188 and 40.

31. Ibid., 45.

32. Ibid., 22.

33. Ibid., 45.

34. Ibid., 46.

35. Sean Miller, *Strung Together: The Cultural Currency of String Theory as a Scientific Imaginary* (Ann Arbor: University of Michigan Press, 2013), 157.

36. Ibid., 208.

37. Whitehead, *Process and Reality*, 40.

38. Ibid., 213.

39. Ibid., 184.

40. Ibid., 44.

41. Ibid., 25.

42. Ibid., 290.

43. Salvator Cannavo, *Quantum Theory: A Philosopher's Overview* (Albany: State University of New York Press, 2009), 30.

44. Robert Sokolowski, "Meditation," in *The Human Search for Truth: Philosophy, Science, and Theology: The Outlook for the Third Millennium; International Conference on Science and Faith, May 23–25, 2000* (Philadelphia: St. Joseph's University Press, 2002), 48.

45. Whitehead, *Process and Reality*, 165–67.

46. Negri, "Specter's Smile," 12.

47. Walter J. Burghardt, *Justice: A Global Adventure* (Maryknoll, N.Y.: Orbis Books, 2004), 74–75.

48. Ibid., 79.

49. Stephen B. Scharper, "The Ecological Crisis," in *The Twentieth Century: A Theological Overview*, ed. Gregory Baum (Maryknoll, N.Y.: Orbis Books, 1999), 219.

50. Morton, *Ecology Without Nature*, 74–75.

51. Negri, "Specter's Smile," 11.

52. Ibid.

53. Derrida, "Marx and Sons," in *Ghostly Demarcations*, 231.

54. Ibid., 262.

55. Negri, "Specter's Smile," 14–15.

56. Kohn, *How Forests Think*, 55.

57. See Ian Angus, "Latin America Faces the Global Ecological Crisis," *Climate and Capitalism*, August 19, 2010, http://climate andcapitalism.com/2010/08/19/latinamerica facestheglobalecologicalcrisis.

58. Derrida, "Marx and Sons," 241.

59. Scharper, "Ecological Crisis," 219–27.

60. In the city of Los Angeles alone, where I now reside, are numerous organizations, such as Pando Populus and Community Home Energy Retrofit Project, that are actively transforming the sustainable landscape of Southern California and aiming at having a positive impact globally.

61. John Sniegocki, *Catholic Social Teaching and Economic Globalization: The Quest for Alternatives* (Milwaukee: Marquette University Press, 2009), 35.

62. Leonardo Boff, *Cry of the Earth, Cry of the Poor* (Maryknoll, N.Y.: Orbis Books, 1997), 103.

63. Sniegocki, *Catholic Social Teaching*, 61.

64. Boff, *Cry of the Earth*, 86–87.

65. Ibid., 69.

THE HUMMINGBIRD SPIRIT AND
CARE OF OUR COMMON HOME

An Afro-Theo-Ethical Response to Laudato Si'

Teresia M. Hinga

Since 1989, Christians all over the world have marked and celebrated the *season of creation.* This is the period, which starts on September 1, globally marked as the world day of prayer for creation. It culminates on October 4, the feast day of St. Francis of Assisi. An optional focus in the church's liturgical calendar, this is a period in which Christians are reminded in a special way to appreciate the gift of life in its multiple forms: human, animal, and plant. It is also a period in which all are invited to tune in to nature, both animate and inanimate, and to give thanks for its awesomeness, its diversity, its beauty, and, at times, its ambiguity and mystery.

This chapter engages the work of two exemplars of our time, namely, Professor Wangari Maathai and Pope Francis. Inspired by African and Christian theo-ethical sensibilities, respectively, the two call us to become better stewards of ourselves and of the gifts nature has bequeathed to us.

In the 1970s, Maathai founded the Green Belt Movement, a grassroots women's movement whose goal was and still remains an environmental reclamation and protection by planting trees. She was convinced that in the reckless cutting down of trees (one of the ways to desecrate the environment), humanity is digging its own grave. Consequently, through word and deed, she urged all to appreciate the gifts of nature and work urgently and proactively to "replenish the earth" by embracing spiritual values "for healing ourselves and the world."[1] Maathai would therefore endorse marking the season of creation as a gentle reminder to all of *our duty* to be stewards of creation.

Similarly, Pope Francis reminds us of our duty to take care of Earth, our common home, in his 2015 encyclical *Laudato Si'*, written three decades after the founding of the Green Belt Movement. Reading this encyclical in 2015, as an African and as a Christian, I had a palpable but welcome sense of déjà vu as I recalled the determined and even heroic work of Maathai, who had since been awarded the Nobel Peace Prize (2004) but who had passed on in 2011, a few years before Pope Francis's encyclical.

Quite independently of each other, though inspired by the African and Christian ethical sensibilities, respectively, the two came to the same conclusion. Namely, the care of Planet Earth, our common home, is an urgent moral imperative of our time. Both urge a retrieval[2] of values embedded in the African and Christian traditions that would help us become better stewards. Such values, in the words of Maathai, would help humanity "replenish" and "heal the earth" while at the same time "healing ourselves." In bringing the ecological thought and practice of these two exemplars to the attention of readers, my intention and hope is that more people will take heed of their urgent message and take urgent action toward reclaiming and implementing the seemingly forgotten but much-needed ecofriendly values, thought, and practice embedded in African and Christian theo-ethics.

Starting first with an analysis of Pope Francis and his call in the encyclical for a heightened ecological theo-ethical consciousness and the scaling up of better ecofriendly practices, we recall that by deliberately adopting the name Francis, the pope signified his intentions to model his life and leadership on the values held dear by Francis of Assisi.[3] In the same spirit, he cites Francis of Assisi in the very title of the encyclical, which echoes Francis's call to praise the Lord, the maker of it all. In the encyclical, Pope Francis continues to develop in detail what is required to take care of our common home.[4] He makes a strong and persuasive case, calling all to treat the earth with respect and to approach it with the spirit of awe and of gratitude as an urgent moral imperative.

In the encyclical, the pope urges all to embrace what he calls *integral ecology*, based on the view that *all is interconnected*.[5] Since all is interconnected, he argues, failure to be stewards, say, in caring for animals, nature, rivers, or soil, is not only injurious to the species or other aspects of nature thus ignored and quite often desecrated by us. It is also injurious to humans since all is interconnected. As he puts it: "If everything is related, then the health of a society's institutions have consequences for the environment and the quality of human life. . . . Every violation of solidarity and civic friendship harms the environment."[6]

The call through the encyclical to embrace integral ecology implies several things. First, it recognizes and celebrates the human capacity to perceive and respond to the reality and the beauty of creation in all its interconnectedness with a sense of awe and appreciation. Referring to the gospel of creation embedded, for example, in the Genesis stories, Pope Francis calls our attention to this capacity to see beauty in nature. The capacity is expressed by the storyteller in Genesis 1, who presents the story in the form of a hymn, a song. It celebrates that all of nature in its goodness is the result of wonderful artisanship by an awesome creator who deserves praise and worship.

The Genesis 1 story of creation told in the form of a hymn also celebrates the fact that humans are made with the capacity to sing such a song. It is the capacity of humans to gaze at creation and appreciate its beauty, to embrace it in a manner akin to falling in love. It leads to the name or label of nature lovers, when the human appreciation of nature becomes more palpably tangible, consistent, and intentional. The capacity to relate to nature in this manner is a defining feature of what it means to be human, a defining feature that is poetically captured by the notion in Genesis 1 that humans are special since they are made in God's image.

At one level, then, Pope Francis's *Laudato Si'* is an invitation to reawaken and to exercise this capacity in humans so that it is more active and intentional. It is an invitation to see intrinsic value in nature and to be able to sing not only in honor of God the creator but also to sing in honor and appreciation of creation, singing, for example, a hymn to "Brother Sun" and "Sister Moon" and to "our Sister, Mother Earth,"[7] as Francis of Assisi commendably did in the *Canticle of Creation*. Commenting on *Laudato Si'* and its call for humans to reawaken and practice a Franciscan contemplative approach to spirituality, Douglas Christie observes:

> The contemplative gaze, that long, slow, loving way of regarding the deepest realities—our own identity as created in the image and likeness of God and the created world as God's sacramental gift to us—is increasingly being supplanted by a quick, superficial, and evasive glance that leaves us unable to see and respond to the things that matter most to us with real thoughtfulness or feeling. It is in this sense that the Pope is suggesting to us that the environmental crisis unfolding in our midst reflects a spiritual crisis, a kind of moral-spiritual blindness that impacts every dimension of the life in the world.[8]

Given this prior spiritual crisis, Douglas concurs with Pope Francis in pointing out that any viable response to the ecological crisis calls for profound spiritual renewal. To quote Douglas: "What would it mean for us to examine seriously the habits of thought and practice that have contributed so much to the ongoing destruction of the environment? What would it mean for us to rekindle the sense of what Poet Denise Levertov describes simply as 'primary wonder,' an openhearted response to all living beings rooted in respect and reverence? Or what Francis describes as a 'loving awareness?'"[9]

Thus, the human capacity to appreciate nature and its maker is not coincidental or mechanical. It is intentional on the part of the Creator, who deliberately says: "Let us make humankind in our image" (Genesis 1:26–27). Being made in God's image is therefore a gift that activates in humans the capacity to gaze at nature with awe and to marvel at it. It was a capacity palpably manifested by St. Francis centuries ago. More recently, this gift came to the fore during the solar eclipse of August 21, 2017, when thousands camped outside and kept vigil across the United States, waiting to witness with awe and to marvel at the eclipse, an enduring but fascinating mystery of nature.

Moreover, creation is not only a gift for us to enjoy and admire reverentially, or solely that something with which to enter into a loving relationship. Nature is also a gift from which we are permitted to benefit. In God's hospitality and generosity, humans have "user rights," or more accurately, user "privileges," but not ownership rights since, as the psalmist aptly puts it, "the world (and all in it) is the Lord's" (Psalm 24). Now, while the first chapter of Genesis accentuates human privilege vis-à-vis the rest of creation, the second story of creation (Genesis 2:15) points out that humans were indeed gifted the earth to till it (e.g., for their benefit). In addition to this gift, humans were also tasked with a duty to keep it—that is to say, we have a duty to take care of it, a duty that the other-than-human creatures do not apparently have. The capacity and the duty thus to care for self and for the rest of creation becomes also a defining feature of what it means to be human. According to the biblical accounts, therefore, humans have a privilege to access and benefit from nature but also a duty of stewardship.

In this context, then, nature is not exclusively of user value to humans (e.g., not exclusively a resource to use, let alone exploit and abuse). As Jesus explains to those inordinately concerned about their individual welfare: "The lilies of the field and the birds of the air" (Luke 12–27) are not merely of user value to humans. Rather, they are of intrinsic value and are worthy of

God's care (and, by extension, our care). Despite the fact that "they neither sow nor reap," they wonderfully grow in due time, as it is their nature. The shared Earth is therefore our common home, and all living things are our *most valued copartners* in this home, a significance often unacknowledged by us.[10]

Genesis 2, this time in poetic story form, reminds humans not only of the privilege of being able to till the land and eat of its fruit but also that humans have the duty to be keepers of it. Pope Francis, citing this second account of creation, reminds us that we are called to be home (earth) keepers as a matter of moral duty. Pope Francis's encyclical is a reminder of what the authors of Genesis sought to convey a long time ago: that humans have agency, and that this kind of agency is ideally expressed in their capacity to fulfill moral duties, in this case the duty of stewardship.

Humans are unique also in that they have the capacity for intellectual curiosity and thus the capacity to explore nature, not only with a view to enjoying it aesthetically but also with intention to unravel and try to understand its complexities and mysteries. Thus, during the recent solar eclipse, as described previously, while the majority were enjoying and marveling at the spectacle (created by the peculiar, mysterious, and rare dance between Brother Sun and Sister Moon, as Francis would say), many scientists were in search for clues regarding this enduring mystery of nature. That capacity to be curious, to explore and unravel nature's mysteries, is also an aspect of being human and is itself a mark of the privilege that humans have, a privilege poetically referred to as being made in the image of God.

This capacity in humans enables them to build on prototypes from nature and to create new entities. For example, airplanes are able to hold their own in the air in a manner similar to birds, whom humans have studied for clues. Studies such as these act as springboards for humans' own innovations. One is here also reminded of how studies in genetics have allowed for a better understanding of how genes work, and this understanding has led to some major innovations and the creation of new organisms by genetically modifying the existing organisms' genes to produce the much-debated GMOs (genetically modified organisms).[11] At other times, humans manifest the capacity to create de novo, seemingly without prototypes, coming up with bold new inventions: for example, "artificial intelligence" in entities such as Watson and Siri.

This capacity to innovate and to invent seems to have accelerated in recent years, with 2007 being the peak year, according to Thomas Friedman. During that year, many innovations and inventions arrived in the world simultaneously and scaled up extremely rapidly in what, according to him, seems to be an instantiation of Moore's Law.[12] As he put it: "There are vintage years in wine and vintage years in history, and 2007 was definitely one of the latter." According to Friedman, 2007 is a vintage year because apart from the iPhone, "a whole group of companies emerged in and around that year. Together, these new companies and innovations have reshaped how people and machines communicate, create, collaborate, and think."[13]

Now, while humans have dramatically and palpably exercised their God-given creativity and capacity for intellectual curiosity and innovation, the innovations and inventions in science and technology, which are themselves an occasion to wonder and marvel, have not made visible the human uniqueness of stewardship. In fact, the opposite seems to be the case. The technological breakthroughs become simultaneously causes for concern since they seem to contradict or undermine the human capacity and duty to take care of the earth, our common home.

It is this concern that led Pope Francis, having observed the multiple intersecting ways in which Earth, our home, is compromised, to write *Laudato Si'*. In this encyclical, he reminds us to be grateful and to celebrate the gift of creativity and even the genius that humans have. However, he says, we must also be aware of the imperative to take care of Earth and protect it from damage by our innovativeness.

As he writes in *Laudato Si'*: "Humanity has entered a new era in which our technical prowess has brought us at a crossroads. We are the beneficiaries of two centuries of enormous waves of change: steam engines, railways, the telegraph, electricity, automobiles . . . modern medicine, information technology and, more recently, the digital revolution, robotics, biotechnologies and nanotechnologies. It is right to rejoice in these advances and to be excited by the immense possibilities which they continue to open up before us, for 'science and technology are wonderful products of a God-given human creativity.'"[14]

Unfortunately, as the pope also points out, humans have for the longest time confused this *gift* of agency, creativity, and capacity to respond to moral imperatives and duties with a misplaced sense of superiority and power over the rest of creation. According to Pope Francis, this misplaced and deadly sense of superiority, particularly in the Western contexts whose worldviews are shaped by the Bible, is largely a result of misreading and misinterpretation of the Genesis stories of creation cited earlier. The phrase "Let us make the human in our image and let them have dominion over the rest of creation" has been read to suggest that, by divine decree, the human is superior to the rest of the created world, which she or he can therefore treat as a mere resource for herself or himself. This has led to an enduring and troubling dualism and hierarchy in which humans posit themselves to be different and higher than the other-than-human animals. A "little less than angels," says the psalmist, who states the human status in humbler terms than contemporary anthropocentrists (Psalm 8:5). The misplaced sense of superiority and the consequent anthropocentrism has led to mind-sets and practices radically detrimental to the earth and, by extension, detrimental to those who call it home, including, ironically, ourselves.

As Pope Francis describes it: "Modern anthropocentrism has paradoxically ended up prizing technical thought over reality, since 'the technological mind sees nature as an insensate order, as a cold body of facts, as a mere 'given,' as an object of utility, as raw material to be hammered into usable shape; it views the cosmos similarly as a mere 'space' into which objects can be thrown with complete indifference."[15]

It is in this context that Pope Francis wrote *Laudato Si'*, which became a passionate reminder that whatever capacities we have are gifts from God and should be exercised with humility and a revived sense of duty and reverence for each other and our common home.

Pope Francis concludes:

> Modernity has been marked by an excessive anthropocentrism which today, under another guise, continues to stand in the way of shared understanding and of any effort to strengthen social bonds. The time has come to pay renewed attention to reality and the limits it imposes; this in turn is the condition for a more sound and fruitful development of individuals and society. An inadequate presentation of Christian anthropology gave rise to a wrong understanding of the relationship between human beings and the world. Often, what was handed on was Promethean vision of mastery over the world, which gave the impression that the protection of nature was something that only the faint-hearted cared about. Instead, our "dominion" over the universe should be understood more properly in the sense of responsible stewardship.[16]

Reading Pope Francis through African eyes gives me an intriguing sense of déjà vu when he refers to the gospel of creation implicit in the biblical stories that describe the world as an awesome, living, interconnected, and interdependent whole. I am reminded of the African indigenous worldview described by R. Sambuli Mosha, an African scholar who espouses indigenous African belief and ethical systems. The four defining features of this worldview are paraphrased here as follows:[17]

1. belief in God, the awe-inspiring maker of it all (interestingly called Ruwa, i.e., Sun by the Chagga of Tanzania, the ethnic group in which Mosha belongs);
2. belief that there is an intrinsic unity between the individual and community;[18]
3. belief that the universe is a living, interconnected, and interdependent whole;[19] and
4. belief that all is not only interconnected but is in constant process of formation, reformation, and transformation.

Mosha describes these aspects of the African worldview as part of his analysis of the multiple and interlocking crises (poverty, environmental degradation, violent conflicts) that seem to be ubiquitous in Africa and, indeed, globally. In his diagnosis and analysis, Mosha suggests that we would navigate these crises (or prophylactically preempt them) in more viable and efficacious ways if only we could tune in better to this African worldview and practice the ethics and values that flow from it. In his diagnosis of root causes, he identifies the seeming abandonment of the African worldview and its ethics as a root cause of these crises.

In his book *The Heartbeat of Indigenous Africa*, Mosha seeks to understand the Chagga people's responses to questions of existential concern, the search for basic necessities of life, the ultimate meaning, and wholeness. Commenting on reasons that motivated him to write this book, he writes:

Five main reasons motivate me to try to answer the three questions above. The most important one is what I view as a serious human and cosmic crisis in Tanzania and in most of the world. We are part of a world rich in natural resources, knowledge, information, science, and technology, yet about fifty percent of the world population goes hungry every day. Most Tanzanians and world leaders and politicians are "well educated," but justice and peace continue to escape us and billions of people are not anywhere close to a life fully alive, fully human. There is, in my opinion, a deepening world spiritual crisis that can, in my opinion, be lessened in part by learning

a lesson from the wisdom of our [African] ancestors. Their holistic
approach to life and world, and their emphasis on a life of virtue . . .
is a model that we cannot afford not to take seriously.[20]

Similarly, determined to diagnose root causes of what she refers to as
Africa's legacy of woes, Professor Wangari Maathai suggests that the root
causes of these woes have to do with the legacy of colonialism, including
colonialism of the mind. Africa seems to have learned excessive anthropocentrism and radical individualism courtesy of the colonial legacy. Such
individualism and erroneous anthropology, based on erroneous readings
of biblical texts, were presented to the Africans as the more superior worldview. For their enchanted and rather "Franciscan" perception of the world
around them, Africans and many indigenous peoples elsewhere were repri-
manded for being nature worshippers. For seeing nature and the universe
as living and pulsating with anima, moya, or spirit, they were dismissed as
superstitious animists. In fact, Africans themselves came to reject their own
seemingly superstitious and culpably "nature worshipping" inclinations as
incompatible with the newly found, ostensibly "superior" worldview and
civilizations.

Maathai laments that in accepting the thesis that there was nothing of
value in their indigenous worldviews and the beliefs and ethical values that
flow from them, it is as if Africans have been suffering from what she calls
"the wrong bus syndrome." Taking the wrong bus seems to have taken the
continent, and indeed the world, in a direction far away from the flourishing of the shared earth as home of humans and other-than-humans.

Commenting on the spiritual and cultural crisis, which in her view
paves the way for environmental crisis, Maathai writes: "Through this analysis of the intersections of culture, the degradation of the environment, and
political corruption, I realized it was necessary to enlarge the Green Belt
Movement's conception of conservation to include a recognition of cultural
heritage and the consequences of its loss, how and why culture was important, and how its neglect manifested itself in the ways the public reacts to
the environment."[21]

In her opinion, a reason why Africans have neglected or even abandoned their cultural heritage, and with dire consequences, is because they
seem to have accepted the view that their cultures are inferior, useless,
or even demonic. In accepting this view, it is as if Africans have taken
the wrong bus, which could only lead to problems. The solution is to get
off the wrong bus and get on the right one. This implies retrieving and

applying indigenous values by which we can replenish the world and heal ourselves.[22]

She explains,

> In my own personal journey, I realized that not only was I on the wrong bus, but everyone else was, too—and that one of the main reasons why we had gotten on the wrong bus was because we had lost our cultures. My analysis led me to conclude that if people are denied their culture, they are vulnerable to being exploited by their leaders and to being exploiters themselves. The reawakening of *kwimenya* can provide individuals with deep psychological and spiritual clarity. . . . A new appreciation of culture gives traditional communities a chance, quite literally, to rediscover themselves, revalue and reclaim who they are, and get on the right bus.[23]

It is this erroneously condemned African worldview that, in retrospect, Professor Wangari Maathai saw as the inspiration for her award-winning Green Belt Movement, an ecological reclamation project with the aim of planting trees. As a biologist by academic discipline, she initially did not quite bother to consider the ethical and even spiritual dimensions of her work. As she explains in her book *Replenishing the Earth*, her campaigning for environmental reclamation through planting trees did not originally concern itself with the significance of religion or any form of spirituality. Later, however, she came to realize that her work was rooted in African spirituality and its ecofriendly overtures. In her own words:

> Upon reflection, it is clear to me that when I first began this work in 1977, I wasn't motivated by faith or by religion in general. Instead, the motivation came from thinking literally and practically about how to solve problems on the ground. . . . Women . . . lacked clear drinking water, adequate and nutritious food, income, and enough energy for cooking and heating. So, when the questions were asked during the early days, I'd answer that I didn't think digging holes and mobilizing communities to protect or restore the trees, forests, watersheds, soil, or habitats for wildlife . . . was spiritual work or only relevant to the religious.[24]

Much later, she began to realize and to appreciate that the work of the Green Belt Movement was driven by passion and vision but also by certain intangible core values that she itemized and which I paraphrase here as follows:

1. *Love for the environment*: a love that propels one to protect animals and their habitats, and to show appreciation for the environment and nature in tangible ways.

2. *Gratitude and respect for Earth's resources*: valuing all that the earth gives us, and because of that valuation, not wanting to waste any of it, and therefore practicing the three *R*s: reduce, reuse, recycle.[25]

3. *Self-empowerment and self-betterment*: the desire to improve one's life and life circumstances through the spirit of self-reliance, and not wait for someone else to do it for you. This encompasses the thought that the power and resources to change are within you, and that one has "the capacity to provide oneself with the inner energy that's needed."[26]

4. *The spirit of service and volunteerism*: this is the value that is "at the forefront of the Green Belt Movement." "It is the giving of self that characterizes prophets, saints, and many local heroes.[27] It puts a priority on doing one's part to achieve the common good: both for those who are near and dear and for strangers who may be in faraway places." Such service should also include other-than-humans with whom we share life and, indeed, the planet.[28]

On closer scrutiny, these values reflect and flow from the African indigenous worldview as described by Mosha. Though Maathai does not mention the word *God*, she does speak of the imperative to acknowledge what she calls "the source" of it all. The interconnectedness of everything demands that we take care not only of our immediate neighbors but of others, including those that are other-than-humans, however remote and far-flung from us they may be.

Maathai reminds us that the duty to serve, to love one another, and to respect and be grateful for nature presupposes the fact that as humans we have indeed the capacity to respect and love one another and to care for nature. Seemingly echoing the biblical, but also indigenous Africa's "gospels of creation" embedded in the African cosmovision and stories of origin, Maathai writes:

Human beings have a consciousness by which we can appreciate love, beauty, creativity, and innovation or mourn the lack thereof. To the extent that we can go beyond ourselves and ordinary biological instincts, we can experience what it means to be human and therefore different from other forms of life. We can appreciate the delicacy of dew or a flower in bloom, water as it runs over the pebbles, or the majesty of an elephant, the fragility of the butterfly, or a field of wheat or leaves blowing in the wind. Such aesthetic responses are valid in their own right, and as reactions to the natural world they can inspire in us a sense of wonder and beauty that in turn encourages a sense of the divine. [Such] consciousness acknowledges that while a certain tree, forest, or mountain itself may not be holy, the life-sustaining services it provides—the oxygen we breath, the water we drink—are what make existence possible, and so deserve our respect."[29]

143

In her view, then, if we are to even make a small dent in addressing the multiple intersecting crises that haunt the African continent and, indeed, the globe, we need to recognize the prior crisis of the wrong bus syndrome.[30] We need to acknowledge that in our recently acquired (or aggrandized) anthropocentrism, we have abandoned the indigenous way of looking at nature with reverence and now look at nature as a mere resource for us. Maathai reminds us that there was a time when we looked at trees and saw more than timber or looked at elephants and saw more than ivory to make our trinkets and jewelry. Sadly, that is all we see now: timber and ivory. In our anthropocentric frenzy and greed, we cut trees with seeming abandon and kill elephants (and other species of animals, such as sea otters) to the point of extinction.

Maathai's strong and passionate proposal, therefore, is that if we are to have any measure of success in replenishing the earth, it is imperative that we get off the wrong bus and reclaim and embrace the less anthropocentric perspectives exemplified in the African worldview, which inspire "spiritual values for healing ourselves and the world."[31]

My sense of déjà vu, as an African Catholic ethicist, then, lies in my recognition of the palpable resonance between the call for ethical metanoia in the face of the ecological crises found in *Laudato Si'* and the similar call from Africa's ethicists based on afro-theo-ethics. I realize that just as Maathai is pleading with us to get off the wrong bus and to retrieve African values hitherto abandoned that will help us heal the earth and heal ourselves, so, too, the encyclical is calling for us to get off the anthropocentric bandwagon in order to retrieve the values embedded in the biblical gospel of creation and to read the Bible in non-anthropocentric ways that foster an integral ecological consciousness and practice. The encyclical is calling us to apply biblical values in ways palpably exemplified by the life of St. Francis, who, according to Pope Francis, embodies the very opposite of anthropocentrism.

Maathai and many others who find her analysis persuasive would fully embrace Pope Francis's call. She recognizes, however, that there are countless interlocking and acute crises and challenges facing Africa, and, indeed, the world. A sense of powerlessness, despair, and being overwhelmed can be the ultimate roadblock to our getting off the bandwagon and getting on the right bus toward enhanced flourishing. She recognizes that often people feel overwhelmed and discouraged, or are tempted to be in denial or become too afraid to do anything. Borrowing a parable from Japan, she tells the story of the hummingbird.[32] According to the story, a wildfire once caused a panic among animals. Except, that is, for one little hummingbird. The animals were all scared and thought there was nothing they could do. The little hummingbird, however, decided to do something about it. She flew back and forth, fetching drops of water in her tiny beak and trying to put out the blazes. The bigger animals thought she was being ridiculous since she had such a tiny beak and the fire was monstrous. But she would not be discouraged, and she told the others: "I am doing the best I can!" Maathai concludes that the hummingbird was a role model for her, and that through her Green Belt Movement, a seemingly lilliputian project, she was trying to replenish the earth one tree at a time. She was like the hummingbird. She invited her audience (now all of us) to emulate that hummingbird and not to be totally paralyzed by the magnitude and enormity of the challenges facing us, including, but not limited to, the challenge of climate change and allied crises. The multiple fires, some accidental and others deliberately started, some literal and others metaphorical, that are raging seemingly ubiquitously around the world make Maathai's call for us to become hummingbirds enduringly urgent, relevant, and timely. Like an ideal African leader, Maathai eschewed lighting destructive fires, seeking instead to be a hummingbird determined to fight the burning blazes (specifically the fire of environmental degradation) the best way she could. Her not-so-little hummingbird act was to plant trees. Others may have other strategies to implement the hummingbird spirit.

I conclude with the thought that if we all do like the proverbial hummingbird, cumulatively and multiplicatively, our acts will stop the multiple raging fires or prevent them from flaring up in the first place. And then, we shall indeed have reason to sing and praise the Lord and with Francis call out with joy and appreciation, Laudato Si'!

Notes

1. The language here is borrowed from the title of one of Wangari Maathai's books in which she makes the case for a retrieval of indigenous ecofriendly values of Africa. The title of the book is *Replenishing the Earth: Spiritual Values for Healing Ourselves and the Earth* (New York: Doubleday, 2010).

2. Pope Francis's call for retrieval of values embedded in the Christian tradition reminds me of the emerging debate around what has been referred to as the Theology of Retrieval, while Maathai's call reminds me of the retrieval encouraged through the idea of *Sankofa*, particularly among African Americans who consider the role of African spiritualities and values in their lives. Such a retrieval, however, as Jean Mac Ela cautions, should not be confused with a mere "exhumation of the past"; see Ela, *African Cry* (Eugene, Oreg.: Wipf and Stock, 2005), 128. For a discussion of the Theology of Retrieval, see W. David Bushcart and Kente Eilers, *Theology as Retrieval: Receiving the Past, Renewing the Church* (Westmont, Ill.: Intervarsity Press, 2015), and for an application of the notion of Sankofa in Womanist thought, see Kali Sherita Robinson Meyers, "Sankofa Healing: A Womanist Analysis of the Retrieval and Transformation of African Ritual Dance" (M.A. thesis, Georgia State University, 2015), https://scholarworks.gsu.edu/rs_theses/48.

3. Francis of Assisi was named patron saint for those who promote ecology by Pope John Paul II in 1979. For details, see Warner Keith, "Retrieving Saint Francis: Tradition and Innovation for Our Ecological Vocation," in *Green Discipleship: Catholic Theological Ethics and Environment*, ed. Winright Tobias (Winona, Minn.: Anselm Academic Christian Brothers Publications, 2011), 19.

4. In chapter 1 of *Laudato Si'*, Pope Francis itemizes and discusses the multiple intersecting ways in which our common home is compromised. These include multiple forms of pollution, a waste and throwaway culture, loss of biodiversity, global inequalities, and the deadly impact of anthropogenic climate change. For details, see Pope Francis, *Laudato Si': Encyclical Letter of the Holy Father Francis on Care of Our Common Home* (Nairobi: Pauline's Publications Africa, 2015), 16–37.

5. For a detailed analysis of theo-ethical implications of the notion that all is connected, an idea that is prevalent in *Laudato Si'*, see Vincent J. Miller, ed., *The Theological and Ecological Vision of Laudato Si': Everything is Connected* (London: Bloomsbury, 2017), 12–21. See also chapter 3, suitably titled "Ecology: The Science of Interconnection."

6. Pope Francis, *Laudato Si'*, 81.

7. For the full text of the canticle, see https://www.catholic.org/prayers/prayer.php?p=3188.

8. Douglas Christie, "Becoming Painfully Aware: Spirituality and Solidarity in *Laudato Si'*," in Miller, *Theological and Ecological Vision*, 120.

9. Ibid.

10. Scientists speak of the specific role of each and every species in the balancing out and even in enhancing the flourishing of all. Some species, called keystone species (e.g., bees), are considered key to the flourishing of the ecosystems despite the fact that humans may not even know or appreciate these key roles. For an analytical discussion of ways in which species other than humans are intrinsically valuable players in our common home, see Terrence P. Ehrman, "Ecology: The Science of Interconnections," in Miller, *Theological and Ecological Vision*, 68. In this chapter, he discusses how humans have over-hunted the sea otters, a keystone species that feeds on sea urchins, thus controlling their population. Consequently, the sea urchin

population has become disproportionately larger and disproportionately consumed the kelp (under the sea forests), leading to what are referred to as "Urchin Barrens." In turn, this "desertification" under the sea has led to the extinction of the sea cow, which depended on kelp for fodder.

11. A recent ethical debate related to humans' capacity to modify genes pertains to the new development of the science and technology to enable gene editing. The question as to whether even to continue with the research that enhances this technology to a point where it is applicable to humans is on the table, with some countries having banned the research midstream. For a detailed commentary on the ethical challenges raised by this technology, see Jeantine E. Lunshof's "Gene Editing is Now Outpacing Ethics," *Washington Post*, December 12, 2017, https://www.washingtonpost.com/news/theworldpost/wp/2017/12/12/bioethics/?utm_term=.d51485724911.

12. See Thomas Friedman, *Thank You for Being Late: An Optimist's Guide to Thriving in the Age of Accelerations* (New York: Farrar, Straus and Giroux, 2016), esp. chapter 3.

13. For further details, see chapter 2, aptly titled "What the Hell Happened in 2007?" According to Friedman, innovations and new technologies in or around that year include iPhone and Kindle, while storage for computer data expanded exponentially with the invention of "the Cloud" (ibid., 20–22).

14. Pope Francis, *Laudato Si'*, 59.

15. Ibid., 67.

16. Ibid.

17. Paraphrased from Sambuli Mosha, *The Heartbeat of Indigenous Africa* (Shrewsbury, Mass.: Garland Publishers, 2000), 7–15.

18. John Mbiti captured this thought well in the oft-cited idea that while in Western circles the proposal about what defines the persons is expressed by Descartes in the phrase "I think therefore I am," in African circles the prevailing thought is that "we are, therefore, I am." For a detailed discussion of this idea and its implications for the ethical imperatives in interpersonal relationships, see J. Mbiti, *African Religions and Philosophy* (Portsmouth, N.H.: Heinemann, 1969), 106.

19. This is reminiscent of the notion of integral ecology discussed earlier in this essay.

20. Mosha, *Heartbeat of Indigenous Africa*, 2.

21. Wangari Maathai, *Challenge for Africa* (New York: Anchor Books, 2009), 17.

22. Maathai makes the case for this retrieval, reclamation, and application of indigenous values in her book *Replenishing the Earth* (New York: Doubleday, 2010).

23. Maathai, *Challenge of Africa*, 171. *Kwimenya* means "self-knowledge or self-awareness."

24. Maathai, *Replenishing the Earth*, 13.

25. Referred to as *Mottainai* in Japan.

26. Mosha would see this capacity for self-propelled transformation as evidence that we are in the process of formation and transformation.

27. Mbiti would see here an instantiation of the African philosophy of being (as cited earlier): "I am because we are."

28. Paraphrased from Maathai, *Replenishing the Earth*, 14–16.

29. Ibid., 17ff.

30. Maathai, *Challenge of Africa*, 6.

31. For details, see Maathai, *Replenishing the Earth*.

32. Here is a link to her parable of the hummingbird, inviting us to embrace the hummingbird spirit with resilient hope and courage: https://www.youtube.com/watch?v=IGMW6YWjMxw.

AN ECOLOGICAL THEOLOGY FOR ASIA

The Challenges of Pope Francis's Encyclical Laudato Si'

Peter C. Phan

Environmental or ecological degradation, as part of a cluster of economic and social problems, was listed among the six most serious threats to global security and peace in the twenty-first century by the United Nations' High-Level Panel on Threats, Challenges and Change in 2005.[1] While ecological degradation through depletion of natural resources; the destruction of ecosystems, habitat, and wildlife; and pollution has long been studied as a scientific issue, it has only recently been investigated from the viewpoints of global security and peace and from cultural, anthropological, and religious perspectives. Furthermore, it has been recognized that ecological destruction, though a direct result of the globalization of what is called "the technocratic paradigm," has deep roots in modern anthropocentrism. Consequently, the solutions to ecological degradation must not be limited to science, technology, and economics, essential as these are, but must also be based on social, cultural, and religious convictions and values so that an "integral ecology" may emerge.

Given the religious nature of the ecological crisis, it comes as no surprise that religious leaders have drawn from their own resources to contribute to its solution. Among these, pride of place is to be given to Pope Francis, whose *Laudato Si': On Care for Our Common Home* is the first papal encyclical devoted exclusively to the issue of ecology.[2] Of course, earlier popes have not been unconcerned about this threat to the survival of humanity and the cosmos. In the opening paragraphs of his encyclical (nos. 3–6), Francis recalls the teaching of his predecessors John XXIII, Paul VI, and Benedict XVI on the moral obligation to safeguard the environment. However, all of their statements on ecology are obiter dicta, and none of the earlier documents of Catholic social teaching offers a sustained treatment of the subject.[3]

In a sense, *Laudato Si'* encapsulates the twin foci of Francis's pontificate, which are implied in his choice of "Francis" as his name. Three days after his election to the papacy on March 13, 2013, he explained the reason for his choice: "Francis was a man of poverty, who loved and protected creation." Protection of the environment and love for the poor are the two basic themes of the encyclical, and they are strictly intertwined since, as the pope insists, it is the poor who suffer the most from ecological destruction: "The deterioration of the environment and of society affects the most vulnerable people on the planet" (no. 21). The encyclical is an urgent clarion call to the whole world to heed the cry of the poor and the cry of the devastated Sister Earth, which, in Francis's arresting description, "is beginning to look more and more like an immense pile of filth" (no. 21).

It is still too early to tell, but all the signs seem to indicate that *Laudato Si'* is fated to meet with the same fierce opposition as Pope Paul VI's *Humanae Vitae*, which condemns "artificial contraception." The difference is that this time opposition comes from the opposite side of the ideological spectrum, that is, conservatives, especially in the United States, who believe that global warming is a scientific hoax perpetrated by anticapitalistic ultra-leftists to destroy profitable fossil fuel industries and to curb the globalization of the Western technocratic paradigm of production and consumption.[4]

Of course, deniers of climate change in wealthy countries of the first world can easily avoid its deleterious effects on their health and environment by having multinational corporations export ecologically polluting industries to third world or majority world countries, where they can operate cheaply and unencumbered by the legal constraints and financial costs imposed on their manufacturing industries in their own developed countries. In the process, they damage the environment, as *Laudato Si'* notes, "leaving behind great human and environmental liabilities, such as unemployment, abandoned towns, the depletion of natural reserves, deforestation, the impoverishment of agriculture and local stock breeding, open pits, riven hills, polluted rivers and a handful of social works that are no longer sustainable" (no. 51).

The intent of this essay is not to summarize and evaluate the encyclical as a whole, which is unnecessary, as there is already a good number of studies, both popular and scholarly, that offer a summary and a critical analysis of it.[5] Rather, my task is to read *Laudato Si'* with Asian eyes, from the Asian perspective, and this I will do by raising three questions. First, which ideas of the encyclical would hold the greatest interest and thus have the greatest relevance for Asians? Second, are there any aspects of the teaching of the encyclical that would be enriched by incorporating the teachings of the Asian Catholic Church and insights from the philosophical and religious traditions of Asia? And third, what are the most urgent remaining ecological issues that still need to be addressed?

Laudato Si': An Encyclical for Asia?

In a broad sense, the question of whether the encyclical is directed to the people of Asia should be responded affirmatively since Pope Francis addresses not only Catholics and other Christians but also all of humanity since "the environmental challenge we are undergoing, and its human roots, concern and affect us all," and since "all of us can cooperate as instruments of God for the care of creation, each according to his or her own culture, experience, involvements and talents" (no. 15). But there is a special sense in which the people of Asia will find *Laudato Si'* to be of particular relevance for them in light of both its teachings on environmental protection and the ecological situation of their continent.

It is interesting to note that in Asia there is no leading politician or prominent business leader who would deny the reality of climate change and ecological destruction. All it takes for them to dispel any thought of climate change as a scientific and political hoax is to step outside their offices into the street in any Asian metropolis, and they would be choked by smoke-filled air, assaulted by acrid smell, overwhelmed by wilting heat, and contaminated by disease-bearing water. In calling for environmental protection in Asia, Francis is thus preaching to the choir. However, the scientific information he provides on global warming (chapter 1) is no less useful, his discussion of the "human roots of the ecological crisis" (chapter 3) no less enlightening, his message about "integral ecology" (chapter 4) no less apposite, and his call for "ecological conversion" and "ecological education and spirituality" (chapter 6) no less urgent, given the fact that in all the areas in which human life is adversely affected by ecological degradation, Asia is no doubt the most vulnerable continent.

Unfortunately, because of the lack of scientific education, many Asians— like most people in the majority world—are not intellectually equipped to understand *why* climate change and its attendant ecological catastrophes occur. They tend to view natural disasters—floods, typhoons, hurricanes, drought, torrential and prolonged rains, ice storms, heat waves, and other weather-related excessive phenomena—as unavoidable natural cycles, or worse, accept apocalyptic interpretations of them as God's punishment for human sins. Thus, they are unable to see, as Pope Francis puts it, "the human roots of the ecological crisis" and that "a certain way of understanding human life and activity has gone awry, to the serious detriment of the world around us" (no. 101). As a consequence, they fail to acknowledge their own responsibility for ecological destruction and to take up the task of protecting the environment.

By presenting a scientifically accurate yet highly accessible explanation of how climate change results from human activities (chapter 1), *Laudato Si'* makes a great contribution—normally not expected of a religious document—to the diffusion of the much-needed understanding of the *causal connection* between the release of greenhouse gases (carbon dioxide, methane, nitrogen oxides, and others) into the atmosphere, the depletion of the ozone layer, global warming, the melting of polar ice, and rising sea levels, on the one hand, and human activities such as the burning of fossil fuel (coal, petroleum, and gas), deforestation, the dumping of industrial and nuclear waste and chemical products, and the increasing use of fertilizers, insecticides, fungicides, herbicides, and agrotoxins, on the other. Unless this causal connection between global warming and human activities is clearly understood and acknowledged, communal efforts "to resolve the tragic effects of environmental degradation on the lives of the world's poorest" (no. 13) in "a new and universal solidarity" (no. 14) would be impossible. Catholics, especially those who do not possess the requisite scientific knowledge—in fact, a majority of Asian Catholics—are not able to verify for themselves the fact of global warming, particularly over against the denial of it by powerful interest groups. For them, the affirmation by the pope, the highest teaching authority of the church, that "our common home is falling into serious disrepair" (no. 61) serves as a rich and helpful source of information and an incentive for concerted action to promote an "*integral ecology*" (no. 137).

Thanks to Pope Francis's clarion call "to hear *both the cry of the earth and the cry of the poor*" (no. 49), we are now encouraged to pay attention to the catastrophic impact of global warming and climate change on the Asian poor, especially in three areas. First, there is loss of safe habitable land. It was recently reported that 35 million people who live in the delta area of Bangladesh would be displaced and lose their livelihood if the global sea levels rise by one meter (3.3 feet).

Second, lack of access to fresh water and the pollution of water is widespread. While 97.5 percent of Earth's water is found in its oceans, only 3 percent is fresh water. During the twentieth century, due to the threefold increase of the human population, industrialization, and irrigation of agriculture, water consumption jumped sevenfold, and it is predicted that by 2025, two-thirds of the world's population will experience water shortages. Sixty percent of the world's population live in Asia, yet only 36 percent of the world's fresh water is available to them, and water scarcity drives up its price for the poor. (It was reported in 2002 that in Pakistan, water costs 1.1 percent of the people's daily wage, whereas in the United States, water costs only as little as 0.006 percent.)

Furthermore, as Pope Francis points out, "the quality of water available to the poor" is toxic: "Every day, unsafe water results in many deaths and the spread of water-related diseases, including those caused by microorganisms and chemical substances. Dysentery and cholera, linked to inadequate hygiene and water supplies, are a significant cause of suffering and of infant mortality. Underground water sources in many places are threatened by the pollution produced by certain mining, farming, and industrial activities, especially in countries lacking adequate regulation or controls. It is not only a question of industrial waste. Detergents and chemical products, commonly used in many places of the world, continue to pour into our rivers, lakes and seas" (no. 29). To those living or visiting Asia, sadly the pope's description of water pollution is all too familiar.

Water scarcity not only has caused conflicts in the Middle East over the Tigris-Euphrates Rivers and in Africa over the Nile but is also a source of potential conflicts in Asia: between Pakistan and India (the Indus River), between India and Bangladesh (the Ganges and the Brahmaputra Rivers), among Thailand, Myanmar, and China (the Salween River), and among Thailand, Cambodia, Laos, and Vietnam (the Mekong River). The melting of the glaciers on the Himalayas, which is caused by global warming, will affect the waters of the Ganges, Brahmaputra, Irrawaddy, Mekong, Salween, Yangtze, and Yellow Rivers. It has been said that in international economy and politics water promises to be in the twenty-first century what oil was in the twentieth century. Finally, the pope goes on to note that "the control of water by large multinational businesses may become a major source of conflict in this century" (no. 31). Transnational water has become a highly profitable commodity, and private companies have attempted to capture the "water market." Needless to say, privatizing water for profit further deprives the Asian poor of their right to safe water.

Third, there is loss of biodiversity. According to many scientists, in our time the earth is experiencing the sixth greatest extinction of life since life began 3.8 billion years ago. In 2015, the extinction of species was taking place one thousand times faster than at the end of the Ice Age, and this unprecedented loss of biodiversity is compounded by global warming. *Laudato Si'* points out that "each year sees the disappearance of thousands of plant and animal species which we will never know, which our children will never see, because they have been lost forever. The great majority become extinct for reasons related to human activities" (no. 33). In Asia, much of the biodiversity found in tropical countries is disappearing at an alarming rate. For example, the orangutan, which lives only in Indonesia and Malaysia, is facing extinction by illegal logging and the clearance of their habitat for palm oil plantations. Golden-headed langurs and black-crested gibbons are disappearing in northeastern Vietnam.

Loss of biodiversity occurs not only on land but also in the sea. *Laudato Si'* notes: "Oceans not only contain the bulk of our planet's water supply, but also most of the immense variety of living creatures, many of them still unknown to us and threatened for various reasons. What is more, marine life in rivers, lakes, seas and oceans, which feeds a great part of the world's population, is affected by uncontrolled fishing, leading to a drastic depletion of certain species" (no. 40). *Laudato Si'* points out that "carbon dioxide increases the acidification of the ocean and compromises the marine food chain" (no. 24). In Asia, in a single year, the Yellow River can dump into the South China Sea 751 tons of heavy metals along with 21,000 tons of oil. In addition to acidification, climate change also contributes to the deoxygenation of seawater. Recent ocean models project that there will be a decline between 1 and 7 percent in the global ocean oxygen in this century, which has a negative impact on fish and other marine organisms.

Loss of biodiversity in the oceans is also caused by fishing with giant deep-sea bottom trawlers, which is heavily subsidized by governments and which strips the oceans bare. A study by the International Union for Conservation of Nature in 2012 found that 12 percent of all the marine species in the tropical eastern Pacific Ocean were threatened with extinction. In addition, mining for copper, manganese, nickel, cobalt, and rare metals on the floor of the Pacific Ocean at 2.5 miles beneath the surface will also do irreparable damage to marine life. Two marine ecosystems are especially at risk: the coral reefs and the mangrove forests. *Laudato Si'* notes: "Many of the world's coral reefs are already barren or in a state of constant decline" (no. 41). Coral reefs, which are comparable to the great forests on dry land, protect coastlines from destruction by waves and tropical storms, and provide habitats and shelter for many marine organisms. Like coral reefs, mangrove forests provide food and shelter for fish. Tragically, over the past forty years, millions of acres of mangrove areas have been destroyed. In Asia, Thailand has lost 27 percent of its mangrove forests, Malaysia 20 percent, the Philippines 45 percent, and Indonesia 40 percent.

From these brief considerations of the disastrous impact of global warming on Asia, and especially the Asian poor, in three areas, namely, habitable land, access to healthy water, and biodiversity, it is clear that *Laudato Si'*, though not specifically written for Asia, is highly relevant to Asia. As the encyclical argues, not only has the "environmental, economic, and social ecology" been degraded (nos. 139–42), but the "cultural ecology" (nos. 143–46) and the "ecology of daily life" (nos. 147–55) have been seriously harmed. These three ecologies constitute what *Laudato Si'* terms "integral ecology," which must be preserved by means of a worldwide and concerted effort (chapter 4). As *Laudato Si'* points out somberly, ecological destruction has led to a decline in the quality of human life and the breakdown of society: "The social dimensions of global change include effects of technological innovations on employment, social exclusion, an inequitable distribution and consumption of energy and other services, social breakdown, increased violence and a rise in new forms of social aggression, drug trafficking, growing drug use by young people, and the loss of identity" (no. 46). Furthermore, ecological degradation has also led to "global inequality" between the rich countries of the Global North and the developing and poor countries of the Global South (nos. 48–52). A quick survey of the Asian contemporary social and economic scene will confirm Pope Francis's succinct litany of the challenges Asia is facing as the result of ecological degradation.

"The Great Sages of the Past": Toward an Interreligious Ecological Theology

In calling for the restoration of integral ecology, Pope Francis appeals not only to the Judeo-Christian biblical tradition, with its emphasis on the universe as God's creation (nos. 76–83), universal communion (nos. 89–92), and the common destination of goods (nos. 93–95), but also to the wisdom of Saint Francis of Assisi, as expressed in his celebrated *Canticle of the Creatures* (no. 87), whose opening line, *Laudato Si'*, serves as the title of the encyclical. Furthermore, introducing a theological novelty, he cites the teaching of the ecumenical patriarch Bartholomew (nos. 7–9) and twenty-one episcopal conferences, including those of the Philippines (no. 41), Japan (no. 85), and the Federation of Asian Bishops' Conferences (no. 116).

The Federation of Asian Bishops' Conferences

It is noteworthy that the Federation of Asian Bishops' Conferences (FABC) is probably the first official church body in the Catholic Church to be deeply concerned with ecology.[6] Already in 1988, at the Eleventh Bishops' Institute for Interreligious Affairs in Sukabumi, Indonesia, it was stated that "the ecological question or the harmony and balance of the natural environment in relation to the life of man is a fundamental one. The destiny of humankind is inextricably bound up with the way they cultivate the earth and share its resources. Harmony and peace call for respect for the earth. She is the mother of whose dust we are made and to whose womb we shall return. The usurpation of the fruit of the earth by some and the deprivation of others of the same results in the rupture of harmony among peoples."[7]

Among the institute's many pastoral recommendations, there is one regarding the environment: "Respect for nature and compassion for all living things are ingrained in the Asian religions and cultural traditions. Today in Asia owing to many factors, the natural environment with which man should be in harmony is being wantonly destroyed through deforestation, industrial pollution, depositing of nuclear wastes, etc. Christian life and witness should manifest greater sensitivity to nature and to all sentiments. Hence we recommend that Christians join forces and cooperate with all movements of followers of other religions and secular groups engaged in maintaining balance and harmony in our ecosystem, and protecting nature and its riches from destruction."[8]

Concern for the environment recurred as a constant refrain in the FABC's Plenary Assemblies and in the various documents of its offices in the ensuing years. At the Sixth FABC Plenary Assembly, "Christian Discipleship in Asia Today" in 1995, it is stated in the final statement: "Ecology is once again brought to our pastoral attention. And urgently so, since we see in the countries of Asia the continuing and unabated destruction of our environment. . . . Life, especially in a third world setting, is sacrificed at the altar of short term economic gains. The Lord, the Giver of Life, calls our discipleship in Asia into a question on the time bomb issue of ecology. Choosing life requires our discipleship to discern and act with other faiths and groups against the forces of ecological destruction."[9]

Note that the FABC's approach to ecology is framed in terms of "harmony" and "wholeness," which are said to be characteristic ideals of Asian peoples: "When we look into our traditional cultures and heritages, we note that they are inspired by a vision of unity. The universe is perceived as an organic whole with the web of relations knitting together each and every part of it. The nature and the human are not viewed as antagonistic to each other, but as chords in a universal symphony."[10] It is out of this sense of universal harmony and wholeness that concern for ecology is born and nourished. Indeed, there is a fourfold harmony to be achieved: with God, with oneself, with others, and with nature. A disturbance in any one of these four relations brings about disharmony in the other three; conversely, harmony in any one of them strengthens harmony in the other three. Thus, harmonious ecology is rooted in harmonious relation with God, with oneself, and with others. By the same token, there cannot be harmony with God, with oneself, and with others without harmonious ecology. Indeed, the idea of harmony is so central to Asian thought and life that the Theological Advisory Commission (now Office of Theological Concerns) has produced a seventy-page document titled *Asian Christian Perspectives on Harmony*, in which ecological degradation figures among the most destructive forces causing disharmony in Asia.[11]

Ecology was also discussed at the FABC's Seventh Plenary Assembly in 2000 with the theme "A Renewed Church in Asia: A Mission of Love and Service."[12] The Tenth Plenary Assembly in 2012, with the theme "A New Evangelization," notes how the ecological issue was brought to worldwide attention by the monumental disaster in Japan caused by a tsunami on March 11, 2011: "Our Assembly has likewise noted the unabated abuse of creation due to selfish and shortsighted economic gains. Human causes contribute significantly to global warming and climate change, the impact of which affects the poor and the deprived more disastrously. The ecological concern, the care for the integrity of creation, including intergenerational justice and compassion, is fundamental to a spirituality of communion."[13]

As important as these FABC documents are, they are not cited by *Laudato Si'*. Instead, the encyclical quotes three other lesser-known texts. The first is a brief statement of the Colloquium on Faith and Science held in Tagaytay, the Philippines, by the FABC Office of Education and Student Chaplaincy in 1993 titled *Love for Creation: An Asian Response to the Ecological Crisis*.[14] The statement provides a helpful analysis of the ecological problem in its scientific, cultural, political, theological, and pastoral dimensions. The second document is the pastoral letter on ecology of the Conference of Catholic

Bishops of the Philippines, whose title *What Is Happening to Our Beauti-ful Land* is echoed in the title of the first chapter of *Laudato Si'*: "What Is Happening to Our Common Home." The letter begins with a graphic list of the ecological damages that have been done to the forests, seas, and land of the Philippines and ends with a recommendation of activities that can and must be undertaken by individuals, churches, and the government "to respect and defend life." The third document is a rather lengthy letter of the Catholic Bishops of Japan titled *Reverence for Life: A Message for the Twen-ty-First Century from the Catholic Bishops of Japan* (January 1, 2001). Chapter 3, titled "Life and Death," discusses eight issues, one of which being the environment. It recalls Rachel Carson's prophetic voice warning the world in 1962 about the "silent spring" and ends with the following beautiful words, which *Laudato Si'* quotes (no. 85): "God cares even for the flowers of the field, dressing each with beauty and loving it. To sense each creature sing-ing the hymn of its existence is to live joyfully in God's love and hope."[15]

So far we have only examined the teachings on ecology of the Catholic Church in Asia. However, the "Great Sages of the Past," to whom *Laudato Si'* refers (no. 47) and from whom we can acquire "true wisdom, as the fruit of self-examination and generous encounter between persons" (no. 47), include also the spiritual masters of Asian religions. *Laudato Si'* explicitly calls for a dialogue and collaboration among religions for the defense of Earth, a call repeatedly made by the FABC: "The majority of people living on our planet profess to be believers. This should spur religions to dialogue among themselves for the sake of protecting nature, defending the poor, and building networks of respect and fraternity" (no. 201).

Among the many causes of the ecological crisis, Pope Francis high-lights what he calls "the globalization of the technocratic paradigm," which "exalts the concept of a subject who, using logical and rational procedures, progressively approaches and gains control over an external object" (no. 106). In this case, the "external object" is the material world, which tech-nocracy tries to dominate by means of "a technique of possession, mastery and transformation" (no. 106). At the basis of this technocratic paradigm is the conception of the material world and everything existing therein as valuable only to the extent that they can be made to serve human needs and wants, and not as valuable in themselves, by their independent existence and autonomous value. This conception is called "excessive anthropocentrism" (no. 1). To counter the technocratic paradigm and excessive anthropocen-trism, the pope develops philosophical and theological arguments derived from Christian sources (chapter 20). Starting from the Christian belief in

God's creation of nature or the universe, Francis affirms the existence of a "universal communion": "All of us are linked by unseen bonds and together form a kind of universal family, a sublime communion which fills us with a sacred, affectionate and humble respect" (no. 89). The pope goes on to emphasize that "universal communion" includes the material universe: "Everything is related, and we human beings are united as brothers and sisters on a wonderful pilgrimage, woven together by the love God has for each of his creatures and which also unites us in fond affection with brother sun, sister moon, brother river and mother earth" (no. 92).

Here I would like to extend Francis's reflections on universal communion by invoking the Buddhist and Daoist perspectives. Admittedly, Pope Francis's belief in a personal God and in God's creative act is fundamentally different from the nontheistic and noncreationist stance of Buddhism and Daoism. Yet, despite this difference, these two Asian religious traditions offer insights into reality that strengthen and enlarge the pope's position. In brief, the technocratic paradigm can be countered by the Buddhist notion of "interdependent/ dependent co-arising/origination" (Sanskrit: *pratītyasamutpāda*) and excessive anthropocentrism by the Daoist view of universal harmony.

The Buddhist Wisdom

There has recently been a significant production of scholarship, both general handbooks and specialized monographs, on Buddhism and ecology as well as a proliferation of Buddhist sociopolitical and spiritual associations of environmental activism.[16] This interest in ecological thought and practice in Buddhism has been dubbed the "Greening of Buddhism." In her helpful overview of the history and development of this movement, Stephanie Kaza acknowledges that "Buddhist environmental thought is both ancient and brand new."[17]

Buddhist ecological thought is ancient because it is rooted in the fundamental teachings of the earliest traditions of Buddhism, though, of course, these teachings need to be reinterpreted to meet the threat of environmental destruction. In Theravada Buddhism, for instance, there is the central notion that suffering (*dukkha*) is caused by desire of and attachment to things (*tanha*) born out of the ignorance of the impermanence of all beings. A remedy against desire and attachment and hence suffering is the practice of compassion (*karuna*) and loving-kindness (*metta*), which is extended not only to all humans but also to all animals, plants, and even natural elements. The Noble Eightfold Path itself, which is intended as a guide for the individual to achieve enlightenment and liberation from suffering (*nirvāna*), is interpreted as ways to prevent and relieve the suffering and destruction of not just individual beings but also the entire physical environment.

In particular, the precepts included in four paths, namely, right view, right speech, right action, and right livelihood, have been reformulated to promote protection of the environment. Right view implies not only the correct understanding of the impermanence of things and the connection between ignorance of this essential nature of things and suffering but also a correct understanding of the causal correlation between certain human activities such as the use of fossil fuel and climate change. Not telling lies under right speech proscribes not only falsehood-telling but also misleading advertising to promote ecologically destructive consumerism. Not taking life under right action includes not only not killing human life but also doing no harm (*ahimsa*) to all living beings and things. Right livelihood commands avoidance not only of life-killing professions but also acquisition of unnecessary things. The remaining four paths—right effort, right mindfulness, right concentration, and right resolve—can also be interpreted in a way that is conducive to ecologically responsible living insofar as they train the individual mind to gain true insight into the nature of reality as suffering, impermanence, and interdependence.

The impermanence and interdependence of all things on one another bring us to the ecological thought present in Mahayana Buddhism. Central to this Buddhist tradition is the concept of "interdependent/dependent arising/origination" (*pratītyasamutpāda*), by which is meant that all things (*dharma*) do not exist as independent and permanent realities or "selves" but are constantly changing or "co-arising" (*samutpāda*) dependently (*pratītya*) on other things, which are also co-arising dependently on the things that co-arise dependently on them. The doctrine of interdependent origination is expressed in the following terse formula: "When this is, that is; This arising, that arises; When this is not, that is not; This ceasing, that ceases."[18] As a result of interdependent origination, there is nothing that is permanent, nothing that is substantial.

This doctrine is also expressed by the concept of "emptiness" (*śūnyāta*), or "no-self" (*ānatman*), which maintains that no-self is independent of other selves. The Indian Buddhist philosopher Nāgārjuna points out that to say that a thing is "empty" is to say that it is dependently originated, marked by three characteristics: transient, unsatisfactory, and without inherent existence. Another representation of this Mahayana concept of the interdependence of all beings is the Jewel Net of Indra, which stretches through all space and time and connects an infinite number of jewels in the universe, with each jewel being infinitely multifaceted and reflecting every other jewel in the net.

In terms of ecological thought, the Buddhist concept of interdependent origination implicitly rejects the technocratic paradigm that views the world in terms of subject-object for the purpose of domination and exploitation. Interdependent origination—as the term implies—affirms universal and mutual conditioning among all things. No being can exist without the other: one person without all other persons, humanity without ecology, and, vice versa, ecology without humanity.

This interdependence of all things is dramatically expressed by the Vietnamese Buddhist monk Thich Nhat Hanh. In a short post titled "Clouds in Each Paper" on Awakin.org dated March 25, 2002, he writes:

> If you are a poet, you will see clearly that there is a cloud floating in this sheet of paper. Without a cloud, there will be no rain; without rain, the trees cannot grow: and without trees, we cannot make paper. The cloud is essential for the paper to exist. If the cloud is not here, the sheet of paper cannot be here either. So we can say that the cloud and the paper inter-are.
>
> "Interbeing" is a word that is not in the dictionary yet, but if we combine the prefix "inter" with the verb "to be," we have a new verb, inter-be. Without a cloud, we cannot have paper, so we can say that the cloud and the sheet of paper inter-are.
>
> If we look into this sheet of paper even more deeply, we can see the sunshine in it. If the sunshine is not there, the forest cannot grow. In fact nothing can grow. Even we cannot grow without sunshine. And so, we know that the sunshine is also in this sheet of paper. The paper and the sunshine inter-are. And if we continue to look we can see the logger who cut the tree and brought it to the mill to be transformed into paper. And we see the wheat. We know that the logger cannot exist without his daily bread, and therefore the wheat that became his bread is also in this sheet of paper. And the logger's father and mother are in it too. When we look in this way we see that without all of these things, this sheet of paper cannot exist.[19]

Because of interdependent origination, humanity and ecology "inter-are." "Interbeing" is the only mode of existence possible, not only among humans themselves but also between humanity and ecology. The animals and the material world are not just "objects" for us humans as "subjects" to

160

manipulate, dominate, and exploit. Their value and worth are not measured by their usefulness to humans; rather, they possess their autonomous value in themselves because they and we co-arise interdependently. Without them we cannot exist, and without us they cannot exist. They and we "inter-are."

The FABC Theological Advisory Commission in its document *Asian Christian Perspectives on Harmony*, cited previously, explains how in the Mahayana tradition the historical Buddha becomes identified with the goal he reached, namely, *nirvāna*, the Ultimate "No-Self," or Absolute "Emptiness," by destroying the twelve causes producing suffering. It goes on to say: "The human task is to follow the example of the historical Buddha and to reach this ultimate state of emptiness, which is stillness, quietness and limitless rest, but the dynamic stillness which reaches out in compassion to all living beings still in the throes of suffering."[20]

Despite profound resonances between Buddhist basic teachings, both in Theravada and Mahayana traditions, and contemporary ecological thought, it would be wrong to think that Buddhism is a religion of "nature" and immediately and inevitably leads to environmental protection activities.[21] (It is equally wrong to imagine that Christianity, with its theology of creation and incarnation, naturally leads to the kind of ecological concerns as evinced by Pope Francis.) There is always a gap between theory and practice, or, more concretely, between what believers say and what they do. But this is no argument against the teachings of Buddhism per se; rather, it calls for a concerted effort by believers of different traditions to draw from their own religious sources on ecological responsibility, to enrich their own insights with those of other religions, and to help each other live up to their beliefs.[22]

The Daoist Wisdom

As mentioned earlier, the FABC regards harmony and wholeness as characteristic ideals of the Asian way of life. Daoism is both a philosophical school (*daojia*) and a religious practice (*daogiao*) that is distinguished from Confucianism and Buddhism (*fojiao*). The classics upon which Daoism is founded are the *Dao de jing*, also known as the *Laozi*, and the *Zhuangxi*. The defining concept of the Daoist religion is the Dao itself. Literally meaning the "way" or the "path," the Dao refers to the proper course of human conduct, especially as taught by the ancient sages. It soon came to be understood as the metaphysical basis of the natural order itself, primordial yet eternally present. In its primordial state, Dao is described as "nothingness," null and void. But the Dao also manifests itself and becomes present in the sensible world through *qi* (literally, breath, steam, vapor, or energy). *Qi*, both energy and matter, is the basic building block of all things in the universe, responsible for movement and energy, and is the vital substance of life. Daoist rituals and religious practices aim at preserving this *qi* by combating the forces of aging, illness, and death. The goal, at once temporal and spatial, is to bring the various parts of the body back into unified harmony and thus to achieve immortality.

As with Buddhism, there are certain fundamental insights into humans and the natural world and basic ethical concepts in Daoism that can provide a consistent theoretical framework for an ecological ethics. Notable among these are the twin set of ideas *de* (virtue) and *dao* (way), and *wuwei* (nonaction) and *ziran* (nature). Taken together, these two sets of concepts create an aesthetic order in which no one thing is assessed as better than another, everything (*de*) possessing its distinctive significance within the context of the whole (*dao*). As Karen L. Lai puts it succinctly: "The realization of each individual is meaningful only the context of its relatedness and responsivity to others within the whole (*dao*). The affirmation of the value of individual beings *within the environmental context* feeds into a complex holism that emphasizes both the integrity and interdependence of individuals."[23]

A corollary of this ontological aesthetics is a decided rejection of anthropocentrism. Daoist environmentalism opposes any dualism that holds humans as discontinuous with, independent of, superior to, and even opposed to the environment. Instead, Daoism promotes both integrity or individuality (*de*) and holism or harmony (*dao*) in defining the individual. It sees the self as self-in-relation and self-in-context. In this combined integrity and holism, the whole is not simply the sum of its parts, nor is the whole more than its parts. Rather, the individuals cannot be what they are unless they are in harmony with the whole, and the whole cannot be what it is unless it is made up of the parts.[24]

Again, it is not necessary to delve into all the intricate philosophical and cosmological speculations and alchemy of Daoism here. Suffice it to note for our present purposes that central to Daoism as a religious practice is the ethics of "noncontrivance" (*wu wei*). According to Zhuangxi, the Dao acts spontaneously in individuals, society, and nature. Similarly, humans must respect and submit to natural changes. In this way, they and the world can become one. By contrast, contrivance should be avoided because it is counterproductive and contrary to the spontaneity (*tzu-jan*) of the Dao. The ethic of noncontrivance means that humans must not act against nature; rather, human action, like the Dao's, must be nonpurposive, nondeliberative, and yet continuously transforming, as natural as water flowing downward and fire rising upward.

Clearly, such ethic of noncontrivance and spontaneity runs counter to the kind of anthropocentrism that makes humans the center or the summit of creation and technological domination of nature the goal of knowledge. Even though Daoist thought and practice are not based on the belief in God the Creator, they provide a powerful stimulus to "hear the cry of nature itself; everything is connected" (no. 117).

Going Forward and Further

In his evaluation of *Laudato Si'*, Donald Dorr says that the encyclical "is an exceptionally important document, which will surely rank with the Vatican II Pastoral Constitution on the Church in the Modern World (*Gaudium et Spes*)."[25] That is not a hyperbole, in light of both contents and methodology. In terms of methodology, the encyclical starts with a clear, accessible, and accurate presentation of the scientific data on the ecological crisis, without which theological elaborations would be no more than abstract speculation. As mentioned earlier, *Laudato Si'* offers a very helpful introduction to the ecological crisis and provides people with inadequate scientific education the means to articulate the causal connections between human activities—individual and corporate—and global warming. Furthermore, the fact that Pope Francis quotes the teachings of episcopal conferences is a welcome departure from the earlier view that they do not constitute a proper teaching authority of the hierarchical magisterium.

In terms of contents, again, according to Dorr: "Francis's account of an integral ecology represents a major breakthrough in Catholic social teaching."[26] Dorr goes on to list eleven areas where such breakthrough occurs: (1) a rich Bible-based theology of ecology, (2) a comprehensive account of the major environmental issues, (3) the affirmation of human activities as causing the ecological crisis, (4) the strong link between "the cry of the earth" and " the cry of the poor," (5) the danger of the "technocratic paradigm," (6) the proposal of an alternative economy, (7) the "ecological debt" of the rich countries, (8) recognition of the contributions of local cooperatives and indigenous communities, (9) encouragement to adopt ecologically friendly practices, (10) emphasis on the need for enforcement measures at the national and international levels, and (11) the need to pressure politicians to take radical enforcement measures.[27]

On the debit side, Dorr notes three areas where *Laudato Si'* could be improved: the population issue, the theology of the "Cosmic Christ," and an evolution-based theology of creation in the form of the "New Story."[28] With regard to the Asian context, the first issue obtains pride of place, and I will briefly develop the first area, leaving aside the second and the third. *Laudato Si'* mentions the "reduction in the birth rate" and "certain policies of 'reproductive health'" (no. 50) and views them as ways in which rich countries try to avoid facing the consequences of their consumerist lifestyle on the environment by blaming it on the birth rate in the majority world. The encyclical goes on to quote the *Compendium of the Social Doctrine of the Church* of the Pontifical Council for Justice and Peace: "While it is true that an unequal distribution of the population and of the available resources creates obstacles to development and a sustainable use of the environment, it must nonetheless be recognized that demographic growth is fully compatible with an integral and shared development" (no. 50).

In light of the demographic explosion in Asian countries such as India, China, the Philippines, Indonesia, and Vietnam, and especially in the poorest countries of Asia, such a treatment of the impact of demographic explosion on the environment is little short of being cavalier. Perhaps *Laudato Si'* is still hampered by the teaching of *Humane Vitae*, but the ecological crisis in 2018 is quite different from that in 1968 and should have provided an occasion for a serious reexamination of Pope Paul VI's admittedly noninfallible teaching on birth control. At any rate, what Pope Francis said on January 19, 2014, on his way back to Rome from the Philippines to the effect that one need not reproduce like rabbits in order to be good Catholics is a good place to start an open and honest discussion of "responsible parenthood."

With the publication of *Laudato Si'*, no one can accuse the leadership of the Catholic Church of turning a blind eye to an issue on which the survival not only of the human family but of Planet Earth itself depends. Pope Francis has sounded a clarion call for an "ecological conversion," a call addressed to the whole of humanity, but also one that Asia will need to heed and respond to actively and promptly because being a continent of the poorest of the poor, it has to respond to the cry of the earth to make a decent human life possible for its own people. The pope's message is not a lone voice. It has been anticipated in many ways by the Asian bishops, not to mention many Asian theologians. Furthermore, Pope Francis's message about an integral ecology can be enriched by incorporating the wisdom of the "Great Sages" of Asia, in particular as embodied in Buddhism and Daoism. Thus, an Asian interreligious ecological theology can be formulated to encourage and accompany concerted efforts to save and "care for our common home."

Notes

Part of this chapter is drawn from my "Pope Francis's *Laudato Si'* and Ecological Theology: Call to Action for the Catholic Church in Asia," in *Asian Christianities: History, Theology, Practice* (Maryknoll, N.Y.: Orbis Books, 2018), reproduced with permission.

1. See *Toward a More Secure World? The Report of the High-Level Panel on Threats, Challenges and Change* (2005). The report lists six threats: (1) economic and social threats, including poverty, infectious diseases, and environmental degradation; (2) interstate conflict; (3) internal conflict, including civil war, genocide, and other large-scale atrocities; (4) nuclear, radiological, chemical, and biological weapons; (5) terrorism; and (6) transnational organized crime.

2. Pope Francis, *Laudato Si': On Care for Our Common Home*, with commentary by Sean McDonagh (Maryknoll, N.Y.: Orbis Books, 2016), henceforth *Laudato Si'*.

3. Of special note is John Paul II's World Day of Peace message: *Peace with God the Creator, Peace with All Creation* (January 1, 1990). For an extensive discussion of the earlier papal magisterium on the ecological crisis, see Kevin W. Irwin, *A Commentary on "Laudato Si'": Examining the Background, Contributions, Implementation, and Future of Pope Francis's Encyclical* (Mahwah, N.J.: Paulist Press, 2016), 1–93.

4. Prominent among opponents to the encyclical are the leading figures of the U.S. Republican Party, such as veteran climate change deniers James Inhofe and Rick Santorum, and the leaders of fossil fuel industries such as Arch Coal.

5. See, for example, Donal Dorr, *Option for the Poor and for the Earth: From Leo XIII to Pope Francis* (Maryknoll, N.Y.: Orbis Books, 2016); John Fleming and John Ozolins, *"Laudato Si'": A Critique* (Redland Bay, Queensland: Conner Court, 2016); Elizabeth-Anne Stewart, *Preaching and Teaching "Laudato Si'": On Care for Our Common Home* (Amazon Digital Services, 2016); Irwin, *A Commentary on "Laudato Si'"*; Nellie McLaughlin, *Life's Delicate Balance: Our Common Home and "Laudato Si'"* (Dublin:

Veritas Publications, 2016); Anthony Kelly, *Laudato Si'* (Adelaide: ATF Press, 2016).

6. For a collection of the FABC's and its various offices' documents, see Gaudencio Rosales and C. G. Arévalo, eds., *Documents from 1970 to 1991*, vol. 1 of *For All the Peoples of Asia: Federation of Asian Bishops' Conferences* (Maryknoll, N.Y.: Orbis Books, 1992); Franz-Josef Eilers, ed., *Documents from 1992 to 1996*, vol. 2 of *For All the Peoples of Asia: Federation of Asian Bishops' Conferences* (Quezon City, Philippines: Claretian Publications, 1997); Franz-Josef Eilers, ed., *Documents from 1997 to 2001*, vol. 3 of *For All the Peoples of Asia: Federation of Asian Bishops' Conferences* (Quezon City, Philippines: Claretian Publications, 2002); Franz-Josef Eilers, ed., *Documents from 2002 to 2006*, vol. 4 of *For All the Peoples of Asia: Federation of Asian Bishops' Conferences* (Quezon City, Philippines: Claretian Publications, 2007); and Vimal Tirimanna, ed., *Documents from 2007 to 2012*, vol. 5 of *For All the Peoples of Asia: Federation of Asian Bishops' Conferences* (Quezon City, Philippines: Claretian Publications, 2014).

7. Rosales and Arévalo, eds., *Documents from 1970 to 1991*, 320.

8. Ibid., 323.

9. Eilers, ed., *Documents from 1992 to 1996*, 11.

10. Rosales and Arévalo, eds., *Documents from 1970 to 1991*, 319.

11. See Eilers, ed., *Documents from 1992 to 1996*, 237–38. The entire document is found on 229–98.

12. See Eilers, ed., *Documents from 1997 to 2001*, 7.

13. Tirimanna, ed., *Documents from 2007 to 2012*, 45. See also Vimal Titimanna, "The FABC and Ecological Issues," *Asian Horizons* 6, no. 2 (June 2012): 287–308.

14. See Declaration of the Colloquium sponsored by the Federation of Asian Bishops' Conferences (Tagaytay, January 31–February 5, 1993). Unpublished.

15. A new and revised version of this text was issued on January 1, 2017. Chapter 3, titled "Threats to Life," in which environmental issues are discussed, has been much enlarged. It describes the changes in environmental

problems and cites *Laudato Si'* extensively in developing an "integral ecology."

16. The following works are most helpful. On religion and ecology in general, see Roger S. Gottlieb, ed., *The Oxford Handbook of Religion and Ecology* (Oxford: Oxford University Press, 2006); Dale Jamieson, ed., *A Companion to Environmental Philosophy* (Oxford: Blackwell, 2001); and J. Baird Callicott and James McRae, eds., *Environmental Philosophy in Asian Tradition of Thought* (Albany: State University of New York Press, 2014). On Buddhism and ecology in particular, two works stand out: Mary Evelyn Tucker and Duncan Ryūken Williams, eds., *Buddhism and Ecology: The Interconnection of Dharma and Deeds* (Cambridge: International Society for Science and Religion, 1997) and Stephanie Kaza and Kenneth Kraft, eds., *Dharma Rain: Sources of Buddhist Environmentalism* (Boston: Shambala, 2000). All these works contain abundant bibliographies.

17. See Stephanie Kaza's "The Greening of Buddhism: Promise and Perils," in Gottlieb, *Oxford Handbook of Religion and Ecology*, 184–206; here, 202. See also Kaza, "Acting with Compassion: Buddhism, Feminism, and the Environmental Crisis," in Callicott and McRae, *Environmental Philosophy*, 71–98, and Kaza, "American Buddhist Response to the Land: Ecological Practice at Two West Coast Retreat Centers," in Tucker and Williams, *Buddhism and Ecology*, 219–48. See also *Buddhism and Ecology: The Interconnections of Dharma and Deeds*, ed. Mary Evelyn Tucker and Duncan Ryüken Williams (Cambridge, Mass.: Harvard University Press, 1997).

18. For a helpful explanation of "interdependent origination" in Buddhist thought, see Richard Gombrich, *What the Buddha Thought* (London: Equinox, 2009), 129–43, and Paul Williams with Anthony Tribe, *Buddhist Thought: A Complete Introduction to the Indian Tradition* (London: Routledge, 2000), 62–72.

19. See Thich Nhat Hanh, "Clouds in Each Paper," March 25, 2002, http://www.awakin .org/read/view.php?tid=222. See also Thich Nhat Hanh, *The Wisdom of Thich Nhat Hanh* (New York: One Spirit, 2000), 233–52.

20. Eilers, ed., *Documents from 1992 to 1996*, 260.

21. For a critique of the view that the Buddhist idea of "emptiness" and oneness of all things with nature make Buddhism an environmentally friendly religion, see Simon P. James, "Against Holism: Rethinking Buddhist Environmental Ethics," in Callicott and McRae, *Environmental Philosophy*, 99–115. Instead of speaking about Buddhism as an environmentally friendly philosophy on account of its metaphysical concepts of emptiness, James argues that Buddhism is so because it commends a way of life, a set of virtues, in particular *karunā*, that promotes ecological responsibility.

22. Stephanie Kaza has also enlisted feminist thought to enrich Buddhist and environmental thought and practice. See Kaza, "Acting with Compassion: Buddhism, Feminism, and the Environmental Crisis," in Callicott and McRae, *Environmental Philosophy*, 71–98.

23. Karen L. Lai, "Conceptual Foundation for Environmental Ethics: A Daoist Perspective," Callicott and McRae, *Environmental Philosophy*, 173–95; here, 183; emphasis original. In addition to Lai's essay, see also the essays on Daoist ecology in this volume by R. P. Perrenboom, "Beyond Naturalism: A Reconstruction of Daoist Environmental Ethics," 149–72; Alan Fox, "Process Ecology and the 'Ideal' Dao," 197–207; Sandra A. Wawritko, "The Viability (*Dao*) and Virtuosity (*De*) of Daoist Ecology: Reversion (*Fu*) as Renewal," 209–24; and James Miller, "Ecology, Aesthetics and Daoist Body Cultivation," 225–43.

24. For a study of Daoism and ecology, see N. J. Girardot, James Miller, and Liu Xiaogan, eds., *Daoism and Ecology: Ways Within a Cosmic Landscape* (Cambridge: Center for the Study of World Religions, 2001) and *Daoism and Ecology: Ways Within a Cosmic Landscape*, ed. N. J. Girardot, James Miller, and Liu Xiaogan (Cambridge, Mass.: Harvard University Press, 2001). For a brief overview, see James Miller, "Daoism and Nature," in Gottlieb, *Oxford Handbook of Religion and Ecology*, 220–35.

25. Dorr, *Option for the Poor*, 436.

26. Ibid., 436.

27. Ibid., 437–38.

28. Ibid., 439–43.

painting 3 José Ernesto Padilla, *TitoArt 12*. Oil on canvas, 20 × 16 inches. Private collection. Used with kind permission by Gladys Soto.

PLASTICITY AND CHANGE

Rethinking Difference and Identity with Catherine Malabou

Clayton Crockett

> The biggest problem we face is a philosophical one:
> understanding that this civilization is already dead.
>
> —THE INVISIBLE COMMITTEE

Introduction

Some readers might remember Van Jones, an African American lawyer who fought against police brutality in the Bay Area of California and then founded an environmental movement, Green for All, that linked the issues of social and racial justice with environmental issues. In 2009, Jones was appointed special advisor for Green Jobs, Enterprise, and Innovation for the White House Council on Environmental Quality by the newly elected president, Barack Obama. After only a few months on the job, Jones was targeted by conservative media figures and politicians for his participation in a radical socialist organization, Standing Together to Organize a Revolutionary Movement, and for allegedly signing a petition for 911Truth.org. Amid the controversy, Jones chose to resign rather than continue on in his position, and some observers criticized the Obama administration for not standing up for Jones. His 2008 book, *The Green Collar Economy*, makes the case for linking the exploitation and impoverishment of human beings with the exploitation of the environment. Jones argues that "we must create a new, 'green-collar economy'—one that will create good, productive jobs while restoring the health of our planet's living systems."[1]

In the heady days of the 2008 election of President Obama, many people agreed with Jones that a new green economy would restore American prosperity and help resolve economic inequality while at the same time resolving our environmental problems. This was a pipe dream, sacrificed to the reality of power politics and the unholy mess called Obamacare, both in its corporate compromise of a single-payer system and the political resistance and reaction to its passage. At the same time, we need to listen to the ideas of people such as Van Jones, who later went on to found another campaign, Rebuild the Dream.[2] I do not think we can rebuild the American dream, and I am not sure we want to, but I think that Jones is right to link economic inequality and environmental destruction together.

Climate change is already affecting everyone and everything, but it harms the most vulnerable most and first. In our understanding of human existence and its technological civilization, as well as our practices of economic capitalism, everything has to change. We know this, or essays and books like this one would not be read. The most real aspect of existence is change, what Buddhism calls anicca, or impermanence. Buddhism argues that there is no substantial permanent identity, whether of the self, the world, or even God. We live in a world that appears to be stable, at least in terms of the trajectory of technological development and human consumption, but this apparent stability is a lie. Every organism, every species, and every society is caught up in a dynamic process that exists in a metastable state, that is, a state that is not an equilibrium.

In concrete political terms, the desire for social change often comes up against what philosopher Jacques Derrida calls an aporia between the specific identities that are deployed in the struggle and the general situation of improvement that is called for. An aporia is a tension or a problem without an apparent solution, and this aporia concerns the struggle between the need to develop connections of solidarity among different groups and the need to preserve distinct social and political identities among and between these same constituencies. We should beware any simple listing of these markers in whatever order—class, race, gender—even if we cannot escape what they connote and how they shape our existence for better and for worse.

On the one hand, we need as much human solidarity as possible to confront the urgent environmental situation we face, one that can and will kill us sooner or later. As the title of Naomi Klein's latest book puts it, *This Changes Everything*. According to Klein, "our economic system and our planetary system are now at war."[3] We all need to recognize that the greatest threat to human existence in large-scale civilizational terms is neoliberal corporate capitalism, and we need to organize against it however we can. On the other hand, we need to be suspicious about the "greenwashing" of differences among distinct groups. *Greenwashing* is a term that refers to the practice of corporate appropriation and labeling of supposedly environmentally friendly practices so that our consumption can continue unabated. A greenwashing of social differences should raise suspicions that this is another ploy to redirect attention away from the fundamental issues of sex, race, and class. It may be that our world is crumbling ecologically, but we can be sure that the people who are suffering and will continue to suffer the least will be people who are male, who are white, and who are rich. And we can already see that the people most exposed to environmental devastation are poor, are nonwhite, and are women.

In this essay, I want to engage with Catherine Malabou, a contemporary French philosopher, to navigate some of the issues of identity and difference that divide and untie us in an ecological context. I appeal to Malabou's conceptions of plasticity and change to cut across some of the problems of the theoretical and practical oppositions between identity and difference in social and political terms. Malabou is a philosopher of change, and she understands change in relation to what she calls plasticity. I develop these ideas in the body of this essay, and I will also compare and contrast Malabou's idea of change with Alfred North Whitehead's notion of process toward the end. These ideas are intended to help us think through some of the difficult issues associated with how our gendered, racialized, and class inequalities persist within an important environmental context.

In this essay, I argue that in a world threatened by severe climate change, we need a political theology of material change as well as a political ecology of change that attends to the mutual substitutability and transformation between what we call essence, Being, ultimate reality, or God and what we designate as specific forms of life or being. Life is the name for the inviolable that is exposed to violation, which is one way that Malabou designates the feminine, as we will see later in the essay. Earth is a name for our planet that is increasingly marked by an awareness of this volatility and fragility. Genuine and radical change involves risking these grounding distinctions between ultimate and conventional reality; it involves risking who and what we are without obliterating any and all distinctions.

Postmodern Differences

Postmodernism is sometimes the name given to describe recent trends in French philosophy, more technically called poststructuralism. After the predominance of existentialism in the work of Jean-Paul Sartre and Albert Camus after World War II, French philosophy experienced a newer movement known as structuralism in the 1950s and 1960s. Structuralism was less popular in the English-speaking world, but it focused on how biological, linguistic, and social structures shape our experience of reality. The next wave of French theory was called poststructuralism, because it developed a critique of the limits of the ideas of structure and structuralism.

The most common way to characterize this French poststructuralist philosophy is to claim that it is a philosophy of difference. In different ways, Gilles Deleuze, Michel Foucault, Julia Kristeva, Jacques Derrida, and Jean-François Lyotard all appear to champion difference over identity, representation, continuity, and totality. For English-speaking readers of these philosophies, identities are constructed rather than essential elements of our being, and differences are what is primary. Some readers celebrate and others lament these philosophies and their potential for social change. To a great extent, our sexual, racial, and class identities are constructed and reconstructed rather than simply given.

At the same time, there is a limit to this affirmation and celebration of difference. As Linda Martín Alcoff explains in her book *Visible Identities*, identities such as race and sex cannot simply be deconstructed or performed out of existence or into another existence.[4] There is an incorrigibility to racial and sexual identity. Furthermore, critical race theorists such as George Yancy focus on the effects of whiteness as a lens through which to objectify, racialize, and stigmatize black and other nonwhite bodies. In his book *Black Bodies, White Gazes*, Yancy treats "the white gaze as a racist socio-epistemic aperture" that "sees" black bodies as dangerous, threatening, and potentially rebellious objects that need to be disciplined.[5] There is a sense in which the objectification and exploitation of human bodies by the white male gaze mimics the objectification and exploitation of the natural world by this same European gaze and activity. As Charles H. Long, a historian of religion at the University of Chicago during its late twentieth-century period of prominence in the study of religion, writes: "The basic problems that confront us as a nation today result from the fact that we have not taken the integrity of nature seriously. The exploitation of our natural resources and of blacks and other racial minorities stems from this fact."[6] So just as Van Jones links economic and racial injustice to environmental devastation, Long affirms that the exploitation of minorities and the exploitation of nature are part of the same attitude. Modern European peoples spread technical civilization and democratic ideals, while at the same time they wrought violence, slavery, and genocide in their colonial endeavors.

In social terms, we confront a tension between global appeals to solidarity and the concrete differences of marginalized and oppressed peoples understood in terms of class, race, and gender. The horizon of our ecological crisis can be used to support or to undermine both sides of this tension. We may diminish the significance of these ethnic and gendered identities in our appeal to a unified ecological front, or we may lose focus on the imminent threat of climate change and its impact on our species as we are divided by issues of class, race, gender, and sexuality. The point is to refuse this implication of either/or and to seek at least a theoretical solution to this aporia.

Malabou's Plasticity

The poststructuralist affirmation of difference over against identity continues to inform many of these discussions and intellectual and political struggles, at least for intellectuals working in fields influenced by contemporary French philosophy. My turn to the philosophy of Catherine Malabou in this chapter is meant to show how difference and identity are both grounded in change, and how change is an expression of material plasticity in her work. I think that *change* is a better context in which to grapple with these difficult theoretical and practical issues.

My reorientation of difference and identity around change is not a grandiose solution but a modest suggestion that a reorientation of theoretical discussions and debates around change might help us reconceptualize and reformulate some of these urgent practical issues in more productive ways. Malabou is a student of Jacques Derrida, and her dissertation consists of an interpretation of Hegel and the Hegelian dialectic that presses beyond the stereotypical poststructuralist critique of Hegel's philosophy as totalizing. In her book *The Future of Hegel*, Malabou notes that Hegel says that the dialectical self-formation of the subject is plastic: "The relation between the subject and predicates [in philosophical discourse] is characterized by 'plasticity.'" This "process of self-determination," she writes, "is the unfolding of the substance-subject."[7] Plasticity characterizes the determination of the subject that forms itself out of its own substance. But what is plasticity?

According to Malabou, we need to think about plasticity, which derives from the Greek verb *plassein*, in at least three distinct ways: first, as the ability to give or shape form, as in an artwork of sculpture; second, as the capacity to receive form, to be formed, which is also part of this sculptural process; and third, there is a destructive or explosive element of plasticity, the auto-annihilation of form itself, which is indicated by the use of the word *plastics* (in French *plastique*) to designate an explosive substance. As she points out in *The Future of Hegel*: "Plastic on its own is an explosive material with a nitroglycerine and nitrocellulose base that can set off violent detonations."[8] Plasticity is the philosophical concept that Malabou evokes, and it is the idea that is most associated with her philosophy.

After her work on Hegel, Malabou shifts gears and begins to focus more explicitly on the brain. She was astounded to discover the significance of neuroplasticity in contemporary brain studies and wrote *What Should We Do with Our Brain?* as a way to pivot and directly engage with the philosophical and political significance of this work. Neuroplasticity has to do with the differentiation and transdifferentiation of cells, including adult stem cells. She says that most adult stem cells are multipotent, and they "specialize, in order to produce all the types of cells in their tissue of origin that normally die." But some adult stem cells, like skin stem cells, are pluripotent; they "can transform themselves into different types of cells," which means that they "transdifferentiate," or literally "change their difference."[9]

In this short book, Malabou critiques the ideological deployment of neuroscientific concepts in workplace networks of horizontal connectivity as well as the association of plasticity with the flexibility that characterizes twenty-first-century neoliberal capitalism. She argues instead for a conception of plasticity that is closer to resilience, where resilient "reconfigurations and . . . becoming[s] are made up of rupture and resistance."[10] We need a biological alter-globalism that gives us tools to resist capitalist ideology. Malabou claims that "to exist is to be able to change difference while respecting the difference of change: the difference between continuous change, without limits, without negativity, and a formative change that tells an effective story and proceeds by ruptures, conflicts, dilemmas."[11] Our brains are not just telling us to obey; they are also telling us to resist—to change, to become different.

Plasticity is about change, about the way that change manifests itself dialectically. I am less concerned with the exegetical accuracy of Malabou's interpretation of Hegel than with how she develops her own conceptions of plasticity and change. I suggest that we cannot understand what Malabou means by plasticity unless we see how plasticity is all about change. As the editors of a recent collection on Malabou's work assert: "Malabou seeks to philosophically recover form by grasping it as always already in restless motion. She is foremost a philosopher of change."[12] And change is not only about biology and neurology, or philosophy and dialectics, but also about politics and social change. Malabou affirms a biological materialism that she also associates with what is called "new materialism." In *Plasticity at the Dusk of Writing*, she claims that "it is my opinion therefore that we should certainly be engaging deconstruction in a new materialism."[13]

The New Materialism is a nonreductionist materialism of complexity and process that is influenced by the philosophy of Alfred North Whitehead, Maurice Merleau-Ponty, and Gilles Deleuze. New Materialism includes thinkers such as Rosi Braidotti, Manuel DeLanda, Donna Haraway, Isabelle Stengers, William Connolly, and Jane Bennett.[14] This New Materialism specifically emerges in the late 1990s, and it advocates a dynamic materialism where being is not stable or static. As Rick Dolphijn and Iris van der Tuin explain: "Manuel DeLanda and Rosi Braidotti—independently of one another—first started using 'neo-materialism' or 'new materialism' in the second half of the 1990s, for a cultural theory that does not privilege the side of culture, and focuses on what Donna Haraway (2003) would call 'natureculture' and what Bruno Latour simply called 'collectives.'"[15]

Many of these readings, including those of Braidotti and DeLanda, stress the compatibility of Deleuze's philosophy with the physics of complexity. Existence is already in process, and these dynamic processes drive systems to a state of chaotic complexity that is not at equilibrium. Materialism is not about the smallest building blocks of nature, whether atoms or quarks or strings, but the energetic transformation of reality by means of physical, chemical, biological, psychological, and social interactions. As Jane Bennett explains, attention to the intrinsic "vitality of matter" counters "the image of dead or thoroughly instrumentalized matter [that] feeds human hubris and our earth-destroying fantasies of conquest and consumption."[16] Matter is not dead or static; it is intrinsically dynamic and transformational.

Malabou is more influenced by Hegel, Heidegger, and Derrida than Whitehead, Merleau-Ponty, and Deleuze, but she advocates a biological New Materialism that has important resonances with these better-known conceptions of New Materialism. For Malabou, material form is more significant than the flows of matter-energy, but we should not view them oppositionally. Later in this chapter, I will compare and contrast Malabou's understanding of change with that of Whitehead and suggest that perhaps our understanding of Whitehead has to change, too.

Changing Difference

In her book *The Heidegger Change*, Malabou ignores the standard interpretations of Martin Heidegger's philosophy and reads him in a fresh and compelling way. She focuses on three German terms: *Wandel* (change), *Wandlung* (transformation), and *Verwandlung* (metamorphosis), and traces their persistence through much of his work. Malabou claims that "the triad W, W, & V would then be what confers on Heidegger's thought its power and vigor, and what at the same time makes it good for something and fit for something else, an energy greatly needed in the world of today."[17] Malabou reads these three terms not only as a way to understand change *in* Heidegger's philosophy but more importantly as a way to *change* it.

The three terms for change—W, W, and V—constitute an exchange, and an exchange where Heidegger's entire philosophy changes from what it is to what it can become for us, which is what makes it fantastic. This triad of change is for Malabou a way to rethink the ontological difference, Heidegger's celebrated difference between Being (itself) and (particular, determinate) beings. What is the nature of being? Change. Being changes, it transforms, and it metamorphosizes itself, both the Being of being and the beings that transform themselves. Change is the transformation of form, or what Malabou calls, in *What Should We Do With Our Brain?*, the transdifferentiation of form. According to Malabou, "Heidegger characterizes metaphysics as a 'form' that changes from epoch to epoch by being re-formed, even as he just as much promises 'the other thinking' to be *transformation* in the literal sense—a *passage* or *transition* to another form."[18]

If we read and think about Heideggerian Being, we usually assume that the Being of beings does not change, even if beings do. But the good news here is that "the good old beings of metaphysics are no more." Malabou says that "*there is an exchange between being and beings that is not an incarceration of the ontological difference, but its liberation.*"[19] This liberation concerns change as the transformation of form, the exchange of Being and being in a seemingly impossible exchange that is radical, real, and revolutionary.

Malabou reads an economics of exchange at the heart of Heidegger's thought. She claims that "a proximity between Heidegger and Marx indeed exists, and it doubtlessly lies in the possibility of the ontological and economic coinciding within the definition of exchange, of exchange and mutability, of the metamorphosible and displaceable character of value, and of the impossibility of transgressing all this plasticity."[20] In this context, which is both economic and ontological at the same time, every modification of Dasein (the *there* of Being, or the being who asks the question of Being) is intrinsically revolutionary. She says that the genius of Heidegger consists "in having inscribed the possibility of revolution not in a future event to come but in the fact (so modest, slight, and tiny) of *being-there, of still being there after the accomplishment that was never accomplished.*"[21] Every slight change is the manifestation of transgressive power, because it affects the being of change itself, *form*, which is the change of Being itself.

Being is plastic, because it changes form. It is also metamorphic, it changes Being itself, because Being itself is change, or exchange. There is an exchange of being that transforms existence in every being there, every Dasein. "Existence itself surpasses metaphysics," writes Malabou, and "*we started a revolution without at all realizing we were.*"[22] The more we focus in on micro-level events, the more we realize how transformative any singular moment or act can be, even if we feel more and more helpless in the face of large-scale political and environmental events.

It is not that we abandon the macro level and focus solely on the micro level, although that is tempting. It is about seeing the exchange between the two and holding onto change. Change is about the transformation of difference, because difference and identity are grounded in change. Change is plasticity, because it is not just about differentiation of an immutable essence but about transdifferentiation. It is about changing difference.

What Should We Do with Our Body?

In *What Should We Do with Our Brain?*, Malabou says that our brains are telling us to resist the flexibility that is prescribed by the ideology of neoliberal capitalism: "What we are lacking is *life*, which is to say: *resistance*. Resistance is what we want."[23] In a New Materialism there is no dualism between brain and body. Our bodies are telling us to resist, revolt, insurrect—change. Change the difference that we are. Stasis is not the idea of nature; "energetic explosion is the idea of nature," including the auto-destruction of form, which is the lesson of destructive plasticity.[24] Malabou says that life is about resistance and resilience, not flexibility, because change is not adaptation to this or that condition of global capitalism; it is the ability to change conditions, to blow up. If we are too flexible, "if we didn't explode at each transition, if we didn't destroy ourselves a bit, we could not live. Identity resists its own occurrence to the very extent that it forms it."[25] The formation of identity is not simply the play of differences but the resistance of plasticity that creates it. Identity and difference are grounded in change.

We think that human culture is an exception to nature, but this is a false dichotomy. In an essay on Darwin, Malabou points out the plasticity of the process of natural selection and argues that we need to think social selection in more plastic terms. Darwinian variability attests to the existence of biological plasticity, which "designates the quasi-infinite possibility of changes of structure authorized by the living structure itself; in other words, the structural law of changing structure."[26] Appropriating Deleuze's interpretation of Nietzsche's eternal return, Malabou argues that selection is a "process of repetition" that "produces its own criteria as it operates" to select for differences rather than similarities.[27] This is a form of social selection that better accords with Darwinian natural selection. For Malabou, both social and natural selection meet at the level of epigenetic plasticity, a place where the genetic envelope and epigenetic variability coincide. Here the lessons of neural plasticity help "articulate the two types of selection and present a coherent theory regarding a certain continuity between nature and society."[28]

This is an insight that has been easier for theorists influenced by process thought to appreciate, and one that has sometimes been more difficult for scholars working in areas affected by Continental philosophy. At the same time, we should not assume a static caricature of "postmodernism" as if it lacks the ability to change. Malabou is just one of the many Continental philosophers who are attending to the natural sciences, bringing their insights to bear on discourses of deconstruction, language, and political power. As is often the case in such vital matters, feminist theorists are leading the way.

In her book *Changing Difference: The Feminine and the Question of Philosophy*, Malabou directly reflects on complex issues of gender and sexuality from the standpoint of her identity as a woman philosopher and her viewpoint of plasticity. She argues that "to construct one's identity is a process that can only be a development of an original biological malleability, a first transformability. If sex were not plastic, there would be no gender."[29] In an essay titled "The Meaning of the 'Feminine,'" Malabou develops her own thought in relation to that of Luce Irigaray and Judith Butler. She cautiously endorses Irigaray's notion of the feminine as "the fold of the lips to one another, a withdrawal that is so easy to force open, to breach, to deflower, but which at the same time also marks the territory of the inviolable."[30] There is a sense in which the feminine for Malabou consists in the inviolable; "without the feminine, the inviolable cannot be thought."

Due to its essential fragility, the idea of the feminine as the inviolable exists within a context of its actual violability. She says that "no doubt woman will never become impenetrable, inviolable. That's why it is necessary to imagine the possibility of woman starting from the structural impossibility she experiences of not being violated, in herself and outside, everywhere."[31] But this situation leads Malabou to a problem, because to name the inviolable as the feminine "we run the risk of fixing this fragility, assigning it a residence and making a fetish out of it." At the same time, "if we resist it, we refuse to embody the inviolable and it becomes anything at all under the pretext of referring to anyone."[32] To name the inviolable as the feminine is to "interrupt a void in difference," whereas to refuse to name the inviolable is "to refuse to interrupt a void in difference." Both stances are equally justified and problematic. It is similar to the aporia with which I began, because the specification of feminine difference risks fetishizing it, while the generalization of the inviolable beyond the feminine risks diffusing and emptying it within the context of patriarchal masculinity.

Malabou complicates the already-complicated relationship between the feminine and woman. She says that the terms of this relation need to be displaced, and she refers to her analysis of the exchange between Being and beings in her book *The Heidegger Change*. "Being and being change from one into the other," she writes—"that's the plasticity of difference."[33] Being (here the feminine) and beings (in this case women) "exchange modes of being." This substitutability exceeds metaphysics, because both Being and beings change in their exchange. If "substitutability is the meaning of Being," then "transvestitism comes with difference."[34] Being is not incarnated in embodied beings, but bodies manifest Being as change even as they change Being by exchanging it.

Malabou opens up the question of the feminine to the transformation of Being, and the change in difference that female beings make. This is a kind of transvestitism because the woman does not remain unchanged. She refers to a point in her Heidegger book where she and her translator, Peter Skafish, decided that the word *essence* in Heidegger's philosophy is a kind of "*going-in-drag*."[35] If gender is a *genos*, a genre or an essence, and essence is always going-in-drag, then that suggests a kind of transvestitism of Being and beings, a clothing across the heart of existence. Malabou concludes that "while the feminine or woman (we can use the terms interchangeably now), remains one of the unavoidable modes of ontological change, they themselves become passing, metabolic points of identity, which like others show the passing at the heart of gender."[36] Tracing the feminine leads us to a passing that is inscribed at the heart of gender.

179

There is no question that Malabou is a woman philosopher, that she *passes* for a woman philosopher, but it is not entirely clear what either of these signifiers means. She says that "if I'm a philosopher it is at the price of a tremendous violence, the violence that philosophy constantly does to me and the violence I inflict on it in return."[37] Philosophy is figured as masculine here, as the object of a "fierce quarrel" whose outcome is "ever more uncertain and unexpected," that produces "an absolute solitude."[38] Woman's liberation is essentially tied to the liberation of all of us, in our shared and unshareable absolute solitude, even those of us who do not pass as women. If Being were not change, there would be no possibility for liberation. In the context of the urgent threats to our ecological civilization, seizing on an alternative involves reflecting on the Malabou Change.

Here change cuts across the stereotypical opposition between identity and difference, and we should understand that both difference and identity are grounded in change. If we could not change, we could not be. Our differences are not essentially who we are, and neither are our identities. We are change, and this change that we are involves gender, it involves race, and it involves social and political divisions of class and caste. This is an incredibly abstract argument in many respects, but seeing social conflicts in terms of change might be more productive than a focus on differences that threatens to dissolve all distinctive identities or an emphasis on stable identities that threatens to divide us from each other.

Process and Change

Many philosophers and theologians interested in ecology and nature are influenced by the philosophy of Alfred North Whitehead. Whitehead elaborates a metaphysics of process that grapples with the extraordinary developments in quantum physics early in the twentieth century. His process philosophy cuts across the common division of entities into natural and artificial processes, or human and nonhuman entities. His perspective helps reorient a view of reality that sees transformation and becoming at the heart of existence, and his emphasis on novelty counters our modern Cartesian obsession with truth and precision. Many environmental and ecological theorists have been influenced and inspired by Whitehead's thought.

Is there a Whitehead Change? Can Whitehead change? Whitehead presented his Gifford Lectures in 1927, and *Process and Reality* was published two years later. Heidegger's *Being and Time* was also published in 1927, and it has been nearly impossible to read these two incredible works together, which in some ways are so similar and in others absolutely incompatible. Certainly, Whitehead had an affinity for science and mathematics that Heidegger deplored as the forgetting of the question of Being. At the same time, just as time is the meaning of Being for Heidegger, process is the nature of reality for Whitehead. To what extent is process compatible with change as theorized via Malabou?

According to Whitehead, there are two basic kinds of things that exist in the world: eternal objects and actual entities. Actual entities are the particular things that make up our world, while the eternal objects are more abstract principles that intersect with and affect actual entities. A red patch of wool, for example, would be an actual entity in Whitehead's terms. Red, however, is an abstract eternal entity, because it supplies the essential color by which we characterize this patch of wool. In comparing Whitehead to Heidegger, we might say that actual entities are beings, while eternal objects are more fundamentally ontological, although this translation is a distortion of both Whitehead and Heidegger.

An eternal object is a pure potential, a "potentiality for 'ingression' into the becoming of actual entities," whereas these actual entities are "the final real things of which the world is made up."[39] It might seem that actual entities are all about becoming and change, whereas the eternal objects persist as pure forms of potentiality. But this would be wrong, because Whitehead clearly states that actual entities do not change. He says that "the doctrine of internal relations makes it impossible to attribute 'change' to any actual entity. Every actual entity is what it is, and is with its definite status in the universe, determined by its internal relations to other actual entities. 'Change' is the description of the adventures of eternal objects in the evolving universe of actual things."[40]

Actual entities do not change; only eternal objects effect change. This distinction appears to limit change rather than liberate change for both

Being as eternal object and determinate beings as actual entities. The question is whether one can exchange actual entities with eternal objects. If not, then the overall situation of things changes, but specific things do not change, and the pure potentialities themselves also refuse to change.

At the level of the actual entity of Whitehead's text, there is no Whitehead Change, because he limits change to the work of eternal objects on actual entities. Change refers to "a history of local change," or "some kind of nexus of actual occasions," but it is "not an actual occasion." Whitehead says that "the fundamental meaning of the notion of 'change' is 'the difference between actual occasions comprised in some determinate event.'"[41] This difference is an event. Change occurs at the level of the event, including the sense of an event. An event is a nexus of actual occasions.

One problem with this understanding is that there is no such thing as an isolated actual occasion or actual entity; there are always multiple actual entities and actual occasions. This fundamental multiplicity is the reason for change, because change is precisely the difference between actual occasions. If this is the case, then the notion of a singular actual occasion is a fallacy of misplaced concreteness, because there is never just one actual entity. Every actual entity becomes what it is, flashes into existence for an instant and then undergoes a "perpetual perishing."

The question, then, becomes whether this perishing of actual occasions in turn changes the status of eternal objects. If not, then there is no Whitehead Change because there can be no exchange. But if the change that entities make in their perpetual perishing can in their turn ingress (or counter-ingress) into eternal objects in a movement of exchange, then this gives us a very different Whitehead. A shift in perspective along these lines, however unfaithful to the letter of his ideas, opens us up to the possibility of a Whitehead Change, because we perceive a substitutability between and among what Whitehead calls actual entities or occasions and eternal objects.

I am using Malabou's interpretation of Heidegger in *The Heidegger Change* to suggest a parallel understanding of Whitehead. Whitehead's philosophy of process gives us a metaphysics and a language to think about the nature of reality as change beyond any simple division between nature and human society. At the same time, I claim that Whitehead's philosophy itself must change, too, if it is to be useful for us today. And I have suggested all too briefly that it might be possible to read a Whitehead Change that is compatible with Malabou's Heidegger Change.

181

Conclusion

182   In general, as I indicated at the start of the essay, we need tools to develop a sophisticated political theology of material change and a political ecology of change that has practical effects. A political theology of change attends to the transformation, metamorphosis, and substitutability of and between what we call essence, form, Being, ultimate reality, the inviolable, the feminine, or God and what we call determinate forms of life. Our life together on this planet is threatened by our inability to imagine and envision another way of being, and this problem is both practical and theoretical, theological, and philosophical.

In *We Have Never Been Modern* and other works, Bruno Latour argues that Western modernity names a condition that installs a false separation between the realm of human politics and the realm of nature. This split induces a schizophrenic divide between scientists who investigate natural laws and politicians who prescribe laws to human societies. In his book *Politics of Nature*, Latour states that most of the contemporary discourse on political ecology "merely rehashes the modern Constitution of a *two-house* politics in which one house is called politics, and the other, under the name of nature, renders the first one powerless."[42] We need to let go of the idea of a separate world of Nature so that we can help fashion a "collective"—that addresses the "progressive composition of the common world."[43]

The problem with the idea of nature is that it suggests a mute entity rather than a collective of agencies. Our human agential world becomes the sole site of ethics and value, because such values are denied to nonhuman objects. For Latour, "political ecology does not speak about nature" because nature refuses the possibility of political ecology.[44] We have to dissolve the very concept of nature if we want a genuine political ecology of change.

In her book *Making Peace with the Earth*, Vandana Shiva says that peace is only possible if we can eliminate the state of separation of humanity and nature, which affects the separation of humans from humans, women from men, and nature from nature. "Separation is at the root of disharmony with nature and violence against it," she writes.[45] Our profound interconnectedness belies this false sense of separation and its concomitant violence. According to Shiva, "making peace with the earth involves a shift from fragmentation and reductionism to interconnectedness and holistic thinking, a shift from violence and exploitation to non-violence and dialogue with the earth."[46] In other words, we need a planetary *change*. That is, we need to change our understanding and interaction with what we call Earth, and this incredible transformation that is ongoing must change our understandings and relations with one another.

It is not that we can simply posit a natural harmony in the beginning from which humans then became alienated, and to which we can return. This idea of an original harmony is a myth. But the separation that Shiva focuses on is the idea that this separation is a natural and ultimate division, the split between humanity and what we have called nature. But this idea of absolute separation is also a myth, and it founds a certain project and practice of humanism that must be overcome. Nonhuman animals, objects, and systems are also agents, as Latour points out, and we have to recognize this enlarged sense of agency, which encompasses the entire earth and beyond.

In her book *Meeting the Universe Halfway*, Karen Barad affirms this multiplicity of agency all the way down to the subatomic level. She advocates an agential realist ontology in which "the world is an ongoing open process of mattering through which 'mattering' itself acquires meaning and form through the realization of different agential possibilities."[47] Quantum entanglement demonstrates this process of mattering in a complex and counterintuitive way, where these tiny interrelations constitute the beings that we and all other beings we know are. Ontology is relationality, it is being-in-relation, as Catherine Keller affirms. In *Cloud of the Impossible*, Keller says that entanglement constitutes a fold, and these folds and foldings form an ontology of relation. "A universe of unbounded, decentered connectivity cuts or contracts perspectively into each creature," according to Keller. "Each creature is a fold," and "a fold becomes a tangle when it doubles." When two particles or creatures interact, they become entangled.[48] Radical entanglement and relationality imply change, because an agent, being, or creature cannot remain what it is, or even be what it is, without this process of entangled folding.

An entity is a fold of sorts, but it is the result of relational processes of folding, enfolding, and unfolding. Here I am reading Keller as resisting the quasi-Platonic implications of some of Whitehead's philosophy, because there is no such thing as an eternal (unchanging) object. These foldings change, because to be in relation is to be exposed to change, to not being who we are or what we think we are. In the beginning is ongoing change, being-in-relation. Sometimes the changes make us, and sometimes they break us, but these changes give us a chance to be, to become, to transform, to live.

According to the Invisible Committee, anonymous authors of *The Coming Insurrection* and *To Our Friends*, we need to achieve a thinking to match the level of our global epoch. I have claimed in this essay that Malabou's philosophy can assist us in this effort. This epoch in which we—but as Derrida asks, who "we"?—find ourselves "contains something global from the outset." At the same time, "the epoch must be sought deep within each person. That is where 'we' meet up, where real friends are found, scattered over the globe, but walking the road together."[49] Despite the urgency of the global situation in ecological, political, and psychological terms, I want to express some of this gratitude to all of our readers who are *real friends*, gratitude for this chance to change together, no matter how impossible or insufficient it might be.

Notes

1. Van Jones with Ariane Conrad, *The Green Collar Economy: How One Solution Can Fix Our Two Biggest Problems* (New York: HarperCollins, 2008), 1.

2. Rebuild the Dream is a nonprofit organization dedicated to reforming the economy into one that works for everyone, including the poor, minorities, and the disadvantaged. http://www.rebuildthedream.com.

3. See Naomi Klein, *This Changes Everything: Capitalism vs. the Climate* (New York: Simon and Schuster, 2014), 21.

4. See Linda Martín Alcoff, *Visible Identities: Race, Gender and the Self* (Oxford: Oxford University Press, 2005). See also her book *The Future of Whiteness* (Cambridge: Polity, 2015).

5. George Yancy, *Black Bodies, White Gazes: The Continuing Significance of Race* (Lanham, Md.: Rowman and Littlefield, 2008), 14.

6. Charles H. Long, *Significations: Signs, Symbols, and Images in the Interpretation of Religion* (Aurora, Colo.: Davies Group Publishers, 1995), 160.

7. Catherine Malabou, *The Future of Hegel: Plasticity, Temporality, and Dialectic*, trans. Lisbeth Durling (London: Routledge, 2005), 11.

8. Ibid., 9.

9. Catherine Malabou, *What Should We Do with Our Brain?*, trans. Sebastian Rand (New York: Fordham University Press, 2008), 16.

10. Ibid., 76.

11. Ibid., 79.

12. Brenna Bhandar and Jonathan Goldberg-Hiller, "Introduction," in *Plastic Materialities: Politics, Legality, and Metamorphosis in the Work of Catherine Malabou* (Durham: Duke University Press, 2015), 3.

13. Catherine Malabou, *Plasticity at the Dusk of Writing: Dialectic, Destruction, Deconstruction*, trans. Carolyn Shread (New York: Columbia University Press, 2010), 61.

14. In addition to works by the authors mentioned previously, see Rick Dophijn and Iris van der Tuin, *New Materialism: Interviews and Cartographies* (Ann Arbor, Mich.: Open Humanities Press, 2012), and Diana Coole and Samantha Frost, eds., *New Materialisms: Ontology, Agency, and Politics* (Durham: Duke University Press, 2010).

15. Dolphijn and van der Tuin, *New Materialism*, 93.

16. Jane Bennett, *Vibrant Matters: A Political Ecology of Things* (Durham: Duke University Press, 2010), ix.

17. Catherine Malabou, *The Heidegger Change: On the Fantastic in Philosophy*, trans. Peter Skafish (New York: State University of New York Press, 2011), 2.

18. Ibid., 21.

19. Ibid., 157; emphasis original.

20. Ibid., 277.

21. Ibid., 278; emphasis in original.

22. Ibid., 279; emphasis in original.

23. Malabou, *What Should We Do with Our Brain?*, 68.

24. Ibid., 73.

25. Ibid., 74.

26. Catherine Malabou, "Darwin and the Social Destiny of Natural Selection," *Theory@ buffalo 16: Plastique: Dynamics of Catherine Malabou* (2012): 144–56 (quote on 144–45).

27. Ibid., 153.

28. Ibid.

29. Catherine Malabou, *Changing Difference: The Feminine and the Question of Philosophy*, trans. Carolyn Shread (Cambridge: Polity Press, 2011), 138.

30. Ibid., 34.

31. Ibid., 140.

32. Ibid., 35.

33. Ibid., 36.

34. Ibid., 37.

35. Ibid., 39.

36. Ibid., 39–40.

37. Ibid., 140–41.

38. Ibid., 141.

39. Ibid., 23 and 18.

40. Alfred North Whitehead, *Process and Reality*, ed. David Ray Griffin and Donald W. Sherburne, corr. ed. (New York: Free Press, 1978), 58–59.

41. Ibid., 73.

42. Bruno Latour, *Politics of Nature: How to Bring the Sciences into Democracy*, trans. Catherine Porter (Cambridge, Mass.: Harvard University Press, 2004), 18–19.

43. Ibid., 59.

44. Ibid., 21.

45. Vandana Shiva, *Making Peace with the Earth* (London: Pluto Press, 2013), 11.

46. Ibid., 13.

47. Karen Barad, *Meeting the Universe Halfway: Quantum Physics and the Entanglement of Matter and Meaning* (Durham: Duke University Press, 2007), 141.

48. Catherine Keller, *Cloud of the Impossible: Negative Theology and Planetary Entanglement* (New York: Columbia University Press, 2015), 153.

49. The Invisible Committee, *To Our Friends*, trans. Robert Hurley (Pasadena, Calif.: Semiotext(e), 2015), 15.

PRISMATIC IDENTITIES IN A PLANETARY CONTEXT

Whitney A. Bauman

> From a distance, we all have enough / And no one is in
> need / And there are no guns, no bombs, and no disease /
> No hungry mouths to feed.
>
> —JULIE GOLD

Introduction: The Danger of Distance

The theology and lyrics to the song "From a Distance," popularized by Bette Midler, are precisely what this essay argues against. Who needs a "God that watches us, from a distance?" Is this the same God watching genocides, species extinction, climate weirding, the lack of concern for black lives in the United States (and other countries), the AIDS crisis, torture, starvation, and the violence against animals in factory farms safely from His living room armchair? An ecotheology of this "distant" god is bolstered by the "earth rise" image of the "little blue ball" spinning through space. The image is an object of our technological gaze looking back on a unified globe: where all of human histories and all of geo-evolution has happened. This detached, distant view, which glosses over the particularities of embodied becoming, is the global view. Gayatri Spivak contrasts this with the planetary view. She writes, "If we imagine ourselves as planetary subjects rather than global agents, planetary creatures rather than global entities, alterity remains underived from us; it is not our dialectical negation, it contains us as much as it flings us away. And thus to think of it is already to transgress."[1]

The planetary view, then, is a way to connect differences together into a larger planetary community rather than enforcing a single view on the entire planet. Ecocritic Ursula Heise's use of Google Earth instead of the Earthrise image also draws the difference between the planetary and the global into focus. Adopting a Google Earth metaphor for thinking about our planetary identities (humans and earth others) enables us to zoom in and out, to see how various terrains are connected, to focus on the particular and get a "wider" view all at the same time. Furthermore, such a view is achieved through technology—placing humans, nature, and technology as all part of the same planet.[2] All are tangled up together in various arrangements, apparatuses, or collectives. As theologian Mayra Rivera notes about our tangled, enfleshed worlds: "This world is a labyrinth of incarnations. To be a body is to be tied to the world, not beyond the specificities of our bodies, but through them. The visible traits of my body affect whether the world recognizes me and receives me or ignores me and wounds me. It constrains my actions—how I move or talk, what I may look at, taste, explore. Social relations leave visible marks on our bodies. Gradually societies may also shape the most fundamental elements of our corporeality. Social norms are always becoming flesh."[3]

We must, then, pay special and particular attention to the ways in which various bodies effect and are affected by the worlds in which we live.

Process thought, object-oriented thinking, and the new materialisms (broadly conceived) encourage us to think theologically not in broad stroke but in pixels and fine print as well as granularly. Redistributing agency and responsiveness to the smallest events of the world and to the largest societies of occasions, we are encouraged to pay close attention both to the particular and to how the particulars relate to one another in the ongoing process of geo-evolution and cosmic expansion. As Bruno Latour notes in "Thou Shalt Not Freeze Frame," thoughts of God should not "take us away" but should open us onto the particularities of life.[4] What this calls for is something like Ivone Gebara's "theology of garbage and noise" rather than a whitewashed, sanitized theology.[5] Again, following Heise's metaphor of Google Earth, we need to both zoom in on particularities and then zoom out to see how the particularities are interrelated at local, regional, and planetary scales. In the brief space I have here, I attempt a close-up theological method by focusing on the spectrum of colors and expanding the ecocritical book *Prismatic Ecology* to a prismatic ecotheology. Such a theology is informed by process, new materialisms, and queer theory (just to name a few theoretical frequencies). What these all have in common is imagining our entire planetary existence as embedded in a single plane of existence where all humans, animals, natures, technologies, ideas, and gods matter together. Not only do these events and objects matter for themselves but they matter for the entire planetary collective wobbling along in a helical motion around a star that is wobbling around a galaxy among other galaxies in an expanding universe.[6] Rather than thinking ourselves as distant from the fray, we humans are embedded, on the spectrum, looking around from our own place on that spectrum. How might an ecotheology proceed prismatically from such a context? The majority of this chapter focuses on just this; however, first let me describe two phenomena that shape this planetary and prismatic perspective: globalization and climate change.

More than anything, globalization and climate change define the contemporary contexts in which we find ourselves at this point in planetary becoming. Most readers have tacit understandings of what these two phenomena mean, but I want to highlight two features of each phenomena important to this chapter and the discussion in this book.[7]

First, globalization, of course, refers to the space-time crunch brought about by the technological increases in speed of transportation, communication, and production. About half of we humans (connected to the internet in some way) can move products, things, and information around the world with the click of a mouse or with the execution of a simple Google search. A smaller number of us are able to move ourselves around the world by air. Wherever we find ourselves, daily life is intersected by planetary flows, and this changes the way we think about ourselves in the world. Historically, whereas it may have been okay to think of oneself in one's local context—as American, or Christian, or Chinese, or Buddhist—today our worlds are all mixed up. We are hybrids on this planet, and our meaning-making practices reflect this: how many Christians practice yoga? How many atheists meditate? How many believers in one or another religion also believe and trust in modern science and medicine? There is no single authority, and so we are left to negotiate our meaning structures without recourse to objectivity.

Second, because we are now looking back on the histories from these globalized perspectives, we can begin to see that there have never been distinct religions, cultures, or "traditions." From interchanges on ancient silk and spice routes, to the *convivencia* in southern Spain, to various eras of colonization, our traditions have always been exchanging with one another. Even modern science itself draws from Indic cultures (mathematics), Chinese cultures (proto-chemistry), the Golden Age of Islam, Christian and Jewish thought, and the many indigenous knowledges of local flora and fauna. In other words, there has never been orthodoxy but always "polydoxy." There has never been a single interpretation of a tradition, event, or fact but always multiple interpretations.

Whereas many of us might understand ourselves through globalization as "culturally" hybrid (though nature and culture are always and already together), the phenomena of global climate change (or what I call *weirding*[8]) places us squarely within a planetary context. First, any illusion of human mastery over "nature" is dispelled with the complex, wicked problem of climate change: we do not know what will happen to us, though we may know likely scenarios (more on this later in the chapter). Managing our way out of this problem (like good stewards) cannot be the whole solution: the managerial metaphor, with its assumptions of human mastery over the natural world, is what helped us get into this trouble in the first place. Second, climate change (along with the contributions of the natural sciences of ecology and evolution) helps those of us moderns who may have forgotten to recognize that we are but one among many creatures on a planet in motion. In other words, the planet is made up of multiple perspectives and agents, and humans are but only one of those perspectives and agents. We humans did very little by way of the evolutionary development of the cerebral cortex or the opposable thumb, yet we have effectively used these features to transform the world (some more than others). Tree transpiration, Earth's orbit around the sun and axial tilt, decomposition, and oceanic carbon banking are all agencies of the planet that have almost nothing to do with human beings: except that they make our very lives possible. So if we are agents among other agents in the world rather than the sole agents on the planet, what might this planetary, prismatic ecotheology and ethic involve?

Color-Filled Thinking: It Is Too Easy to Just Be Green

As with all tropes, "being green" started out in a revolutionary way for a certain time and place but now has both been co-opted in the form of greenwashing and placed in its context as a metaphor for mostly middle- to upper-class, whitish-looking folks of European and English descent. When we think about promoting a "green" understanding of environmentalism, we might conjure up images of a green English-style yard, which were imposed upon the landscapes of the United States and other colonies in an attempt to re-create the "new" world in the image of the mother country.[9] Or we might think of "green" parks, the history of which in the United States conjures up images of the removal of native peoples in order to create recreational spaces for white middle-to-upper-class city dwellers, so that these people might escape the "dirty" (read racially and culturally mixed) cities.[10] One might also think of the rugged "green" and "natural" landscapes that the Boy Scouts of America used to try to prevent the "sissification" of boys in the city.[11] Finally, "green" has affinities with a lopsided view of the world focused on birth, youth, and growth at the expense of death and decay. Death and decay are much harder sells when humans cannot imagine themselves as part of the food chain, yet this side of the circle of life is just as important ecologically, as there is no resurrection without death.[12] In many ways, it turns out that Kermit the Frog might need to reconsider the lyrics to his song and instead sing: "It is pretty easy being green."

In a recent book titled *Prismatic Ecology*, the authors seek to move us beyond "green" (pristine) understandings of nature and explore the whole spectrum of colors for what they might mean ecologically.[13] After all, "green" is only one color in nature, and there is nothing more "natural" than the full color spectrum, so why have we limited our metaphors (and habits) to green thinking? In the chapter on "Brown," for instance, the authors link the dirt with fecal matter and other waste. The humus, the source of all of our nutrients, is, after all, nothing more than decay and waste. "Smelly, rancid, and impure, it is no one's favorite color. We need brown but do not like looking at it. It is a color you cannot cover up, that will never go away."[14] To deny this is to deny the decay that is necessary for all life to continue. How much is spent on a daily basis to remove our waste from our daily sight, to remove the food we eat from its relationship with the earth and other life, and to secure our bodies from the rest of the natural world? Maybe a healthy look at our own waste and its relationship to other bodies could help us think ourselves back into the predator–prey cycle. Instead of pretending there was "an away" to which our garbage is thrown, perhaps we begin to see our own waste as fodder for new life.[15] Perhaps we could create a "cradle to cradle" economy with everything from the waste that comes out of our bodies to the waste that ends up being burned or buried deep underground.[16] Such a recognition of the porousness of our bodies and the constant flows of energy and materials that flow through us helps to ground our bodies in the evolving planetary community.

In yet another chapter, "Orange," the author takes an object-oriented approach to discuss ecological relations. "For color, like any complicated phenomenon, reveals itself to be a multiplicity, a knot in motion that connects different times and places in a structure of only apparent simultaneity. And so, at almost every moment, my orange ecology waxes in and out of being, revealing itself to be merely one orientation to a generalized prismatic archive."[17] This type of understanding of the world (and the individuals therein) highlights the individual-in-relation: similar to the process of Process, or the idea from Gilles Deleuze and Félix Guattari that the virtual is the real, or Mayra Rivera's understanding of flesh quoted earlier.[18] In other words, what is really real is constant movement, exchange, and relationality—exchanges within and between bodies, places, and things. This flow of energy and materials, what we might think of as "virtual reality" in comparison to the concrete bodies and things that make up our daily life, is, in other words, the really real. Any time we mark off a stable entity with a concept—a tree, individual human, dog, computer—we are abstracting from the virtual flow of life (or, as Whitehead might say, we are committing "the fallacy of misplaced concreteness").[19] Much philosophical and religious ink has been spilled to reassure us that reality is made up of stable, enduring bodies, and these more relational, processive, and immanent understandings of reality flip that understanding on its head.

There are no colors without relation, and there is no ecology without relation: "thingness" is an abstraction from these sets of relations, whether an "orange," a "color," a "tree," or an "individual." There is "realness" at every level of this moving life: all the way "up," and all the way "down." As object-oriented philosopher Graham Harman notes, from within this way of thinking, "humans lose their place as the metaphysical core of the universe . . . , but only because *no* object is allowed to occupy that core, including the inanimate sort. Instead, all objects are equally decentered, equally converted into just one object among others."[20] Furthermore, this means that the planet we inhabit is radically multiperspectival. As Catherine Keller notes in *Cloud of the Impossible*: "The individual viewpoint, however, only takes place in its interdependence with the others: the 'more eyes,' the more vision."[21] Such multiperspectivalism demands that we listen closely and deeply to the multiple earth others, both human and non, if we desire to have a better understanding of the worlds in which we live.

Finally, in this decentered relationality, as the chapter "Chartreuse" suggests and as Karen Barad has pointed out elsewhere: all matter is agential.[22] It is not that there are passive objects and active subjects in the world, but rather all things, from the subquantum to the cosmological and everything in between "influence" or "act" upon all other things. In the end, the authors in *Prismatic Ecology* are trying to take us beyond a human-centered approach to the world, and all the mastery that entails, toward a "postgreen, postcolor, posthuman ecology."[23] The "postcolor" is not so much a denial or refusal of our particular embodiment as it is a spectral focus on the relationships of bodies: of our own with others, of the multiple bodies that make up our own, and of the ways in which these "queer" relations can only be understood when we abstract from them and create abjections. As Derrida's "hauntology" points out, there is always a ghost, a specter haunting any solidification of a concept, or here an identity. These specters/hauntings/abjections are what keep these relational selves open and relational to a multitude of becoming. What happens when these specters are completely ignored, repressed, or denied is what we experience as environmental degradation and social injustice. Bodies are literally cut off from their living contexts. When bodies are cut off from living contexts, they begin to suffocate and die. Indeed, much violence against bodies comes as a result of trying to "fit" bodies into strict categories of race, gender, ability, and sexuality. Yet another form of violence is done by ignoring the relationships between bodies, such as those between the elements that make up the bodies of the planet. How these materials are consumed and transformed have different effects on different bodies: oftentimes having the worst effects on the poorest human bodies that are black or brown and upon earth bodies that are not human.

Geographical Mappings of Meaning-Making Practices: Killing Me Slowly with Values

We humans need better mappings that account for the different effects of practices and ideas upon different earth bodies. A good example of this is the effects of fossil fuels. One component of dealing with the colors "brown" and "black" in the ecological imagination is the contemporary fossil-fueled world in which we live. After all, fossil fuels are the death and decay of life "gifted" to future generations. They are, like the humus, the grounds from which new lives, hopes, dreams, and possibilities emerge. However, what happens when humus and fossil fuels become distributed unevenly so that certain places can remain focused on the "green" while others become strip-mined, fracked, deforested, and impoverished? What is happening during this contemporary era of globalization and climate weirding[24] is that a certain segment of the human population (one fifth of the world's human population, perhaps, depending on how you cut the pie) is literally living at such a pace that we are outstripping the reproductive capacities of the planet.[25] Every semester in my Earth Ethics course, I have students fill out an ecological footprint survey and then write an essay on their experience. The ecological footprint, if you are unfamiliar, asks a series of questions about where and how you live, then based on your answers tells you how many worlds we would need if everyone were to live as you do. The secret that I do not tell my students is that by virtue of living in the United States, you can never get less than 1.5–2 worlds. In other words, the entire culture/society we have built in the United States, and which my (mostly young) students were just born into, is itself "out of this world." And, we moderns also live at the expense and to the detriment of other life. As Rob Nixon points out, perhaps the dreams and hopes that emerge from the fast-paced fossil-fueled reality are quite literally out of this world.[26] What is called for, then, are perhaps some spiritual, ethical, emotive, and imaginative cartographies that help us map these inequities.[27]

Many readers are likely familiar by now with the Intergovernmental Panel on Climate Change's assessment reports, which have been published every five to seven years since 1997. Each report includes "emission scenarios" with cones of possibility for what types of things to expect given the particular scenario. There are four basic models—formerly A1, A2, B1, and B2, and now RCP 8.5, RCP 6.0, RCP 4.5, and RCP 2.6—moving in general from "business as usual" in terms of the fossil-fueled expansion and economic growth based on that expansion to transitions toward renewables and equitable economic growth.[28] Interestingly, the reports include social and political changes that need to take place in terms of mitigating and adapting to climate change, ranging from gender equity in education, migration, and reliance on social networks to, in the latest report, "individual and collective assumptions, beliefs, values and worldviews influencing climate change responses."[29] It is here where our spectral cartographies of values, beliefs, and goals begin to matter(ialize) for the planetary community. How can we trace the ways and which flows of energy, information, and materials affect different bodies, well, differently? How can we map the traces of these various flows while paying attention to unintended consequences and inequitable distributions of goods and ills? What on earth might this look like? Will theologians now have to add levels of training that include geographic information systems? Well, maybe not, but we should at least offer those working with geographic information system or even mental modeling software some parameters to work within.[30]

Assuming here that all theology is about theo-anthropology—I am not interested in mapping god; I will leave that to folks who have much more of a direct line than I do—let me offer a partial scenario of a spiritual cartography. Given that this volume comes out of a conference that was hosted at the Center for Process Studies, I figure it is alright to poke fun of the omni-understanding of God a bit, so I will attempt to map some of the effects of omnipresence.

Many, most famously Ludwig Feuerbach, have argued that our articulation of the divine results in making ourselves in the image of that divinity.[31] How has the desire for omnipresence been in part materialized over the course of the fossil-fueled era? How has this desire transformed our modes of transportation and communication: by foot, animal, steam, coal, oil, nuclear energies, and now instantaneously through the virtual realities of the internet? What does the mapping of this theology turned anthropological desire look like? Can we color-code the ecological footprint of belief in an omnipresent god turned desire for some humans to be omnipresent? How has such a desire affected earth bodies differently according to race, gender, class, ability, and sexuality within the human community, and differently according to species beyond the human? How has such a desire affected the "green" of forest ecosystems, the blue of oceanic systems, the brown of earth systems? Note, I am not laying the blame here on theologies of omnipresence but simply trying to analyze how such a belief within a whole system of complex beliefs might materialize in the world around us.

This tendency toward theo-anthropology makes apophasis and negative theologies of the kind Keller speaks of in The Cloud all the more important. If our ideas of God—justice, love, ultimate value, and so forth—become a container, then we have no choice but to move toward that container and become like that god. "If theologians transcend our nonknowing, in the name of Jesus, revelation, or even justice, we practice Christian idolatry."[32] Such closures begin to favor certain bodies over others because privileged bodies background relations in an effort to self-fulfill the idea that they are made in their projected understanding of God's image.[33] For instance, maleness and whiteness get projected onto images of God, and even onto reason, in ways that create violence toward women and people of color. This much the histories of liberation, feminist, and postcolonial theories have shown. Yet, the very ability for privileged perspectives to emerge in the first place depends on all of the relationships that allow for that privilege (historically slaves [or low-wage and "free" labor], other animals, plants, minerals, and the earth's living systems). Thus, we can map the effects of ideas, values, and concepts onto how they affect actual earth bodies differently and begin to question these unequal distributions of goods and ills. If closure cuts us off from our relationality and begins to cipher all relations into material-conceptual containers, then gravity/gravitas will eventually do its work and the weight of injustice will burst open our material-conceptual containers onto the becoming planetary community of which we are a part.

Gravity-Action, Gravitation: Defying Gravity as Usual with a Spectral Ethics of Probability

"We mistakenly think of our flesh as fixed and finite form, a neatly bounded package of muscle and bone and bottled electricity, with blood surging its looping boulevards and byways. But even the most cursory pondering of the body's manifold entanglements—its erotic draw toward other bodies; its incessant negotiation with that grander eros we call 'gravity' . . . suffices to make evident that the body is less a self-enclosed sack than a realm wherein the diverse textures and colors of the world meet up with one another."[34]

As David Abram so poetically puts it, gravity is about the eros of bodies attracting other bodies. Gravity is the attraction that makes our every movement on this earth possible. It is a constraint, but the type of constraint that allows for freedom and proliferation of possibilities in terms of the bodies that fold in and out of one another throughout evolution and on a daily basis. Gravity, then, is a planetary subjection that makes all life possible: we cannot perform our lives without it. Gravity, gravitas, eros opens us onto the multiplicity of living, evolving bodies on this planet. It is in and through these bodies that our own bodies exist and persist, and it is with these bodies that we move forward toward possibilities for our future. Again, according to Mayra Rivera: "Consenting to being flesh implies accepting the social obligations that emerge from our coexistence in the flesh of the world, analyzing social structures not as debates about ideas, positions, or power conceived in abstraction but rather as the mechanism by which societies promote the flourishing of some bodies and stifle that of others, distribute life and death."[35]

Mapping bodies, as was argued for in the previous section, might give us a prismatic view of the effects of our religious, ethical, and other beliefs on the multiplicity of bodies. Once we understand our own bodies in the context of this deeply open and relational reality, as theologian Catherine Keller notes in her explication of the cosmological ideas of Nicolas of Cusa, we begin to see that our context "is a multiverse of perspectives, proliferating, holographically, irresolvable into any fixed proposition."[36] This multiperspectival context and perspective helps us to discern better at any one moment of mapping what our possibilities might be for moving forward toward a different planetary future. Far from slowing us down, gravity-as-eros opens us onto this prism of possibilities and increases our freedom to move spectrally: respecting the way in which all possibilities are interconnected and what it will mean for particular bodies when we begin to move toward some and not others. As we move forward and possibilities become realities (and nonrealities), even the past will be re-membered in different ways from the new grounds we cocreate: just as I argued in the beginning of this chapter that the hybrid effects of globalization enable us to see that polydoxy has always been at play.

The stories about who we are, what ultimate reality is, and what our role in the cosmos might be are always changing. As many have pointed out, some of the stories of Western monotheistic theology helped to support a world of Newtonian mechanics, just as some of the more relational stories of Buddhism, Taoism, and Hinduism have helped physicists think about special relativity and quantum mechanics.[37] Our narratives of the world (whether religious, philosophical, or other) help to reshape the way in which we see and understand the world. Arguably, one strong holdout from a certain type of monotheistic theology is that of the idea of creation ex nihilo. Mary-Jane Rubenstein, in *Worlds Without End*, does a fantastic job of making the rhetorical and conceptual connections between ex nihilo theology and big bang cosmology.[38] Perhaps some understanding of the multiverse might open newly imagined possibilities for the future and give us new eyes with which to see and materialize the world in different ways.

Another contemporary attempt to revisualize and rematerialize the world through cosmological metaphors can be found in the idea of "Rainbow Gravity." In this theory, there is no beginning to the universe: no big bang, no creation ex nihilo. Further, there is a kind of particle-based perspectivism according to this theory. As one article puts it: "The color of light is determined by its frequency, and because different frequencies correspond to different energies, light particles (photons) of different colors would travel on slightly different paths though spacetime, according to their energy."[39] Different frequencies and different paths through space-time mean different embodiments and multiple ways of becoming. This is highly speculative, but speculation is precisely what helps us material-ize in different ways of becoming. We need spectral thinking in order to discern the spectrum of possibilities. Our seizing of alternative possibilities for how we might want to become as a planetary community must include speculation, or we will be adrift in space-time, unaware of the grounds on which we stand.

Gravity helps to position bodies in different ways of becoming, and thus helps to diffract on the pluralistic ethics and politics that become possi-ble in different planetary contexts. In other words, just as there is not one perspective, and just as no one earth body will experience the effects of our enacted beliefs, meanings, and values in the same way, so there cannot be a single, common way of moving forward from the planetary present. What may seem inconsistent from a substance-based metaphysic of separate entities—all with essential natures and teleological purposes—is precisely the disorderly, inconsistent, seemingly hypocritical flip-flopping that is required when acting with uncertainty. Rather than maintaining an ideo-logically consistent framework and forcing the principles that result from that framework onto all places, we need a flexible framework that allows us to open onto the different contours of our geo-locations and the multi-ple perspectives therein. As Tom Boellstorff suggests in his anthropological work on the Indonesian archipelago, an understanding of the "archipelagic self" might better suit us here.[40] I would extend Boellstorff's model to the planetary scale because it has something to tell us about what it means to be human in an era of climate change and globalization: we must be flexi-ble and open to oceanic possibilities that emerge in tricky situations.

Here, at the end of my reflections, let me provide you with a brief exam-ple of how a planetary, prismatic ethic might operate. In speaking with some volunteers for a community health center that deals with everything from abortion to HIV prevention and education and LGBTQ advocacy in Indonesia, one of the organizers told me, after a long discussion of queer theory, that their organization had a sort of double standard when it comes to speaking about LGBTQ identities. When they are trying to change the minds of citizens about the need for equal rights of LGBTQ peoples in a predominantly Muslim (albeit Indonesian-style Muslim) country, then the message is clear: "Baby, LGBTQ peoples were born this way!" When they are holding seminars and consultations with LGBTQ persons, then the message is not so clear: they can speak freely about the fluidity of gender, sex, and sexuality. It is a version of "strategic essentialism" that depends on the "island" or context that one finds oneself in: we all do it, but we do not necessarily own it. Many people who live in "two worlds" due to ableism, sexism, racism, and heterosexism, or any other minority living within a world created by a different majority (or minority) are familiar with this type of double speech that happens internal to the group versus external to those not within the group. To put it into our familiar context: for the general public, "Gay marriage yes!" while for an all-queer audience, "Let's abolish the legal rights and privileges associated with marriage across the board and recognize all types of relationships (romantic and non), free health care for all, and wealth redistribution rather than biological inheritance generation after generation."

A second feature of this type of contextual, planetary ethics is that ideals, principles, and values can be seen as hopes and desires rather than markers of any essential features of embodiment in the world. As Judith Butler notes, words such as *democracy* and *woman* are really political desires and intentions rather than markers of anything essential to ontology.[41] The "universal" declaration on human rights also operates in this political way. The problem with assuming "woman," "democracy," or "human rights" as essential to reality is that such essences seldom account for the variations expressed by those concepts. If you do not exhibit or contain x, then you are not part of the club. Identity politics cascade into multiple points of diffraction because no voice speaks for the experience of what it means to be white, black, male, female, trans, gay, straight, and/or other. Queer studies is in part a way in which to highlight this prismatic and processive understanding of identities.

Hardly a queer theorist, Jürgen Moltmann, following Hans Jonas, recognized this in terms of the imago dei. Bucking the essentialist trend of interpreting the imago tradition, Moltmann suggests that becoming the imago dei is something to work toward in relationship to other humans and the rest of the natural world—it is not a given. If we think of humans, rights, traditions, and other concepts in this way, as imaginative suggestions toward a not-yet-realized reality, or as something we can only attain in certain breakthrough relational moments, then we can understand that changes to identity markers that expand what it means to be woman, human, man, black, brown, white, gay, straight, trans, Christian, Buddhist, and so forth are expansions of these markers, and thereby every expansion becomes a more power-filled understanding of the given concept. In this sense, Latour argues that we should think about ourselves as living in open multiverses (which finds resonance with Mary-Jane Rubenstein's work mentioned previously). He writes, "The word multiverse points to the fully secular series of surprising agents before they are unified by any global view—be it that of Nature or that of God—and before they are assembled in many provisional compositions by the slow and costly process of extension carried out either by chains of reference or by the preaching of transformative messages" (Gifford Lectures, 44–45). Such a shift in thinking from "essence" to "process," from a "universe" to a "multiverse" loses power from those "in the center" and gives it to those ever-expanding concepts, theories, and identities at the edges and margins. Such expansions, in a sense, enable us to diffract these concepts and opens us onto the spectrum of possible becomings within the planetary community.

Notes

1. Gayatri Spivak, *Death of a Discipline* (New York: Columbia University Press, 2003), 73.

2. Ursula Heise, *Sense of Place and Sense of Planet: The Environmental Imagination of the Global* (New York: Oxford University Press, 2008).

3. Mayra Rivera, *Poetics of the Flesh* (Durham: Duke University Press, 2015), 156.

4. Bruno Latour, "'Thou Shall Not Freeze-Frame' or How Not to Misunderstand the Science and Religion Debate," in *On the Modern Cult of the Factish Gods* (Durham: Duke University Press, 2010), 99–123.

5. Ivone Gebara, *Longing for Running Water: Ecofeminism and Liberation* (Minneapolis, Minn.: Fortress Press, 1999).

6. On the collective, see Bruno Latour, *The Politics of Nature: How to Bring the Sciences into Democracy* (Cambridge, Mass.: Harvard University Press, 2004).

7. For a much longer description of these two phenomena in the way that I understand them, see Whitney Bauman, *Religion and Ecology: Developing a Planetary Ethic* (New York: Columbia University Press, 2014).

8. I discuss this further later in the chapter. The term is widely attributed to Hunter Lovins of the Rocky Mountain Institute. It gained more traction with an article by Thomas Friedman titled "Global Weirding Is Here," *New York Times*, February 17, 2010, http://www.nytimes.com/2010/02/17/opinion/17friedman.html. There is now a regular YouTube series with popular climate scientist Katharine Hayhoe called *global weirding*: https://www.youtube.com/channel/UCi6RkdaEqgRVKi3AzidF4ow.

9. Carolyn Merchant, *Ecological Revolutions: Nature, Gender and Science in New England* (Chapel Hill: University of North Carolina Press, 1989), 69–111.

10. Mark David Spence, *Dispossessing the Wilderness: Indian Removal and the Making of the National Parks* (New York: Oxford University Press, 1999).

11. See, for example, Michael Kimmel, *Angry White Men: American Masculinity at the End of an Era* (New York: Nation Books, 2013), 49–50.

12. Val Plumwood, *Environmental Culture: The Ecological Crisis of Reason* (New York: Routledge, 2001), 227.

13. Jerome Cohen, *Prismatic Ecology: Ecotheory Beyond Green* (Minneapolis: University of Minnesota Press, 2014).

14. Ibid., 193.

15. On the psychology of "throwing away," see Kenneth Worthy, *Invisible Nature: Healing the Destructive Divide Between People and the Environment* (New York: Prometheus Books, 2013).

16. William McDonough and Michael Braungart, *Cradle to Cradle: Remaking the Way We Make Things* (New York: North Point Press, 2002).

17. Cohen, *Prismatic Ecology*, 94.

18. Rivera, *Poetics of the Flesh*.

19. Alfred North Whitehead, *Science and the Modern World* (New York: Macmillan, 1925).

20. Cohen, *Prismatic Ecology*, 107; emphasis original.

21. Catherine Keller, *Cloud of the Impossible: Negative Theology and Planetary Entanglement* (New York: Columbia University Press, 2014), 96.

22. Karen Barad, *Meeting the Universe Halfway: Quantum Physics and the Entanglement of Matter and Meaning* (Durham: Duke University Press, 2007).

23. Cohen, *Prismatic Ecology*, 333.

24. See Whitney Bauman, *Religion and Ecology*, and Whitney Bauman, "Climate Weirding and Queering Nature: Getting Beyond the Anthropocene," *Religions* 6 (2015): 742–54. At the time of writing this article, I was unaware of the history of this term. My thanks to the editors of this volume for pointing this out to me.

25. Teresa Brennan, *Globalization and Its Terrors: Daily Life in the West* (New York: Routledge, 2003).

26. Rob Nixon, *Slow Violence and the Environmentalism of the Poor* (Cambridge, Mass.: Harvard University Press, 2013).

27. Thomas Tweed, *Crossing and Dwelling: A Theory of Religion* (Cambridge, Mass.: Harvard University Press, 2008).

28. Rajendra K. Pachauri, Leo Meyer, et al., *Climate Change 2014 Synthesis Report* (Intergovernmental Panel on Climate Change, 2015), 8–9. Can be found online at: https://www.ipcc.ch/site/assets/uploads/2018/02/SYR_AR5_FINAL_full.pdf.

29. Ibid., 27.

30. Such as Mental Modeler: http://www.mentalmodeler.org.

31. Ludwig Feuerbach, *The Essence of Christianity* (New York: Prometheus Books, 1989).

32. Keller, *Cloud of the Impossible*, 113.

33. On "backgrounding," see Plumwood, *Environmental Culture*.

34. David Abram, *Becoming Animal: An Earthly Cosmology* (New York: Vintage Books, 2011), 229.

35. Rivera, *Poetics of the Flesh*, 157.

36. Keller, *Cloud of the Impossible*, 121.

37. Ibid., 135–36; David Kaiser, *How the Hippies Saved Physics: Science, Counterculture and the Quantum Revival* (New York: W. W. Norton, 2012); Bruno Latour, "Facing Gaia: A New Inquiry into Natural Religion," lecture given at University of Edinburgh, February 18–28, 2013.

38. Mary Jane Rubenstein, *Worlds Without End: The Many Lives of the Multiverse* (New York: Columbia University Press, 2014).

39. See Clara Moskowitz, "In a 'Rainbow' Universe, Time May Have No Beginning," *Scientific American*, December 9, 2013, http://www.scientificamerican.com/article/rainbowgravityuniversebeginning.

40. Tom Boellstorff, *The Gay Archipelago: Sexuality and Nation in Indonesia* (Princeton: Princeton University Press, 2005).

41. Judith Butler, *Bodies That Matter: On the Discursive Limits of Sex* (New York: Routledge, 1993).

CULTIVATING LISTENING AS
A CIVIC DISCIPLINE

Krista E. Hughes

Our inability to listen has become a civic crisis. As a society in the United States, we seem to lack both the will and the capacity to listen to the other. We now listen in order to react rather than to understand, raising the question of whether we are really listening at all.

Listening to react or respond assumes an adversarial relationship. We now seem to think the whole purpose of a conversation is to persuade another to our point of view. Set up as such, we dig in our heels, determined to not be persuaded ourselves. Conversations become debates that become arguments, both sides often leaving not only more persuaded of their own positions but even less sympathetic to any others'.

The desire to be "right" is not a new development of the human condition. Well documented, however, is that we now live in media echo chambers that allow us to engage people, ideas, and outlooks that predominantly mirror our own. These echo chambers offer the illusion that we are *not* fundamentally entangled with those unlike ourselves: political others, racial and ethnic others, even other-than-human creatures and the earth itself. In this context, listening openly and nonreactively can be exceptionally difficult.

Much like a spiritual discipline such as meditation or prayer, listening to understand requires intention, steady practice, and ultimately a willingness—yes, even a desire—to be changed. For these reasons, it likewise requires a certain receptive openness and vulnerability that is avoided in a U.S. culture that equates vulnerability with weakness. Yet, the future of our civic life depends on cultivating listening as a civic discipline: one we intentionally practice (perhaps especially at the most challenging times) and in turn one we model and teach to younger generations.

Here I briefly profile three technologies of listening developed for the purpose of cultivating healthy civic encounter. One was developed as a method for use in communities and institutions of higher education. Two were developed by community transformation organizations and are regularly used in their programs. The aim of each technology is to lend insight into another's story and perspective and to find threads of connection. The goal in no case is to persuade or be persuaded (thereby also avoiding the misplaced energies of trying to resist persuasion at all costs).

Bring It to the Table: Connecting the Personal and the Political

Bring It to the Table (http://www.bringit2thetable.org) is both a documentary and a method of conversation developed by Julie Winokur to encourage dialogue between two people who hold differing opinions on controversial social and political topics: gun regulation, abortion and reproductive policies, immigration, same-sex marriage, the NFL U.S. flag controversy, and so forth. Conversation partners sit across a table that is divided by a ribbon. This ribbon acts as a spectrum, and the speaker is asked to place a vase and flower on that spectrum to represent approximately where they stand either politically or on a specific issue: the moderate middle, closer to one of the poles, or somewhere else. Key to the method is that one person asks questions and listens. The questioner-listener may not interrupt, and questions are exploratory rather than interrogatory, intended to elicit insight about the speaker's perspective and how their experience informs it: as the event planning toolkit explains, "People are asked to explain the roots of their beliefs so we understand *why* they believe *what* they believe."[1]

There are several scenarios for conversation: digging into a specific controversial issue, probing where someone stands on the political spectrum and why, or exploring questions "you've always wanted to ask the 'other side'"—and in all cases Winokur provides carefully framed questions such as:

- Where do you stand [on this issue] and why?
- What personal experiences have helped you come to your belief?

- What does the other side get right about the issue?
- How have your views on this issue evolved over time?
- Do you think compromise is possible, and if so, what would it look like?[2]

The first two questions, like the methods discussed later in this chapter, ask the speaker to connect their position to concrete personal experience. Not only does this grounding in the personal take the issue out of a polemical arena, but it often invites people to consider the ways their opinion is influenced, perhaps quite strongly, by the rhetoric of media and the echo chambers of which they are a part. In turn, there is acknowledgment that people with other experiences might legitimately reach different conclusions. Other questions invite the conversation partners to think about points of connection, both the values that motivate certain positions as well as the possibilities for compromise. Because neither of these is especially encouraged, or even acknowledged, in many public disagreements today, conversation partners often leave Bring It to the Table conversations feeling more positive about and appreciative of the people who hold a differing opinion as well as more hopeful about potential solutions.

The focus on storytelling and personal experience encourages a richer, more generative form of listening than a debate-style conversation (seemingly the default these days). I cannot argue with your *experience*, even if we ultimately may disagree on how to interpret that experience. The ground rule that the interviewer may only ask questions and listen is even more key. It can be hard to not interrupt, especially to ask clarifying questions, but just the awareness that one may not interject leads to a deeper form of listening that often surprises the listener. There is something refreshing and hopeful about "hearing another into speech,"[3] even when one disagrees with them.

L.A. Relational Center: Resonance Listening

The Relational Center in Los Angeles, California (http://www.relational center.org), offers a range of grassroots programs in community wellness, youth leadership, and transformative change-making. Their motto, "Spread Empathy. Inspire Leadership. Build Community," conveys their conviction that building people's capacities for empathy and connection is as important for community transformation as policy initiatives and overt civic action.

One of the practices the Relational Center uses to promote both empathy and self-insight is a practice that might be called "resonance listening." In this practice, the storyteller is invited to tell their life story. Rather than providing a chronology, the storyteller is asked to share key moments and events that seem to have particularly shaped who they are today. The story receiver, the listener, may not interrupt. What the listener is invited to do, in addition to listening, is to carefully attend to what parts of the story register viscerally—not cognitive points of connection or agreement but points of bodily *resonance*. The leaders describe this resonance practice as a sort of "collective meditation."

One striking element to notice about the Relational Center's method is the attention they invite listeners to pay to their bodies. Listening is rooted in how the storyteller's story resonates *physically* in the body of the listener. The listener is asked to recall what part of the story registered bodily and simply to state when that was without explanation. This listening, rooted partially in the ear but primarily in the gut- and heart-centers, requires a receptivity and openness that honors our affective, noncognitive responsiveness to others yet avoids reactivity by asking the listener simply to notice it in the moment. It is only after the storyteller has finished that the listener may respond verbally about the experience. Importantly, neither the storyteller nor the listener is asked (or even permitted) to offer reasons or explanations but simply to name the points of resonance. The power is in the telling and the listening—specifically in a mutual acknowledging that resides as much in the affective and emotional as in the cognitive.[4]

Speaking Down Barriers: Poetry and Presence

Speaking Down Barriers in Spartanburg, South Carolina (http://www.speak downbarriers.org), marks its origin in the hearing of a poem. Marlanda Dekine (whose poetry appears herein under the name Sapient Soul) shared a poem at a conference, and Scott Neely (whose paintings appear in this volume) listened. From that singular moment of genuine listening grew a community transformation organization that roots all its community dialogues in spoken word poetry and other forms of creative expression. Like autobiographical storytelling, rooting dialogue first in poetry allows for the expression of deep truths based in deep experiences. Speaking Down Barriers has discovered that poetry is a mode of expression that allows listeners to hear others' personal experience more receptively. Spoken word poetry is emotionally evocative—and therefore compelling. It is also often provocative, aiming to unsettle its listeners and to shift the lens through which they view the world. There may be moments of resonance between artist and listener, but just as likely are moments of ringing dissonance. While this dissonance may repel some listeners, great riches come to those listeners eager to gain a new lens on the world. In sum, while the aim of spoken word poetry is personal expression, not persuasion or argumentation, it offers a powerful portal to transformation for those who are genuinely receptive listeners.

In addition to starting each community dialogue with poetry of some sort, Speaking Down Barriers uses their community agreement[5] to set a tone for engagement that encourages receptive, courageous speaking and listening. Among the guidelines, articulated primarily as first-person commitments, are:

- I will show up and be present.
- I will speak from my own experience.
- I will not be a frequent voice.
- I will speak and listen with unconditional positive regard for the other.
- We meet not to agree but to learn and understand.

Like the two methods profiled earlier, there is an emphasis on speaking from personal experience and an explicit articulation that the point of engagement is not agreement but mutual understanding, thereby preempting efforts to persuade or argue—but also giving permission for disagreement and its inevitable discomfort. All of the commitments work together. "I will show up and be present" encourages participants not only to try to leave other concerns at the door so that they can focus on the conversation at hand but also to stay with the conversation even when it feels difficult or uncomfortable. Engaging others with a disposition of unconditional positive regard, that is, assuming that others are offering their genuine best to the collective effort of community transformation, also helps the group move through uncomfortable points. All of these commitments require an intentional practice, a *discipline*, of open, receptive listening.

Listening as a Civic Discipline

Civic engagement as historically practiced is on the decline in the United States. Younger generations are affiliating in different ways than their elders have, and technology has dramatically shifted modes of personal and communal engagement. Whereas civic participation was once an unquestioned given, the mood among younger generations now is that it is optional. A revitalization of civic engagement may benefit from the cultivation of "disciplines" much like those practiced in wisdom traditions. This sense of the term *discipline* refers not so much to a bending of the will as to recurrent practices that over time teach us something, whether about ourselves or the world or the nature of reality itself. But disciplines do require "self-discipline" in that we must intentionally commit to their steady practice in our lives, for they do not come automatically.

We can imagine a whole range of civic disciplines, from committing to attending zoning board or school board meetings in our own neighborhoods to contacting congressional representatives several times a week. We can decide to participate in public protests whenever one is scheduled for our city; we can participate in voter registration drives; or we can learn how to start an official petition to address a local problem. Next to these, a civic discipline of open, receptive listening may seem weak or inconsequential. But in an increasingly divisive society, its transformative, illumining power should not be underestimated.

While my emphasis in this reflection is on listening, each of the technologies profiled previously also depends on turning conversation partners toward storytelling and speaking from personal experience. It turns out that framing conversations in this way organically orients us toward deeper, more receptive, less reactive forms of listening. This suggests that the craft of storytelling would be a complementary civic discipline to that of listening.

There are perhaps many sociocultural reasons that listening itself has become a lost art. One is certainly that listening carries risk. Actor Alan Alda has said, "Unless I am willing to be changed by you, I'm not really listening."[6] An unwillingness to have our perspective challenged, at the risk that we ourselves might be changed, works in tandem with a refusal to listen well. Our entangled reality reminds us, however, that in contrast to reigning cultural narratives, receptivity is not necessarily passive, and vulnerability is not necessarily weak. Indeed, in the technologies profiled here, the open receptivity of the listener, alongside the generous vulnerability of the storyteller, provide the conditions for connection, growth, and transformation for storyteller and listener alike—and in turn the wider world. Change becomes a promise rather than a threat.

Carefully listening and being genuinely listened to can prompt profound self- and other-awareness. Spiritual disciplines, after all, are about opening oneself to the unknown in the faith that what we receive might transform us in generative, if not always comfortable, ways. What would it mean to learn from sacred practices of receptiveness for the sake of civic flourishing? How might we grow, how might we be transformed if we were to deliberately open ourselves through careful listening to the unknown who is our creaturely neighbor, whether human or other-than-human? In a world that now tends to be more fearful of, rather than delighted by, our entangled differences, it seems that little could be more civically vital than a fiercely steady and tenderly engaged discipline of listening.

Notes

1. *Bring It to the Table: The Toolkit*, 9; emphasis original. https://bringit2thetable.org/purchasefilm (accessed March 8, 2019).

2. Ibid., 11.

3. The phrase "hearing one another into speech" comes from feminist theology foremother Nelle Morton, who proposed it as a method for women to help one another find, honor, and cultivate their own voices in a world that historically had dismissed them (Morton, *The Journey is Home* [Boston: Beacon Press, 1985]). The technologies of listening profiled here may be even more radical, for they all implicitly suggest that we offer this gift of hearing into speech even to those with whom we may vehemently disagree.

4. Representatives of the Relational Center attended the final session of the multiday conversation at the "Seizing an Alternative" conference, which marks the origin of this volume. They led participants in this method of storytelling and listening.

5. Speaking Down Barriers, "Community Guidelines" (Copyright 2018). Handout.

6. Quoted in Howard Fishman, "What 'M*A*S*H Taught Us,'" *New Yorker*, July 24, 2016, https://www.newyorker.com/culture/culturedesk/whatmashtaughtus.

XTOPIA

An Alternative Frame for Ecosocial Justice

Dhawn B. Martin

The news is not good. The integrity of the earth's biosphere is eroding, even collapsing. In July 2017, reports of an enormous iceberg breaking away from Antarctica were "trending." A few days before that headline, a soul-crushing article appeared in *New York Magazine*, titled "The Uninhabitable Earth."[1] Take a moment. Let that soak in.

I confess that I could not make it through the article in one sitting. It was too devastating. Too much. One reviewer of "Uninhabitable" labeled the article "'extinction porn'" due to its grisly, at times less than nuanced, doomsday account.[2] And the details are graphic.

Yet in the midst of terrifying future scenarios, "Uninhabitable" raises important issues. The most salient question it asks is: "Why can't we see it?" More pointedly, why are we humans, particularly humans shaped by a U.S. consciousness, not willing to see the massive scale of ecocatastrophes in their current and emerging expressions? One answer "Uninhabitable" offers is: "'Because the dilemmas and dramas of climate change are simply incompatible with the kinds of stories we tell ourselves about ourselves . . . which tend to emphasize the journey of an individual conscience rather than the poisonous miasma of social fate.'"[3]

In short, the stories we Americans tell ourselves are neither reflective of the communal nor broadly relational. But how might more community-centered narratives help us to better see the world as it is and the world as it might be? This question remains unasked in "Uninhabitable" but is central to my proposal of an *xtopian* frame for social activism. I develop *xtopia*—drawing on theories of utopianism in conversation with Aristotle and feminist theory. The *x* of xtopia serves multiple purposes, as I shall develop it. The primary one is to offer a frame for collective sociopolitical engagement that x's out or challenges policies and narratives that have become static through convention or frozen through caricature.

209

Smoke and Mirrors

> Mirror, mirror, on the wall,
> Who in this land is fairest of all?[4]
>
> —THE QUEEN

In an age of rapid climate change, a more apt query might be: *Mirror, mirror on the wall, who in this land is greenest . . . or coolest . . . or least degraded . . . or most water secure of all?* And yet exchanging one superlative for another, say fairest for coolest, is problematic. For one thing such exchanges obscure the gendered dynamic key to this particular story. "Fairest," in this instance, speaks to the commodity of female beauty as valued in Europe's nineteenth century. The one who is valued most in this tale is Snow White. Here we encounter, for neither the first nor the last time in Western narratives, the linking of land, competition for commodities (the "who" that surpasses all other who's), and constructs of gender, beauty, and race. It is imperative to accentuate these connections if we hope to create communities of ecosocial justice.

But someone might challenge the aforementioned linkages, arguing that Snow White is a dusty relic of outdated injustices. As Sandra Gilbert and Susan Gubar point out in their feminist analysis of Snow White, however, this story perpetuates a "prototype" that illustrates not only "the structure of patriarchy" but also the violence intrinsic to the stark polarities presented between "angelic" Snow White and the wicked Queen.[5] The angelic and fairest, as determined by the *pater familia* voice of the mirror, necessarily expels the wicked. The two frozen and caricatured images cannot exist together. One must destroy the other.

Furthermore, recent political fracases and environmental disasters would beg to differ with efforts to dismiss the "lessons" of Snow White. Take, as one example, the 2017 Texas "bathroom bill" (SB 6). SB 6 seeks to limit use of state-affiliated bathrooms to "persons of the same biological sex." And for the purposes of clarity, the bill defines biological sex as "the physical condition of being male or female, which is stated on a person's birth certificate."[6] This bill links the land of Texas with a simplistic understanding of the relationship between sex, gender, and identity. The "fairest" in this frame would be those who legitimate their identities through state-sanctioned mechanisms, mechanisms put in place by a "mostly white, male, middle-aged" legislature.[7]

As another example, consider Flint, Michigan. As I write this, the water there is still contaminated. Still. As the final 2016 report from the Flint Water Advisory Task Force details: "The facts of the Flint water crisis lead us to the inescapable conclusion that this is a case of environmental injustice. Flint residents, who are majority Black or African American and among the most impoverished of any metropolitan area in the United States, did not enjoy the same degree of protection from environmental and health hazards as that provided to other communities."[8]

When the commodity is clean water, it appears that in the land of Michigan, race and economic power stand paramount in policy decisions. The report names the Flint crisis an "environmental injustice." And that it is. It is also an example of ecosocial injustice, as evident from the task force's correlation of environmental discrimination to race and economic inequalities. Were the residents in Flint snow-white or in a different socioeconomic stratum, would this injustice continue? Doubtful.

In my Texas and Michigan examples, "land" stands for a sovereign political body with defined boundaries. Land as state, and therefore state power, speaks to how power—political, social, and economic—shapes the realities of life-forms inhabiting those boundaries. But in these examples, land also, especially in the Michigan case, represents the ecological. And here we see the inextricable ties binding concepts of land to both the body politic and bodies biological and ecological. Further, the push for state legislatures to exercise their rights, often over and against federal policies (think of Texas and its nonexpansion of Medicaid in defiance of the Affordable Care Act), must be interrogated if the work of environmental justice is to expand. I note the double binding of "land" to governmental policies and environmental conditions to highlight the entangled nature of constructs of power, competition, race, and gender. We humans ignore this entanglement at our own peril.

To discuss the water crisis in Michigan without attending to the economic crisis and racial bigotry engulfing the area is to ignore the layered injustices suffered by those in Flint. If U.S. community members are to address the myriad collusions that perpetuate inequalities and environmental degradation, we must mobilize around "the direct correlation of sustainability and social justice work."[9] To act effectively, we need to acknowledge and attend to the broad swath of policy decisions, inherent biases, and operational inequalities that fuel injustice. Ecosocial justice offers an expansive frame to analyze and act that recognizes the complex nature of injustice.

And yet for most of us, the land of Michigan can seem far away, its troubles the troubles of those removed from our daily concerns. What is more, life is hard as I write in August 2017. As a global community, we are distracted by threats of nuclear engagement with North Korea. We are numbed by the Trump administration's smoke-and-mirror statecraft. As a population, we in the United States are crushed by the hate, racism, and violence that invaded Charlottesville, reminding us that at some point the United States will have to atone for its original sin of slavery. On top of this, in the back of our minds, at least in my mind, looms the picture of an "uninhabitable earth."

The future can feel bleak. And so a few nostalgic souls might yearn for some magical mirror, some vision or narrative of hope. Yet, as with many a heart's desire, there is a double edge. Mirrors, as Snow White pinpoints, often tell or show individuals things that challenge, provoke, or annihilate. Questions multiply, then, for those formed by Western narratives. Should we throw out all mirrors? Do we choose to ignore tales and messages that provoke or stereotype? And by ignoring, do we risk perpetuating injustice or missing opportunities to transform not only ourselves but also the message? Or do we opt to critically engage such stories and systems in the world?

To critically engage, of course, is to analyze the message, the media it uses, the systems it supports and is supported by, as well as its generative or destructive capacity. Now, please do not misunderstand. I do not seek to validate the violent polarities presented in Snow White, or any other narrative that reinforces oppressive hierarchies. But in the spirit of feminist methodology, I suggest a hermeneutic of suspicion, whereby all messages (and the mirrors they hold up to the world) are questioned. This particular hermeneutic is not only one of critique but also of creativity. It searches for the cracks and distortions that potentially open spaces for alternative narratives to be developed. For not all mirrors rank the fairest or whitest of all. Some just might help us to see in different or alternative ways.

The Distortions and Possibilities of Utopia Reconceived

212 In his analysis of and work with expressions of utopianism, scholar Lyman Tower Sargent casts utopias as "distorting mirror[s] in reverse showing how good we could look. Utopia rightly upsets people," he continues, "because it constantly suggests that the life we lead, the society we have, is inadequate, incomplete, sick."[10] That may sound harsh, but recall the earlier examples of Texas and Michigan. Bombarded by racial injustices and ecological degradations, it is imperative to create narratives and social theories that attempt to show all of humanity how we can do and be better, of just how *good* or how *right* our communities could be.

Utopian ideas, be they expressed through narratives, sociopolitical theory, or attempts at creating new forms of communal living, are almost as old as human civilization.[11] Whether articulated in tales of Atlantis, in the Garden of Eden story, in the Chinese tale "The Peach Blossom Spring," in Shaker communities, or in Ursula Le Guin's *The Dispossessed*, a utopic thread seems to pull collective imaginations and practices toward an alternate vision of the way things are, were, or should be.

As most might know, we owe the term *utopia* to Sir Thomas More's wit. Drawing on More's *Utopia*, modern readers have made much of the possible play of the Greek prefixes "ou" ("no" or "not") and "eu" ("good"), creating ou/eu-topia. Utopia in its more literary expressions, then, "has come to refer to a non-existent good place."[12] Nonexistence can suggest an elusive quality to utopias, their capacities to resist easy replication or reductive formula. The negative strands in utopian DNA are also on display in *dystopias*. Writer Jason Heller, reflecting on the popularity of postapocalyptic narratives and their dystopian visions, notes that "the world feels more precariously perched on the lip of the abyss than ever, and facing those fears through fiction helps us deal with it. These stories are cathartic as well as cautionary. But they also reaffirm why we struggle to keep our world together in the first place. By imagining what it's like to lose everything, we can value what we have."[13]

Valuing what we as humans have in a way that invites and welcomes all to flourish, including other-than-human life-forms, is at the heart of ecosocial justice, as I have cast it. But fiction is not the only medium through which this valuing might transpire. Sargent illustrates the breadth of utopianism in his definition of it "as social dreaming—the dreams and nightmares that concern the ways in which groups of people arrange their lives and which usually envision a radically different society than the one" they inhabit.[14]

Sargent's definition helps us identify several key elements to utopian thinking. First, utopian projects are primarily social in nature, stressing relationships. These projects therefore disrupt the problem of "individual consciousness" named in "The Uninhabitable Earth." Utopian frames draw to the fore "social fate" while ignoring neither individual choice nor consciousness. In LeGuin's *Dispossessed*, for example, readers accompany main character Shevek, his choices and thoughts, as he navigates two very different societies, which are literally worlds apart. While Shevek is but one person, he is molded by and molds the different spheres he inhabits. As punctuated throughout this narrative, the personal is the political and communal.

Second, utopian projects can be both imaginative and pragmatic. The social dream developed by a community or author speaks to "not-yet" -realized possibilities. Utopias need not, then, be dismissed, as they often are, as fantastical flights from reality. Visions of not-yet-realized possibilities can ignite productive, practical, and just action. The image of the kingdom of God, as expressed in certain Christian theologies, for example, speaks of a now and not-yet reality. Unlike Eden, which has been lost, the kingdom remains an assured divine promise and possible human undertaking: "Blessed are the peacemakers, for they will be called children of God" (Matthew 5:9, New Revised Standard Version). Note the plural and therefore social nature of the blessing, which binds divine action to human being and doing.[15]

Third, utopian projects are rarely sterile, passionless undertakings. As dreams, as alternatives to the status quo, utopias tap into desire. Utopias speak to mind, body, and heart. As utopian theorist Ruth Levitas suggests, "utopia is the expression of the desire for a better way of being." Identification of a common thread of desire does not aspire to any claims for a universal "utopian propensity," however. Levitas is clear to note that utopian projects are contextual, they "remin[d] us that, whatever we think of particular utopias, we learn a lot about the experience of living under any set of conditions by reflecting upon the desires which those conditions generate and yet leave unfulfilled. For that is the space which utopia occupies."[16]

Utopias are generative precisely to the extent that this "unfulfilled" dream or desire does not paralyze by despair but mobilizes through a vision of a "better way of being" in community.

Fourth, "all utopias ask questions."[17] By creating alternative visions of society, utopian projects challenge practices of the status quo. In short, utopias offer critiques that call societies to reevaluate the hows and whys of their social constructs. The mirror they hold up, however distorted, offers moments for critical reflection and transformation.

These four elements by no means exhaust possible descriptions or experiences of utopias. They do, however, suggest reasons why utopian projects exist. Furthermore, I argue that these elements point to possible strategies for ecosocial justice. Such strategies, as I will fully develop in the last section on xtopia, mobilize individuals and communities that are creative and pragmatic, that stir heart, mind, and body, and that challenge perspectives and policies that foster injustice.

That said, the history, present, and future of utopian projects are not risk-free. Numerous theorists have traced totalitarian threads across utopian plans, particularly where force is used to further the envisioned "better way of being."[18] When force is not an issue, other utopias might entail wish-fulfillment quests, bordering on the quixotic. Force and fantasy, alas, are not the only potential ills of utopia. Le Guin crafts *The Dispossessed* as "An Ambiguous Utopia," leaving open the question of how to determine which societies are truly "better."[19] Mindful of the dangers and ambiguities marring some utopian projects, and yet reticent to dispense with the strategies highlighted earlier, I more fully develop the frame of *xtopia* in the next two sections. I do so in conversation with Aristotle's theories of rhetoric and Michel Foucault's "heterotopia."

Mirrors Cracked

> She looked down to Camelot.
> Out flew the web, and floated wide,
> The mirror cracked from side to side,
> "The curse is come upon me," cried
> The Lady of Shalott.[20]

In Lord Alfred Tennyson's ballad "The Lady of Shalott," readers encounter a linking of constructs of land and gender, with a utopian twist—Camelot. For those unfamiliar with the plot, our dear Lady finds herself confined to a tower room and weaving loom. Her only view of the world is through a mirror, which reflects life outside. While the images in the mirror are active,

Shalott remains frozen. And once she dares move beyond the reflected images, we learn the extent of her curse—death. To move from a vision of utopia to active participation in it is risky in every sense of the word. For The Lady of Shalott reveals both the ambiguities and possibilities borne of utopian dreams.

The contrasts are clear. In part of the mirror readers see a glorious vision of Camelot, governed by knightly virtues. The lore of Camelot invoked by Tennyson's ballad bids us to envision a kingdom that challenges other kingdoms by force of its valor and courtly chivalry. This kingdom is also radiant, located in a lush environment. In another part of the mirror, however, we catch glimpses of Shalott. She sits, perhaps, as a portrait of "perfected" nineteenth-century femininity. She is perfect as long as she is bound to her place and work but death-bearing should she break free. Is the static nature of Lady Shalott imperative to the social order of the utopian Camelot? Would Camelot's structures, its "better way of being," have crumbled if a woman freed from caricature had crossed its borders alive? Shalott's premature death shuts down such questions. The only thing interpreters can say for certain, within the lines of the narrative, is that the mirror cracked. The old way of seeing and being was altered by the desire to move, to actively participate in a different world.

At first glance, Tennyson's poem presents a utopia as distant from liberating action as Shalott is from Camelot. The Lady dies; the ancient utopia appears to go on—business as usual. But what about that cracked mirror? Sargent's description of utopianism as a "distorting mirror" offers a way to interpret that side-to-side crack as an opening to change found in the midst of suffocating chains. This change, if not disruptive, at the very least challenges perceptions and comfort levels. The images reflected in Shalott's mirror prior to her risky act are ones of perfection. Camelot is perfect. The ecological setting is perfect: "The sun came dazzling thro' the leaves." The Lady stuck to room and loom is feminine perfection. But as many of us have likely experienced, and most world religions teach, no human enterprise can bear the work of perfection. Perfection is not only impossible but also tends to trade in static stereotypes. Yet the cracked mirror reflects not perfection but possibility. At the end of Tennyson's ballad, the 1833 version, the people of Camelot are left "puzzled" and unsettled. "They crossed themselves," shocked by Shalott's death barge and her message: The web was woven curiously / The charm was broken utterly, / Draw near and fear not—this is I, / The Lady of Shalott.[21] The charm, the stereotype, was broken. Draw near, she bids her community, this is I. In death, Shalott invites the too-perfect Camelot to see her, to be troubled and even changed by her dream of a better way to be. And who knows just what images were next reflected in that cracked mirror? The possibilities for Camelot, its all-too-perfect environment, and other utopias are left open to interpretation and imagination.

It is this imaginative or creative impulse that can serve as engine for transformation in utopian projects. I turn next, then, to exploration of other creative possibilities pulsing within utopia as frame for ecosocial activism. As a first step in constructing the unique elements of my proposed xtopian frame, I examine the root, topos, and then the prefixes of utopia—the *eu* and *ou*—and others.

The root of utopia is rather straightforward, meaning place. But if we examine topos from the standpoint of rhetoric, another level of meaning develops. Aristotle will prove of use in developing this connection, and for two reasons. First, Aristotle's *Politics* can be seen as standing in ambiguous relation to the idea and pragmatics of "'ideal states,'" as highlighted by Manuel and Manuel in their seminal study, *Utopian Thought in the Western World.*[22] Second, Aristotle's theories on rhetoric deepen the communal and strategic character of the topos in utopia.

As scholar George A. Kennedy highlights, "topos," as a "concept" in Aristotle's work, serves as "the 'place' where topics are to be found that provide the strategies for persuasive reasoning (*Rhet.* 2.23.1–29)." We will return to the importance of persuasion momentarily. For now, though, our focus is on topos as connective place. This place, according to Kennedy, is one of commonality, of relationship, and is even a "'civic space.'"[23] In other words, if you are going to create persuasive arguments or narratives, you need to draw on ideas, experiences, metaphors, beliefs, and dreams that are communally accessible. In *Rhetoric*, Aristotle advises his readers to use "words . . . that are current and ordinary." For, he continues, "people do not feel towards strangers as they do towards their own countrymen, and the same is true of their feeling for language."[24] Rejecting the xenophobia, we can nevertheless develop strategies from Aristotle's emphasis on shared reservoirs of meaning. If utopian projects are social dreams, we might then think of rhetoric as producing social resonances. As Carolyn R. Miller points out, the topos in Aristotle is "particularly rich in connectivity."

What is more, Miller argues that these connections are not simply a rehearsal of previous patterns, but rather they "make possible new combinations, patterns, [and] relationships that could not be seen before."[25] Aristotle notes the productive tension between common and new. "It is therefore well," he remarks, "to give to everyday speech an unfamiliar air: people like what strikes them, and are struck by what is out of the way."[26] Out of the way, but not inaccessible. Topos in its persuasive mode, therefore, speaks to both the communal and creative. In other words, what is common need not be static, exclusivist, or even fully visible or understood but can function as the ground for new paradigms of being and doing.

I am not an expert on Aristotle or rhetoric, but I find Kennedy's and Miller's work compelling. And while rhetoric and utopia might appear miles apart in content and intent, it is important to recall More's *Utopia*. This text dabbles unapologetically in wordplay as a mode of social critique, theological rumination, philosophical discussion, nuanced satire, and persuasive argumentation.[27] I submit, therefore, that analysis of classical Greek uses of topos proves relevant to the current discussion. Furthermore, my rooting of utopia in the strategies of rhetoric binds the concept and vision to exercises of the persuasive as opposed to the coercive. Ecosocial justice will not be attained through force but through persuasive, persistent, and productive action based on respect for all life-forms. It is a collective movement, not an imperial march.

If we accept the proposal that topos can serve as a place of rich, generative, as well as yet-to-be-realized possibilities, how might this proposal shape utopian theories? And can an understanding of topos as "a region of productive uncertainty" render utopias open systems of thought and action?[28] Furthermore, once cast as open systems, might utopias prove robustly resistant to the totalitarian or quixotic? I explore these queries more fully in the last section, where I unpack the specific elements of *xtopia*. But this line of questioning draws us to another query: are *ou* and *eu* the only prefixes that inspire productive social dreaming?

Philosopher Michel Foucault, for one, would answer no, preferring to think through the frame of "heterotopia." As "counter-sites," heterotopias reveal "a kind of effectively enacted utopia in which the real sites, all the other real sites that can be found within the culture, are simultaneously represented, contested, and inverted."[29] Foucault lists several examples of heterotopias, including museums, libraries, and prisons. Each of these examples offers a challenge to policies, practices, or business as usual.

Museums and libraries, as repositories of multiple knowledges, centuries, and images, for example, simultaneously blur borders while erecting them. The challenge they present is to perceived limits, striving toward the "perpetual and indefinite accumulation of time in an immobile place."[30] The intersection of infinite and finite contests and inverts conventional understandings of time and space. Foucault, it should be clear, seeks neither to establish a utopian vision nor to mobilize action toward a particular dream. Rather, Foucault charts an alternative way to perceive and engage cultural constructs. In particular, he dissects those constructs that may, on the surface, appear innocuous but that in their functioning reveal a panorama of biases, hopes, injustices, illusions, and even possibilities.

Three of Foucault's insights contribute to my proposed xtopian frame. The first is a willingness to not only draw on utopia as an established model but to expand that model. This willingness is not simply to play with prefixes but rather to name experiences and conditions unique to a particular place, time, or culture. This leads to a second insight, one shared by other utopian thinkers—that of the profound contextuality of utopian projects. Heterotopias are in relation to "all the other real sites . . . within a culture." Heterotopias, and utopias more broadly, are products of a particular culture. There is no one utopia or one social dream applicable across all time and space. As stated earlier, utopias must tap into social resonances. And lastly, while Foucault notes the diversity of heterotopian projects, he nevertheless classifies them into "two main categories": "heterotopias of deviation" and "crisis heterotopias."[31] It is to the "crisis" mode we turn next, primarily due to its linking of place, gender, and environment.

In Foucault's analytic lens, crisis heterotopias are "privileged or sacred or forbidden places, reserved for individuals who are, in relation to society and to the human environment in which they live, in a state of crisis: adolescents, menstruating women, pregnant women, the elderly, etc."[32] Notice that two of the named populations highlight societal constructs of gender and how these constructs function in or are regulated by society. Of course, women comprise the other two populations as well, the elderly and adolescent. And although Foucault does not pursue the gender dynamic, the construct of "woman" clearly bears multiple burdens in his example. What is more, "women" in this context might—except for a brief period of time—exist in perpetual crisis both to society and the "human environment." Of course, there is no human environment void of other biological or ecological relations. Therefore, it could further be argued that certain constructs of gender place individuals in risky, compromised, or crisis relations to all biological systems within particular cultures.

It is unlikely that Foucault intends such a sweeping conclusion. Nevertheless, he does link heterotopias to "all other real sites," which would include sociocultural constructs of nature, earth, and environment. Indeed, Foucault's "oldest example" of heterotopia is gardens. He references "the traditional garden of the Persians . . . that was supposed to bring together inside its rectangle four parts representing the four parts of the world." Within these socially managed sites humans encounter both the world in its "smallest parcel" and also its "totality."[33] Again, as with museums and libraries, we see how the pairing of the finite and infinite, the parcel and totality, inverts conventional orders. How can the totality of the world "come together" within its smallest part?[34] And yet this was the social dream inspiring those earliest heterotopias. Might the inverting dynamic Foucault attributes to heterotopias also challenge, or at the very least trouble, his own theories? I am thinking specifically of Foucault's limiting of crisis heterotopias to "human environments," a designation that appears to exclude biological and ecological environs. Might we read into this space of crisis a contesting or blurring of boundaries between human and ecological? And why might this blurring matter?

I argue that Foucault's crisis heterotopia, understood as a phenomenon that extends through and beyond sociocultural and human environments, serves as a compelling frame for ecosocial justice. Foucault locates, and therefore limits, crisis heterotopias to "primitive society." And this makes sense, on one level. For the creation of forbidden places, of places where individuals in "crisis" are isolated from the rest of society, does seem an archaic practice. The state of "crisis" was determined by the operating culture. It tended, in Foucault's examples, to be limited to specific groups for specific times. The crisis, in other words, was temporary . . . unless, as suggested earlier, you were a woman. And so we must ask the question, How primitive and how limited were (or are) crisis heterotopias?

As the earlier examples of Texas and Michigan demonstrate, contemporary configurations of land, together with constructs of gender and race, perpetuate injustices of isolation and of "crisis management." Furthermore, contemporary cases of injustices and crisis verge on the perpetual and expansive. Think systemic racism in the United States. Think sexism across international and cultural borders, as evidenced in the #MeToo movement of late 2017. Think ecological exploitations shattering the planet. Might the human species be facing another place and time where the "parcel" and "totality" of the world converge, and in converging challenge our conceptual orders and understandings?

In the current Anthropocene era, I suggest that all humans live in a state of crisis to our ecological environment and vice versa. The crisis is all too pervasive and perpetual, at least for the foreseeable future: global warming, unstable glacial ice sheets, environmental injustices, unpredictable weather patterns, outbreaks of disease, the extinction of species. But, some-one might ask, Is this situation one of Foucauldian heterotopia? Perhaps not. I have stretched the scope of his analysis. And developing the frame of xtopia, not distorting heterotopia, is my goal. But what I hope to accentuate in my reading of Foucault is the constructed and contextual nature of the Anthropocene crisis. As constructed crises, increased global warming, envi-ronmental injustices, and greenhouse gases are human productions. This fact must be acknowledged before communities can engage in meaningful acts of ecosocial justice. The crisis, for the most part, is of the Western and industrializing world's making. And while we in the West may not be able to fix the crisis, accepting responsibility is a first step in the social dream-ing needed to creatively, pragmatically, and honestly face the situation. It is a crucial first step. We will explore other steps and strategies of xtopia in the final section.

Objects in Mirror Are Closer than They Appear

> Between utopias and ... heterotopias, there might be a sort
> of mixed, joint experience, which would be the mirror. The
> mirror is ... a utopia, since it is a placeless place.[35]
>
> —FOUCAULT

Whether cracked or distorting, the mirrors that utopia holds up to commu-nities provide space to imagine and act. A "placeless place" need not be empty or sterile. Through concerted effort and respectful engagement with others, the placeless might become places brimming with possibilities.

More broadly, utopias offer communities chances to dream of alterna-tives, of better ways of being and doing. These dreams, in their classical and contemporary expressions, share overlapping strands: connectivity, contex-tuality, the asking of questions, the activation of desire, and the balance of creativity and pragmatism. The density and complexity of these strands, I suggest, provide insight for effective strategies to mobilize communities. How so? When approached as multilayered projects of thought, action, desire, and imagination, utopias are well equipped to diagnose and tackle practices that engender and racialize ecosocial injustice. In short, the complexity that is ecosocial injustice demands an equally complex frame for analysis and action.

An xtopian frame for ecosocial action builds on the best of utopian impulses. Through this frame communities are invited to draft and enact strategies that are inherently social and connective in nature. Furthermore, these social impulses need be expansive and invitational. Just and welcoming ecosocial practices recognize that isolationist practices not only exacerbate divides but also, and more importantly, fail to understand the entangled nature of our planetary existence. As signs at a 2017 Earth Day rally in San Antonio, Texas, put it: *There is no Planet B*. Failure to include, connect with, and negotiate the hopes, desires, theologies, and ideologies of others will condemn all life to an "uninhabitable" earth. Willingness to negotiate leads to other xtopian strategies, strategies resonant with grassroots organizing.

Equally important to plans that are connective and invitational are plans nuanced in understandings of contextuality and desire. A project that speaks to the dreams and desires of West Texans will likely not resonate as fully with New Yorkers. Key to mobilizing individuals and communities, therefore, are knowledge of and actions driven by the issues most salient to them. Tapping into self-interest and systems of communal desire is an element of xtopian activism, but an element that must be balanced by practices of connectivity. Locating individual desire within the broader landscape and narratives of shared "social fate" is imperative. As any organizer knows, there is power in numbers. Though imperative, this linking of individual fate and social fate can be difficult and exhausting. Communities committed to ecosocial activism, then, need to invest time, energy, and collective resources in fostering a culture of openness to transformation and experimentation.

Experimentation, as evident in the evolution of dystopian literatures and in Foucault's heterotopia, is intrinsic to utopian projects. Within an xtopian frame, business as usual is not an option—especially capitalist practices that prize profit over ecological sustainability. Key to experiments, of course, is the asking of questions. Experiments test existing theories with the untried. Furthermore, experiments risk. They risk inconclusive or ambiguous results. They risk mistakes made and discoveries unearthed. Risk is innate to experiments because questions that challenge preconception or bias drive the mechanics of experimentation. Other aspects of experimentation that can well serve activists are: patience, the ability to give experiments the time they need to fully mature, and a capacity to return to the drawing board to recalibrate methodologies.

In experimentation, another strand of utopian DNA is hinted at—that of creativity. In an xtopian frame creativity bears a double meaning: openness to new things and a capacity to engage in the hard work of developing and sustaining alternative ways of being community. Hard work speaks to the pragmatic element of utopias. Creativity and pragmatism need be seen as two sides of effective thought and action. Foucault's work with heterotopia presents a creative and pragmatic adaptation of utopian models, as discussed earlier. It develops a new frame while not discarding previous markers of utopia. It seeks to describe "real sites" and simultaneously unpack how "placeless places" contest the norms of a given culture. In short, heterotopia provides an interpretive frame. Through this frame readers can rethink libraries or gardens, a rethinking that just might translate into alternative practices, whether or not this possibility was expressed in Foucault's work.

As stated earlier, Foucault's heterotopia, like dystopian models before him, opens the door to experimentation with utopian concepts. It is in this spirit of creativity that I have traced the aforementioned characteristics of an xtopian frame. These characteristics owe much to the literature and study of utopia. There are two additional strategies that distinguish xtopia from other models. One of these strategies, touched on earlier, draws from classical uses of the Greek topos. The other strategy, which I develop next, delves into theological terrains.

I highlighted three elements of Aristotle's concept of topos that, I contend, expand utopian projects. The first element is to recognize the importance of identifying a common space for discussion that is accessible to many. In other words, it is important to craft visions and messages adept in cultivating social resonance. Such adeptness reveals attention to the matters that matter to a community. It is important to note that social resonances need neither trap communities in ruts nor rehearse tired or oppressive tropes. To the contrary, they can offer ecosocial activists opportunities to reframe narratives that emphasize social fate. Recall that Aristotle bases the art of persuasion in languages, images, and visions that are both *everyday* and *unfamiliar*. This creative tension, between the everyday and unfamiliar, invites potential allies to dream, act, and contribute to the development of new strategies. Communities and strategies that welcome and mindfully engage unfamiliar ways of thinking and being are less likely to demand rigid conformity or destructive absolutes.

The second element inspired by Aristotle's concept of topos is emphasis on the art of persuasion. In an xtopian frame this is particularly salient with regard to exercises of power. The powers mobilized by xtopian strategies are those of persuasion as distinct from those of coercion. If there is power in numbers, the so numbered need to intentionally determine the power they desire to embody. An xtopian frame seeks to generate strategies that persuade through their resonances, their clarity, their pragmatism, their openness to change, and their commitment to relational politics and just action. Persuasion works at the level of desire and self-interest, yet this level is never uprooted from its grounding in community, connection, and narratives of social fate. Stated differently, persuasive power is communal power.

The last element works with Miller's description of Aristotle's topos as "region of productive uncertainty." As an xtopian frame for ecosocial justice embraces the unfamiliar, so, too, does it toil within the uncertain. To live and act in accord with uncertainty, with not knowing the final outcome, and with acknowledging the limits of human designs is to resist temptations of the totalitarian. As philosopher Hannah Arendt observed: "Ideologies always assume that one idea is sufficient to explain everything."[36] Xtopian strategies challenge the monolithic totality of ideology through openness to the unfamiliar and uncertain.

Gaining fluency in the languages and ways of the uncertain is central not only to practices of the xtopian but also to my reframing of utopia as a project of ecosocial justice. The prefixes *ou*, *eu*, *dys*, and *hetero* open spaces within sociocultural imaginations to critically examine practices, beliefs, and ways of being. They do so in unique ways. Some are cautionary, as noted by Jason Heller's review of the dystopian. Some challenge through elusive languages, such as Thomas More's ou/eu-topian play. Some, as with Foucault's heterotopia, offer a descriptive lens for analysis. The *x* of xtopia, as I develop it, serves as reminder, marker, and call.

As reminder, the *x* functions to actively hold a place for the uncertain, the unfamiliar, the unforeseen. To hold a place is to be prepared for the unexpected, as much as humanly possible, in a proactive rather than reactive manner. It is to be ready to welcome a new community member, ready to employ an untried but suggested method of organizing, or ready to pay attention to an emerging situation in order to respond thoughtfully. Such placeholding echoes political philosopher William E. Connolly's "guiding principles . . . don't explicate too much; cultivate care; experiment politically."[37] The *x* troubles pretentions to perfection and acts of dominative power.

As marker, x marks the spot not of some hidden imperial treasure chest but of economies and ecologies of interdependence. This x in its crossing out, its cutting of space and place, abounds in symbolic meaning. X marks our complicity in systems of exploitation and oppression. The constructs of land, gender, and race that have shaped past and current U.S. policies have destroyed innumerable human and other-than-human lives. X conjures images of warning. Think of a skull and cross bones, of pirates pillaging the world for individual or communal gain. It can warn us, bid us to go no further on our current path. There is a dynamism to x that also speaks to possibility and not just warning. X speaks to efforts, inevitably cracked and distorted, to experiment with alternative ways of being and doing. These alternatives disrupt, even x out, business as usual and frozen caricatures. The x inspires acts of resistance, but resistance nurtured through the cultivation of care.

As call, the x beckons to acts of desire, to acts of love. It locates ecosocial activism within the wellsprings of compassion and the subversions of love. As theologian Jean Luc Marion avows, "love . . . does not pretend to comprehend." Here, Marion is offering a phenomenological reading of love, divine and human. Divine love is one of excess, an excess that "saturates" and therefore "crosses out our thought."[38] This crossing out is not an eradication of that which is human, human thought, human efforts toward love, peace, justice. Rather, it is a love that through its excess, through its sheer givenness, thaws and destabilizes frozen perceptions of self, God, neighbor, and world. One need not, of course, add a theological turn to xtopian projects. The cultivation of care, as detailed by William Connolly, serves as a guiding principle for reflection and action.

Xtopia offers a layered, open, and flexible frame for ecosocial activism. As a utopian model profoundly attuned to the current Anthropocene crisis, it calls for Western and industrializing populations to acknowledge culpability as a first step. Other steps include crafting strategies for collective action that are complex, nuanced, and daring enough to grapple with the realities of systemic injustice and global warming. An xtopian frame resists temptations to manufacture a one-size-fits-all, easy-fix solution. To the contrary it invites collaboration, connectivity, relation-building, experimental methods, the activation of self- and communal interest as modes of transformative engagement, and practices of compassion and love. The xtopian challenges every human to recall that the objects, subjects, lifeforms, desires, and dreams that diverse cultural mirrors reflect are closer and more entangled than they might appear.

Notes

1. David Wallace-Wells, "The Uninhabitable Earth," *New York Magazine*, July 9, 2017. http://nymag.com/daily/intelligencer/2017/07/climatechangeearthtoohotforhumans.html.

2. Chuck Wendig, Twitter Post, July 10, 2017, 6:19 a.m., https://twitter.com/Chuck Wendig/status/884401770574868481, quoted in Robinson Meyer, "Are We as Doomed as That *New York Magazine* Article Says?," *The Atlantic*, July 10, 2017, https://www.theatlantic.com/science/archive/2017/07/istheearthreally thatdoomed/533112.

3. Wallace-Wells, "Uninhabitable Earth," referencing Amitov Ghosh, *The Great Derangement: Climate Change and the Unthinkable* (Chicago: University of Chicago Press, 2017).

4. Jacob and Wilhelm Grimm, *Little Snow-White*, http://www.pitt.edu/~dash/grimm053.html.

5. Sandra M. Gilbert and Susan Gubar, *The Madwoman in the Attic: The Woman Writer and the Nineteenth-Century Literary Imagination*, 2nd ed. (New Haven: Yale University Press, 2000), 616, 68, and 616.

6. Rep. Lois Kolkhorst, *Senate Bill 6* (S. B. No. 6), section 4, chapter 769, section 769.101, lines 5–6, and section 4, chapter 769, section 769.001, lines 14–16. http://www.legis.state.tx.us/tlodocs/85R/billtext/pdf/SB00006I.pdf, 5, see esp. 2.

7. Alexa Ura and Jolie McCullough, "Once Again, the Texas Legislature Is Mostly White, Male, Middle-Aged," *The Texas Tribune*, January 9, 2017, https://www.texastribune.org/2017/01/09/texaslegislaturemostlywhitemale middleaged.

8. Matthew M. Davis, MD, MAPP, Chris Kolb, Lawrence Reynolds, MD, Eric Rothstein, CPA, and Ken Sikkema, *Flint Water Advisory Task Force: Final Report*, March 2016. Commissioned by the Office of Governor Rick Snyder, State of Michigan, 54.

9. The quote is drawn from a web page describing University of Colorado "Boulder's Eco-Social Justice Leadership Program," http://www.colorado.edu/ecenter/ecosocial.

10. Lyman Tower Sargent, "The Three Faces of Utopianism Revisited," *Utopian Studies 5*, no. 1 (1994): 1–37, esp. 25, http://www.jstor.org/stable/20719246.

11. Ibid., 1–37. More specifically, Sargent names the three faces as "utopian literature . . . communitarianism, and utopian social theory," Ibid., 4. Sargent creates this threefold typology for analysis of utopias. For a fuller analysis of the "three faces" or expressions of utopianism, see the aforementioned article.

12. Lyman Tower Sargent, *Utopianism: A Very Short Introduction* (Oxford: Oxford University Press, 2010), 2.

13. Jason Heller, "Does Post-Apocalyptic Literature Have a (Non-Dystopian) Future?," *Book News and Features Review, National Public Radio*, May 2, 2015, http://www.npr.org/2015/05/02/402852849/doespostapocalyptic literaturehaveanondystopianfuture.

14. Sargent, "Three Faces of Utopianism," 3.

15. For a somewhat extensive review of utopian elements in Kingdom of God imagery and histories, see Mary Ann Beavis, *Jesus and Utopia: Looking for the Kingdom of God in the Roman World* (Minneapolis, Minn.: Augsburg Fortress Press, 2006).

16. Ruth Levitas, *The Concept of Utopia* (Syracuse: Syracuse University Press, 1990), 8.

17. Sargent, *Very Short Introduction*, 5.

18. For more detailed exploration of these dangers, see Sargent, "Three Faces of Utopianism," 21–25.

19. Ursula K. Le Guin, *The Dispossessed: An Ambiguous Utopia* (New York: Harper and Row Publishers, 1974).

20. Lord Alfred Tennyson, "The Lady of Shalott" (1833), stanza 3, https://d.lib.rochester.edu/camelot/text/tennysonshalott comparison.

21. Ibid.

22. Frank E. Manuel and Fritzie P. Manuel, *Utopian Thought in the Western World* (Cambridge, Mass.: Belknap Press of Harvard University Press, 1979), 10.

23. George A. Kennedy, "Reworking Aristotle's Rhetoric," in *Foundations for Socio-rhetorical Exploration: A Rhetoric of Religious*

226

Antiquity Reader, ed. Vernon K. Robbins, Robert H. von Thaden Jr., and Bart B. Bruehler (Atlanta: SBL Press, 2016), 78, 79.

24. Aristotle, *Rhetoric* 3.2, http://classics.mit.edu/Aristotle/rhetoric.3.iii.html.

25. Carolyn R. Miller, "The Aristotelian *Topos*: Hunting for Novelty," in Robbins, von Thaden, and Bruehler, *Foundations for Sociorhetorical Exploration*, 115.

26. Aristotle, *Rhetoric* 3.2.

27. Numerous commentaries on More's *Utopia* point to its "seriocomic mode." Take as an example the lead character of Hythloday, whose name translates to "something like 'non-sense peddler'" (George M. Logan, Robert M. Adams, and Clarence H. Miller, eds., *Thomas More Utopia: Latin Text and English Translation* [Cambridge: Cambridge University Press, 1995], xxv).

28. Miller, "Hunting for Novelty," 115.

29. Michel Foucault, "Of Other Spaces: Utopias and Heterotopias," *Architecture/Mouvement/Continuite*, trans. Jay Miskowiec (October 1984), 3, http://web.mit.edu/allanmc/www/foucault1.pdf ("Des Espace Autres," March 1967).

30. Ibid., 7.

31. Ibid., 4–5.

32. Ibid., 4.

33. Ibid., 6.

34. Ibid.

35. Ibid., 4.

36. Hannah Arendt, "Ideology and Terror: A Novel Form of Government," *The Review of Politics* 15, no. 3 (July 1953): 317, http://www.jstor.org/stable/1405171.

37. William E. Connolly, *Facing the Planetary: Entangled Humanism and the Politics of Swarming* (Durham: Duke University Press, 2017), 55.

38. Jean-Luc Marion, *God Without Being: Hors-Texte*, trans. Thomas A. Carlson, with a foreword by David Tracy (Chicago: University of Chicago Press, 1995), 48, 46.

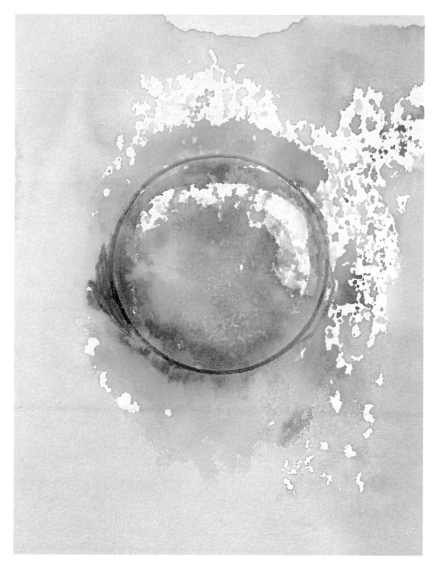

painting 4 Scott Neely, *Ocean Circle*.
Watercolor on paper, 12 × 9 inches. Used
with kind permission by the artist. Photo:
Mark Olencki.

Contributors

SCOTT NEELY serves as minister at the Unitarian Universalist Church of Spartanburg, South Carolina. He is a facilitator and strategist for Speaking Down Barriers, an organization that uses facilitated dialogue to build our life together across the differences that divide us. In April 2015 he presented a TEDx talk on race and racism titled "What Will I Teach My Son?" Neely is an instructor in religion and the humanities at the University of South Carolina–Upstate and Wofford College. A practicing artist, he has led literary and visual community art projects on issues of diversity, race, and religious pluralism.

CATHERINE KELLER practices theology as a relation between ancient traces of ultimacy and current matters of urgency. The George T. Cobb Professor of Constructive Theology in the Theological School and Graduate Division of Religion of Drew University, she teaches courses in process, political, and ecological theology. She has from the start mobilized, within and beyond Christian conversation, the transdiciplinarity of feminist, philosophical, and pluralist intersections with religion. Her most recent books invite at once contemplative and social embodiments of our entangled difference: *Cloud of the Impossible: Negative Theology and Planetary Entanglement* (2014), *Intercarnations: On the Possibility of Theology* (2017), and *Political Theology of the Earth: Our Planetary Emergency and the Struggle for a New Public* (2018).

CRYSTAL TENNILLE IRBY is a doula and identifies as a Black Mother Creative, which is an artist who creates work across multiple artist disciplines that centers on the Black experience, particularly Black women and mothering. She is a 2017 Water Hole Poetry Fellow and the cofounder and director of Writers Well Youth Fellowship Retreat, which is a retreat for Black girls ages 14–19 focused on writing and performance. Crystal is a spoken word poetry grand slam champion, published writer, actress, and current cohost and executive producer of Dem Black Mamas Podcast, a podcast that delves into the unique experience of Black mothers. Most recently Crystal directed and coproduced the Untitled Reconstruction Project, which is a performance based on the 1871 testimony of Spartanburg County residents who were terrorized by the Ku Klux Klan.

MARLANDA DEKINE is Sapient Soul (MSW, LMSW), a poet and licensed social worker residing in South Carolina. She is the author and recording artist of i am from a punch & a kiss, a multimedia project exploring black queer identity, the legacy of white supremacy, and spirituality in the South. Her poetry and thoughts have been shared with *USA Today*, *Sojourners*, SC Public Radio, TEDx, *Facing South*, *Flycatcher Journal*, Spark & Echo Arts, the Brighter Futures' Conference for Child Abuse Prevention, the Children's Trust Prevention Conference, the TogetherSC Nonprofit Symposium, as well as various open mics, poetry slams, and podcasts across the southeast. Marlanda is the founder of Speaking Down Barriers, a nonprofit that provides encounters that transform our life together across the intersections of human difference, facilitating raw, honest dialogue and offering spoken word poetry as its primary tools for healing and justice within the world. Currently, Marlanda teaches with Writers Well Youth Fellowship, a literary retreat for young, Black femme writers ages 14–19. She is also studying poetry with NYU's MFA Low-Residency Writers' Workshop in Paris. She received her BA in psychology from Furman University and her MSW from the University of South Carolina. To hear, watch, or read more, visit sapientsoul.com.

SHARON JACOB is an assistant professor of New Testament at Pacific School of Religion. Jacob earned her bachelor's degree in accounting from Bangalore University and went on to earn her master of divinity from Lancaster Theological Seminary and master of sacred theology from Yale University. She earned her PhD from Drew University. Her research interests include gender and sexuality studies, feminist theory, race and whiteness theory, and postcolonial theory. Her publications include a monograph titled *Reading Mary Alongside Indian Surrogate Mothers: Violent Love, Oppressive Liberation, and Infancy Narratives*. She has also coauthored an essay titled "Flowing from Breast to Breast: An Examination of Dis/placed Motherhood in Black and Indian Wet Nurses," in *Womanist Biblical Interpretations: Expanding the Discourses*, published by Society of Biblical Literature Press. Sharon has also published an article in the Bangalore Theological Forum titled "Reading Mary Alongside Indian Surrogate Mothers." Her forthcoming essay is titled "Imagined Nations, Real Women: Politics of Culture and Women's Bodies. A Postcolonial, Feminist, and Indo-Western Interpretation of 1 Timothy 2:8–15," in *The T&T Clark Handbook of Asian American Biblical Hermeneutics*, published by T&T Clark.

CYNTHIA MOE-LOBEDA has lectured in Africa, Asia, Europe, Latin America, Australia, and North America in theology; ethics; and on matters of climate justice and climate racism, moral agency, globalization, economic justice, eco-feminist theology, and faith-based resistance to systemic oppression. Her most recent book, *Resisting Structural Evil: Love as Ecological-Economic Vocation*, won the Nautilus Award for social justice. She is author or coauthor of six volumes and numerous articles and chapters. Moe-Lobeda is professor of theological and social ethics at Pacific Lutheran Theological Seminary, Church Divinity School of the Pacific, and the Graduate Theological Union in Berkeley. She holds a doctoral degree in Christian ethics from Union Theological Seminary, affiliated with Columbia University.

GAIL WORCELO, SGM, is a cofoundress of Green Mountain Monastery in Greensboro, Vermont, along with the late cultural historian and Passionist priest Thomas Berry. The monastery's mission is "A Single Sacred Community." She leads retreats and programs within the United States and internationally on themes related to evolutionary spirituality.

MARG KEHOE, PBVM, lives in a shanty town in Lima, Peru, and offers a variety of healing opportunities to adults and children in two holistic centers in the area—Centro Nana Nagle and Corazón de Nana.

JOERG RIEGER is distinguished professor of theology, Cal Turner Chancellor's Chair in Wesleyan studies, and the founding director of the Wendland-Cook Program in Religion and Justice at the Divinity School and the Graduate Program of Religion at Vanderbilt University. Among his most recent books are *Jesus vs. Caesar: For People Tired of Serving the Wrong God* (2018), *No Religion but Social Religion: Liberating Wesleyan Theology* (2018), and *Unified We Are a Force: How Faith and Labor Can Overcome America's Inequalities* (with Rosemarie Henkel-Rieger, 2016).

MARY JUDITH RESS, a U.S. Catholic lay missionary with Maryknoll (now retired), has been living and working in Latin America (El Salvador, Peru, and Chile) since 1970. She holds a doctorate in feminist theology from the San Francisco Theological School in California, and master's degrees in political economics from the Graduate School of Social Research in New York and in Spanish language and literature from the Universidad Internacional in Saltillo, Mexico. Dr. Ress's writings include *Ecofeminism in Latin America* (2006), which won second place in best gender issues at the Catholic Press Association of the United States and Canada in 2007; *Lluvia para florecer: Entrevistas sobre el ecofeminismo en América Latina* (2002), *Circling*

232

in, *Circling Out: A Con-spirando Reader* (2005), *Virgenes y diosas en América Latína: La resignificación de lo sagrado* (with Veronica Cordero, Graciela Pujol, and Coca Trillini, 2004), and *Del Cielo al la Tierra: Una antología de teología feminista* (with Ute Seibert and Lene Sjorup, 1994). Her historical novel *Blood Flowers* (2010), a tribute to the four religious women killed in El Salvador in 1980, has been translated into Spanish as *Flores de Sangre* (2014). Her second novel, *Different Gods* (2018), has just been released.

JOSÉ ERNESTO PADILLA (TITO) was an artist whose artwork depicted many familiar scenes and local landscapes that spanned from his growing-up years in his hometown of Yauco, Puerto Rico, to his adult life experiences in the States. In particular those included in this book, with their bright colors, capture the vividness of his life as a teenager on his grandparents' coffee farm. Several other paintings—such as the one on the small houses on the hilltop of one of the most visible neighborhoods called "El Cerro"—and his neoclassical-style drawings in black and white juxtapose more evidently his exuberant mood mixed with melancholy and mild cynicism that permeated his perspective.

ELAINE PADILLA is associate professor of philosophy and religion, Latinx/Latin American studies. Padilla constructively interweaves current philosophical discourse with Christianity, Latin American and Latino/a religious thought, mysticism, ecology, gender, and race. She is the author of *Divine Enjoyment: A Theology of Passion and Exuberance* (2015) and coeditor of *Theology and Migration in World Christianity*, a three-volume project with Peter C. Phan: *Contemporary Issues of Migration and Theology* (2013), *Theology of Migration in the Abrahamic Religions* (2014), and *Christianities in Migration: The Global Perspective* (2015). She has also published numerous articles and chapters, and is currently drafting a manuscript provisionally titled *The Darkness of Being*, in which she explores views on the soul and interiority with implications for race and gender. She is a member of the American Academy of Religion and the Catholic Theological Society of America, where she serves on various steering committees.

TERESIA M. HINGA is associate professor at Santa Clara University in the Department of Religious Studies. She received a bachelor of education degree in English literature and religious studies, and an master's in religious studies from Nairobi University, Kenya. She attained her PhD in religious studies (focusing on gender in African Christianity) from Lancaster University, England. She is a member of the American Academy of Religion, a founding member of the African Association for the Study of Religion, and a founding member of the Circle of Concerned Women Theologians (founded in 1989). Dr. Hinga's research includes examining the roles of reli- gion in the public square as well as exploring the nexus between religion, gender, and sustainability ethics, where she focuses on issues of poverty and food security as well as environmental ethics. Her latest publications include a volume on Afro-theo-ethics titled *African, Christian, Feminist: The Enduring Search for What Matters* (2017), as well as a chapter titled "Of Rainbow Nations, Kente Cloth, and the Virtue of Pluralism: Navigating the Beauty and Dignity of Difference in Search of a Livable Future in Africa," in *Finding Beauty in the Other: Theological Reflections Across Religious Traditions* (2018).

PETER C. PHAN, who has earned three doctorates, is the inaugural holder of the Ignacio Ellacuria Chair of Catholic Social Thought at Georgetown University, in Washington, DC. His research deals with the theology of icon in Orthodox theology, patristic theology, eschatology, the history of Christian missions in Asia, and liberation, inculturation, and interreligious dialogue. He is the author and editor of more than thirty books and has published more than three hundred essays. His writings have been translated into Arabic, French, German, Italian, Polish, Portuguese, Romanian, Serbian, Spanish, Chinese, Indonesian, Japanese, and Vietnamese, and have received many awards from learned societies. He is the first non-Anglo to be elected president of the Catholic Theological Society of America and president of the American Theological Society. In 2010 he received the John Courtney Murray Award, the highest honor bestowed by the Catholic Theological Society of America for outstanding achievement in theology.

CLAYTON CROCKETT is professor and director of religious studies at the University of Central Arkansas. He is the author of a number of books, including *Derrida After the End of Writing and Radical Political Theology.* He is a fellow of the Westar Institute and a member of its Seminar on God and the Human Future.

WHITNEY A. BAUMAN is associate professor of religious studies at Florida International University in Miami. He is the author of *Religion and Ecology: Developing a Planetary Ethic* (2014), editor of *Meaningful Flesh: Reflections on Religion and Nature for a Queer Planet* (2018), and coeditor with Lisa Stenmark of *Unsettling Science and Religion: Contributions and Questions from Queer Studies* (2018). He is currently working on a manuscript that examines the nonreductive materialism of the German Romantic scientist Ernst Haeckel.

KRISTA E. HUGHES is director of the Muller Center and associate professor of religion at Newberry College. A constructive theologian by training, her current work focuses on assisting college and high school students to integrate vocational exploration, ethical inquiry, and civic identity. She has published essays in *Dialog: A Journal of Theology*, *Syndicate Theology*, *Anglo Saxonica*, *Transformative Lutheran Theologies*, and *Apophatic Bodies: Infinity, Ethics, and Incarnation*. She is author of a forthcoming book on Buddhist and Christian resources for grappling with white identity for the sake of racial justice and serves as an antiracism, community transformation facilitator with Speaking Down Barriers.

DHAWN B. MARTIN is the executive director of the SoL Center of San Antonio, Texas, an interfaith education and peace-building center. Her publications include "A Cosmopolitical Theology: Engaging 'The Political' as an Incarnational Field of Emergence," in *Common Goods: Economy, Ecology, and Political Theology*, and "A Provisional Politics: Reclaiming Grace at the Intersections of Religion and Politics," *Crosscurrents* 64, no. 3.

Index